HOME AND FAMILY

CW01457581

Home and Family

Creating the Domestic Sphere

Edited by

Graham Allan
Lecturer in Sociology, University of Southampton

and

Graham Crow
Lecturer in Social Policy, University of Southampton

M
MACMILLAN

First published 1989

Published by
THE MACMILLAN PRESS LTD
Houndmills, Basingstoke, Hampshire RG21 2XS
and London
Companies and representatives
throughout the world

Filmset by Wearside Tradespools, Fulwell, Sunderland

Printed in the People's Republic of China

British Library Cataloguing in Publication Data
Home and Family: creating the domestic sphere.
1. Great Britain. Families
I. Allan, Graham   II. Crow, Graham
306.8'5'0941
ISBN 0–333–48974–8 (hardcover)
ISBN 0–333–48975–6 (paperback)

For Diane

Contents

Acknowledgements

We would like to thank our colleagues in the Department of Sociology and Social Policy at the University of Southampton for their encouragement in the formulation and production of this book. We appreciate in particular the excellent service and support the secretarial and clerical staff in the Department provide despite their increasing workload. Special thanks are due to Lita Cook who word-processed many of the original papers for us. Finally we would like to thank our contributors for their enthusiasm for the project and for their willingness to meet the demands we made of them.

GRAHAM ALLAN
GRAHAM CROW

Notes on the Contributors

Graham Allan is a Lecturer in Sociology at the University of Southampton. His interests include the sociology of the family, informal relationships and research methods. In addition to various papers, he is the author of *A Sociology of Friendship and Kinship*, *Family Life* and *Friendship: Developing a Sociological Perspective*.

Jennifer Craik currently lectures in the Division of Humanities at Griffith University, Queensland, having previously studied at Cambridge University for her PhD. Her research interests include cultural policy, tourism, and political television.

Graham Crow has been lecturing in Sociology and Social Policy at the University of Southampton since 1983. He was awarded his PhD from the University of Essex in 1987 for research into family farming. He has published papers from this work as well as on sociological theory, sociology of the family and community studies.

Fiona Devine is currently employed as a Research Officer at the Policy Studies Institute conducting a survey of employers' recruitment practices towards women scientists and engineers. She is also completing her PhD in sociology at the University of Essex. Her doctoral research focuses on the lifestyles of affluent working-class families in Luton.

Michael Hardey is a Research Fellow at the University of Surrey working on the Alvey DHSS Demonstrator Project. He has recently completed a longitudinal study of low-income households with others on this Project, and is currently engaged in a study of lone parents. He previously studied and worked at the University of Essex.

Joan Higgins is a Senior Lecturer in Social Policy at the University of Southampton and Director of the University's Institute for Health

Policy Studies. Her main interests are health care and comparative social policy. As well as numerous papers, she is the author of *The Poverty Business*, *States of Welfare* and *The Business of Medicine*.

Pauline Hunt, sometime Research Fellow in the Department of Sociology and Anthropology at the University of Keele, has a long-standing interest in the domestic environment dating back to her work as a WEA Tutor Organiser in North Staffordshire in the 1970s. This interest was developed in her book *Gender and Class Consciousness* and in various articles. In 1980 she made two films entitled *The Home: Castle or Cage?* for the BBC as part of an Open University course.

Jennifer Mason is currently a Research Officer at the University of Lancaster working on an ESRC funded study of family obligations and social policy. She received her PhD from the University of Kent in 1987 for a study of marital relationships amongst couples aged 50 to 70. She has published a number of articles from this study.

Marion Roberts is a qualified architect. She has worked in architectural practice and taught social policy and administration. She is currently writing a book on the topic of gender divisions and architectural design, following the completion of her PhD on the same subject. She lives in London.

1 Introduction
Graham Allan and Graham Crow

Ronald Frankenberg has recorded how, as a young researcher in a Welsh village in the 1950s, he 'would often climb a hill and look sadly down upon the rows of houses of the housing estate and wonder what went on inside them' (1969, p. 16). What goes on inside houses is home life, and this is something about which relatively little is known because it is fundamentally a private affair, curtained off from the public gaze. Researchers trying to build up a picture of home life face serious problems of access, so that, in general, 'they can only deduce social process from the information they can collect by questioning people in their homes or elsewhere' (Frankenberg, 1969, p. 16). Since this observation was made other methods of research have become available, and Frankenberg is among those who have pioneered their use (Hunt and Frankenberg, 1981; Hunt, this volume), but with these as with more conventional questionnaires the researcher remains essentially an outsider allowed only temporary and partial access to the private lives which people lead in their homes. Penetrating the veil of secrecy which surrounds home life in order to arrive at a balanced assessment of its nature and significance is no easy matter.

This book has been compiled in the belief that the home deserves to be treated as a central part of contemporary society. Conventionally home life has been understood as the cornerstone of the private sphere, something quite distinct from and secondary to the mainstream activities of the public sphere such as paid work and politics. It is in the home that the everyday routine of domestic life is played out, but the mundane character and private nature of home life conceal the energies that have to be put into its management and the powerful influence it has in shaping people's lives. As the setting in which personal life is located, the home makes a strong claim on people's time, resources, and emotions. In addition the creation of home life inevitably bears the strong imprint of the modern domestic ideal in which 'home' and 'family' are run together (Crow and Allan, 1989). It is this idea of the active construction of the home around the family that explains the title given to this volume, *Home and Family: Creating the Domestic Sphere.*

1

The observation that family relationships are central to people's conceptions of home life is not itself a new one, but it is essential to the understanding of how the home has developed. Historical research has shown how women's lives have revolved around home and family since at least the mid-nineteenth century (Lewis, 1986), and in some instances a good deal earlier (Davidoff and Hall, 1987; Williams, 1987; Rybczynski, 1988). It is nothing new for the home to be considered 'a woman's place' (Roberts, 1985), where she serves as the focal point of family relationships. By contrast men's position in the home has in the past been less significant than women's, at least in terms of time spent in the domestic setting, but there is a good deal of evidence to suggest that over the course of the present century men (as husbands and fathers) have become more home-centred than their predecessors. By the 1960s 'home-centredness' and 'family-centredness' were represented as twin pillars of the 'privatised style of life' of (male) affluent workers (Goldthorpe *et al.*, 1969, p. 163), a finding which Devine's re-study of Luton in the 1980s (this volume) and research elsewhere (see, for example, Holme 1985a) has confirmed for the current decade. Ideas about family life have changed significantly without undermining the centrality of such ideas to the project of creating home life.

Oakley has taken the argument that the ideas of home and family are interconnected a stage further by suggesting that, in one sense at least, the home *is* the family: 'If society has grown more "family-oriented" the family itself has identified more and more squarely with its physical location, the home. "Home" and "family" are now virtually interchangeable terms.' (1976, p. 65). While such a bald statement may need to be qualified to some degree, the contributions to this volume do bear out Gilman's proposition that the home 'is home *while the family are in it*. When the family are out of it it is only a house' (1980, p. 80, emphasis in original). In particular the presence of women is essential to such conceptions of home life, since only they can perform the roles of wife and mother around which 'home' as a set of social relationships is built, issues which Hunt, Mason and Craik address in their chapters. Much may have changed since the turn of the century when Gilman expressed her opposition to such a situation by stating the view that 'A house does not need a wife any more than it does a husband' (1980, p. 75), but the ideology which requires of home life the presence of a wife (and, ideally, mother) remains a powerful one. In consequence, as Hardey notes in his chapter, non-conventional households such as those headed by a single parent find the establishment of home life problematic. In her paper Higgins shows that the same is true for elderly residents of institutions, albeit for different reasons. However this should not be taken to imply that creating and maintaining a home is under any circumstances straightforward, as other contributors to this volume amply demonstrate.

Although the contributions to *Home and Family* focus on a variety of aspects of domestic social relations, there are certain common threads linking them together, and it is the purpose of this introduction to discuss these in broad terms, and to consider their consequences for our understanding of home life. To begin with, the chapters that follow all emphasise the importance of the home as a private place with access restricted to family members and, under certain circumstances, privileged others. The private sphere of the home is marked off from the public sphere of society in terms of who is encountered there, the activities undertaken there, and the styles of behaviour thought appropriate. Secondly the home is a place of security, control and freedom. Being 'at home' means (among other things) that an individual can feel safe and in command, free from the intrusion and direction of others. Thirdly the home is a place of creativity and expression in which activity, even mundane activity such as housework and repair work, takes on special significance. 'Making a home' is a project undertaken for others, most obviously other members of the family, and is therefore highly symbolic. Each of these three themes, the home as a place of privacy, of security, and of creativity, invites examination in greater depth, not least for the reason that what is revealed by doing so is the complexity and contradictoriness of the various elements that go to make up 'the home' in modern society.

THE HOME AS A PRIVATE PLACE

There exists a widespread belief among the population of contemporary Britain that their accommodation should provide them with privacy. Thus Holme's respondents in her study *Housing and Young Families in East London* sought more than anything else 'somewhere to be on their own' (1985a, p. 134), and Bulmer notes that a 'good' neighbour is one who observes 'respect for privacy' (1986, p. 30). Similarly Willcocks, Peace and Kellaher argue that old people have a 'preference for privacy' (1987, p. 3), and that this does not desert them when they move (or are moved) into old people's homes. Moreover lack of privacy is a major source of dissatisfaction among those living in hostels for homeless people (Watson, 1987). In sum, being in a private place is a central part of what it means to be 'at home'.

On the whole, privacy is regarded as a feature of home life to be valued. This has been noted to be particularly so where young parents are concerned (Holme, 1985a; Wallace, 1987). Affording privacy to family relationships is a central function of the home, with the idea of 'normal family life' being built around the nuclear family living independently in its own, separate dwelling (Leonard, 1980; Leonard and Speakman, 1986). The home is first and foremost a place for the immediate family, but in addition it is a place to which relatives and friends may be admitted from time to time. Those friends and relatives invited into the private sphere of the home are in an important sense privileged, since this access is restricted, both in terms of which particular friends and relatives are entertained in the home and in terms of which parts of the home they are permitted to see (Morgan, 1975). The exercise of such control over access to the home helps to maintain the essentially private nature of what is contained in it and of what activities take place there. Restricting access to the home may be used to conceal what is felt to be the failure to live up to the material standards (Allan, 1979) or the standards of behaviour (Burgoyne and Clark, 1984) taken as normal in modern society.

A home of one's own is, then, valued as a place in which the members of a family can live in private, away from the scrutiny of others, and exercise control over outsiders' involvement in domestic affairs. In this sense 'privacy' refers to the power to exclude others, a defensive measure to allow access to the resources of the home to a select and privileged few. However, closer inspection of how access to the home is structured reveals that there can be no simple distinction made between public and private arenas, or between outsiders and insiders; rather, as Allan and Mason both argue in their chapters, it is the case that access to the home varies considerably, with different people allowed varying degrees of access to certain parts of the home at certain times. The distinction between public and private spheres of life is a complicated one to draw, not least where family-type relationships are concerned (Morgan, 1985), and any boundary line between public and private worlds is in consequence at best blurred. In terms of the discussion of the home, and stated crudely, the public world does not begin and end at the front door.

Where the home does serve to provide a more or less private place for the family, this does not necessarily secure privacy for its individual members from each other. Individuals' claims to their own space separate and distinct from the family's space may well be denied even though houses are far more spacious now than when Jackson observed of homes in the traditional working-class community that the 'only place which is private in the way that a professional worker's "study" might be, is the lavatory' (1968, p. 158). Rising standards of domestic facilities may have made it more relevant to speak of the bathroom in this context, but the essential point remains that an individual's ability to secure some degree of privacy is frequently conditional. As Weigert puts it, the private areas of a home 'may only be legitimate and recognised during certain times of the day or certain moods of the family members' (1981, p. 264).

The point about family members having limited access to individual private space within the home has been made with particular reference to women (McDowell, 1983; Francis, 1984; Deem, 1986; Hunt, this volume). It could also be applied to other household members, for example children, whose use of space is subject to parental approval (Hunt and Frankenberg, 1981). When this is borne in mind, there is no particular surprise in Abrams and McCullogh's finding that the degree of privacy available to commune dwellers is 'a good deal more than individual members of many conjugal families enjoy' (1976, p. 185). This is not necessarily something experienced as a problem, particularly where young families are concerned (Holme, 1985a; Devine, this volume). However, both Hunt and Mason in this volume report women's feelings of intrusion by their husbands, bearing out Stacey and Price's contention that 'the private domain has been invaded to the disadvantage of women' (1981, p. 122). In his chapter, too, Hardey notes how single mothers, although free from interference by a partner, also have to strive to keep their own space separate from that of their children.

Where privacy at home is achieved by people, it is not necessarily experienced positively. 'Private' can signify deprivation as well as advantage (Williams, 1976), a point which directs attention towards a side of privatised lifestyles less widely acknowledged than family-centredness but no less real for that. Limitation of contact with others is a prominent, indeed integral, part of privatised lifestyles, but it is something which can be experienced as a lack, especially by women.

This can be appreciated from the many complaints about isolation which are recorded not only among women outside conventional households (although, as Pahl (1985) shows, this is an important phenomenon), but also among women in 'normal' families (Oakley, 1974; Austerberry and Watson, 1985; Leonard and Speakman, 1986). For women, 'Home, as the setting in which most caring is carried out, becomes not so much a haven from the rigours of the labour market, as a prison.' (Graham, 1983, p. 26). A similar perspective informs Craik's description in this volume of the kitchen as 'mother's panopticon'.

Women's domestic responsibilities may make the home a place of captivity (Gavron, 1968), of confinement (Hunt, 1980), the setting where they experience 'the isolation that passes for privacy' (Boys *et al.*, 1984, p. 2). Men without responsibilities in the labour market may also experience the privacy of the home negatively. Binns and Mars refer to the daily life of a long-term unemployed man as being 'grimly' home-centred (1984, p. 674), the product of withdrawal from wider social networks 'into the increasingly non-supportive world of nuclear hearth and home', in short the product of 'retreatism' (1984, pp. 677–8, 684). Similarly it is not really appropriate to describe the situation of old people who lack contact with the outside world as being positively home-centred; a more fitting term, suggesting lives of isolation and boredom, is 'homebound' (Deem, 1985, p. 188). For all of these reasons, and for all of these groups, it may be appropriate to consider the home more of a 'cage' than a 'castle' (Hunt and Frankenberg, 1981).

THE HOME AS A PLACE OF SECURITY, CONTROL AND FREEDOM

There are then contradictions inherent in the pursuit of privacy at home since the exclusion of outsiders can lead to the loss of valued sociable links with friends, neighbours and kin beyond the immediate family, while the creation of home life around the family may work to undermine individual privacy. It can be argued that similar contradictions surround the pursuit of security, control and freedom in the home. The idea of the home as a secure space where a person is not answerable to outsiders is a commonly held one, captured in the characterisation of the home as a 'castle'. Yet an individual is not completely free to act in the home as he or she chooses. This is so in part because each individual member of a family is regulated to some degree by the wishes of other household members, something which is most obvious in the exercise of parental control over children but which is true to a certain extent for everyone, save those who live alone. In addition there exists a tension between the conception of the home as a place for relaxation and freedom from rules and regulations and the need for some element of regularity and predicta- bility in domestic arrangements and routines if the familiarity and order upon which feelings of being in control depend are to be achieved.

The idea of home as 'sanctuary', 'a place of secure retreat' (Moore, 1984, p. 203) is a very old one indeed, and it is one which has grown in importance as the division of life into public and private spheres has progressed. Typically in contemporary society involvement in the public sphere is undertaken for limited periods, after which an individual returns 'home'; it is, for example, from home that people 'go out to work'. Thus, as Heller has noted, 'Integral to the average everyday life is awareness of a fixed point in space, a firm position from which we "proceed" . . . and to which we return in due course. This firm position is what we call "home".' (1984, p. 239). Heller argues that the meaning of 'home' is not only familiarity but also protection and warmth, all of which are essential to feelings of security: ' "Going home" should mean: returning to that firm posi- tion which we know, to which we are accustomed, where we feel safe, and where our emotional relationships are at their most intense' (1984, p. 239). In brief, the word 'home' like the word 'family' conjures up images of 'personal warmth, comfort, stability and security' (Watson with Austerberry, 1986, p. 8). The home is created as a secure territory, and when it is intruded upon by uninvited outsiders this is experienced as an invasion of privacy and a transgres- sion of personal space. These feelings of violation are particularly prominent in reactions to burglary (Walsh, 1980).

It is clear that responsibility for creating an atmosphere of security and order in a home does not fall evenly among members of a household. Women remain primarily responsible for the smooth running of the home and the achievement of comfort and orderliness in the domestic arena, despite the preparedness of many men to 'help' with these tasks, as authors of previous studies have pointed out (Oakley, 1974; Edgell, 1980; Hunt, 1980). Women's responsibil- ity for the day-to-day organisation of the home can be seen to continue even where the husband breadwinner, wife home-maker

ideology on which this division of labour is founded no longer applies
to the reality of the situation, for example among couples where both
spouses are in paid employment (Hunt, this volume), or where
retirement is taking place (Mason, this volume). As with the comparable cases of dual career couples and unemployed husbands the
primary responsibility for home and family stays with the wife
(Edgell, 1980; Harris, 1987; Pahl and Wallace, 1988). Within the
broad framework of the acceptance by women, men and children of
women's responsibility for domestic cleanliness, tidiness and orderliness, there are indications that ideas about domestic responsibilities
do vary to some degree over the course of the life-cycle, and this is a
theme which Devine's chapter develops. In addition, where there is
continuity in the division of domestic responsibilities, this is not
necessarily the result of habitual adherence to established routines;
rather it may be actively brought about by, for example, wives
resisting their husbands' intrusion into what they perceive to be their
sphere. Mason's analysis of the reconstruction of the home in later
life highlights this point.

The unequal distribution of responsibility for the home providing a
secure and comfortable place for the family is reflected in the
differential experience of leisure which is to be found between the
different members of the household. Ideally the home provides a
'peaceful haven' in which leisure can be enjoyed, but, as Deem points
out, the home is also women's workplace and the 'continued presence
of household duties and obligations means that it is difficult for
women to set aside time for leisure at times when others are relaxing
which they can be sure will be uninterrupted' (1986, p. 81). For those
with responsibility for the state of the home, it is not easy to enjoy
'free time' in the same way as it is enjoyed by other household
members. This is particularly true for those leisure activities where
people from outside the household are being entertained in the home
and are thus given an opportunity to judge its appearance (Allan, this
volume). It is not surprising to find disagreements between family
members about what are acceptable standards of cleanliness and
tidiness on such occasions, since women appear to be more suscepti-
ble than men to feelings of being judged on the state of their home by
visitors, and are more likely to prepare a home for inspection by
outsiders in an effort to create the right impression. In their chapters
Hunt and Mason are both concerned to examine the roots of this
important aspect of gender inequality in domestic responsibilities.

A central function of a home is thus to provide a sense of security to those who live in it through its being run according to certain routines. The feeling of being 'at home' and in familiar and predictable surroundings requires the presence of regularity in domestic arrangements. In addition to this sense of security provided by homes being run according to patterns set down by those who live in them, there is a need to consider the contribution made by housing tenure to the way in which the home is experienced as a safe place. Here it appears that a major change has accompanied the growth of owner-occupation, with 'a home of one's own' coming to mean something which is not fully achieved without ownership of a dwelling, whereas previously its principal meaning was that of a dwelling not shared with another family.

The process whereby owner-occupation has come to be seen as a prerequisite for control over the home is a complex one. The idea of home-ownership being a 'natural' aspiration is one that has been encouraged by governments since the 1950s (Crow, this volume), but the expressed preference for owner-occupation over rented property has to be placed against the background of the long-term decline of the rented sector. As Roberts's examination of a post-war council estate in London indicates, high levels of satisfaction among those re-housed by local authorities after 1945 were not uncommon, so that the lower levels of satisfaction reported among today's tenants must be seen in terms of their comparatively restricted choice and the relatively poorer quality of the housing stock now available for rent. In addition, while tenants are more likely than owner-occupiers to express feelings of vulnerability (Holme, 1985a), it needs to be pointed out that the greater 'ontological security' (Saunders, 1984; Saunders and Williams, 1988; Pahl and Wallace, 1988) taken to accrue to owner-occupiers does not necessarily arise out of the fact of ownership in itself. Equally important here is the freedom to undertake certain activities which ownership brings. There is clearly an attraction to owner-occupation where it offers the opportunity to escape from petty regulations such as those relating to hanging washing out to dry (Roberts, this volume), but the growth in popularity of owner-occupation has to be understood more positively in terms of what it permits in the realm of creating one's own home. It is the occupants of a dwelling who make it into a home, and the greater scope for making a home which is allowed by owner-occupation accounts in no small part for home-ownership's popularity.

THE HOME AS A PLACE OF CREATIVITY AND EXPRESSION

In line with being viewed as a social and physical territory controlled by members of a household, the home is also now perceived to be a creative and fulfilling arena. This is so not simply in the sense that the home is the site where family life is continually reproduced, important though this aspect of home life is. In addition the home has become a creative place where a good deal of effort is put into moulding the physical surroundings in which everyday domestic life takes place. Vast industries have been created to cater for people's desires for new furnishings and different styles of decoration, in the process rendering possible home improvements once technically beyond the relatively unskilled individual. The growth in Do-It-Yourself (DIY) in recent years has been dramatic, as Pahl (1984) has shown, with the result that many people have gained a new sense of having created their home environment.

The significance of the project of creating an appropriate environment in which domestic life can take place has grown to the point at which it stands alongside paid work and bringing up a family as a major life interest (Pahl and Wallace, 1988). Pride in the home rests in part on it appearing clean and tidy, as was the case in the past (Roberts, 1985), but in addition to being an indicator of domestic organisation the appearance of the home is also an expression of taste. The desire to create certain atmospheres varies between different rooms, pointing to a link with the gendered division of domestic responsibilities, as Craik shows in her discussion of the kitchen as the realm of 'mother'. Hunt's chapter also highlights the variation in senses of style between classes, with distinct preferences in patterns of home decoration found among working-class and middle-class households. The overall objective of all households may be the achievement of domestic comfort, but there is great diversity among the ways in which it is pursued.

There exist many forms through which domestic creativity is expressed. Given the need for material resources in the process of making a home, those households with access to plentiful resources will be better positioned to achieve their ideal home (Pahl, 1984; Pahl and Wallace, 1988), in contrast to those poor households (such as those described by Hardey in his chapter) which face difficulty in securing even the most basic requirements around which a home is built. Architecture too plays no small part in restricting the possible usages of the home, and although there is usually some scope for people to modify their physical surroundings, the intentions of architects and planners inevitably loom large as a factor shaping home life, a point both Crow and Roberts develop in their chapters. The impact of domestic architecture plays a particularly important part in structuring the home lives of women (Ungerson and Karn, 1980; Boys *et al.*, 1984).

In addition to being influenced by class factors and architectural design, the creation of home life will not be a uniform process because of variations between households in the understanding of what the activities involved in home-making symbolise. Different tasks emphasise to different degrees the development of practical skills, investment in a capital asset, artistic expression, and the provision of service to other family members. Gullestad (1984) suggests that people's accounts of why they undertake home improvement tend to emphasise the practical benefits, in terms of greater ease of housework, improvements in the home's appearance, and increases in the dwelling's value. Standing alongside this are less tangible reasons: 'By decorating their home the family members symbolise their unity, and elaborate on the values of sharing and togetherness in the charged context of hearth and home' (Gullestad, 1984, p. 97). A well-decorated home is a symbol of a united family, representing its ongoing collective effort. As Roberts argues in her chapter, such aspects of the home are also an important basis of prestige within the local community.

When considering the diversity that exists in the meanings attached to the various elements of home-making, it is important not to overlook the simple point that creating the home is essentially an active process which involves forms of work, 'housework' in the broadest sense of that term. The tension between such domestic activity and ideas of home as a place of leisure and escape from work is immediately apparent, and highlights the contradictoriness of the home functioning as both workplace and place of relaxation. Attempts to resolve this problem can be traced back to the nineteenth century. A tradition of writing already existed then which sought to minimise the disruptive impact of housework on family life by encouraging improvements in the technical efficiency with which it was carried out. The chapters by Crow and Craik chart how the present century has seen the elaboration of this theme with the elevation of housework to the status of a respectable 'career' for women, and even to a form of artistic expression. Yet the more that the home is organised along 'rational' lines, the more it is subject to the process of 'disenchantment' (Reiger, 1985) which threatens to undermine its special emotional significance. Higgins's analysis of residential homes in this volume illustrates the more general point that the 'metaphysical' dimension of the meaning of home is one that is notoriously difficult to create and remarkably easy to lose.

THE PLAN OF THE BOOK

The contradictions which emerge from the study of the home reflect the existence of tensions between the uses to which the home is put and the complex character of the social relations which make up domestic life. The home has many uses, as a place of privacy and a place of sociability; as a place of freedom and a place of responsibility; and as a place of leisure and a place of work. Further, as Clark has pointed out, domestic life contains 'intimacy and estrangement; growing together and growing apart; affection and violence; affluence and poverty; experience and inexperience' (1987, pp. 130–1). Overall the diversity of people's experience of the home reflects the diversity of family life which takes place there.

The chapters which follow convey this diversity. Graham Crow's chapter sets out the post-war context in which modern home life has developed, and shows that home life in contemporary Britain is quite different from that of the years following 1945. His argument that there have been important changes both in the material circumstances of the home and in ideas about home life is illustrated by Marion Roberts, who examines how the ideals of post-war planners were put into practice on a London estate built in the early 1950s. The contrast between the architects' intentions and the tenants' actual experiences of their new homes highlights the way in which ordinary families (and in particular the women in them) still had to work hard to create a comfortable home life even in their improved surroundings. The third historical chapter, by Jennifer Craik, analyses the popular thesis that the nature of housework has changed, freeing women from drudgery and heralding a new era of domestic satisfaction. She concludes that while the principal site of housework, the kitchen, has undergone something of a transformation, the anticipated liberation of 'mother' has not materialised.

The next four chapters draw on contemporary empirical research among households in diverse circumstances, and demonstrate that there is a great variety of ways in which the home is experienced in modern society. Pauline Hunt argues that gender inequalities are central to the construction of home life, and notes this to be true of both middle-class and working-class households despite their differences in other respects such as their ideas about domestic furnishing. Fiona Devine's chapter concentrates on working-class families, and highlights the variation in her respondents' experiences of the home over the course of the life-cyle, noting in particular the isolation felt by young mothers. With the approach of retirement representing a later stage in the life-cycle, the theme developed by Jennifer Mason is that of the re-creation of domestic life following the departure of children and the greater presence of the husband in the home. She shows that adjustment to changes in family membership can often be a lengthy process. This point is also of much relevance to the situation of lone parents, as Michael Hardey's analysis of the difficulties of re-creating home life for single mothers brings out, although his chapter also argues that by no means all of these new experiences are negative ones.

The final two chapters cover more general matters relating to issues of the wider society and public policy. Graham Allan's discussion of the boundaries around the home emphasises the negotiated nature of domestic privacy and examines the use to which the home is put. And Joan Higgins's chapter investigates the character of 'home' life experienced by those in institutions. Her analysis of the sense of loss felt when people move permanently into residential settings conveys powerfully the metaphysical significance normally attached to the home.

2 The Post-War Development of the Modern Domestic Ideal
Graham Crow

Being 'at home' means something quite different in the 1980s from what was understood by the term 40 or so years ago. To begin with, the material circumstances in which people lead their home lives have altered dramatically since the 1940s. War-time damage and neglect had added to the problems of the previous decade to leave the country's housing stock seriously run-down and inadequate. From this starting point, developments in the field of housing in the subsequent four decades have inevitably had a major impact on people's domestic lives. Dramatic changes have also occurred in the technology with which homes are equipped, and the spread of ownership and use of modern domestic appliances has heralded new forms of domestic organisation, albeit not necessarily those more egalitarian ones which have frequently been anticipated. Further, changing ideas about family relationships and behaviour in the domestic sphere have played an important part in the evolution of everyday life in the home. People's perceptions and expectations of family life have shifted and, as they have done so, ideas about home life have altered too. This chapter is devoted to charting the major features of these changes that have taken place in home life over the course of the post-war period.

The post-war period is to some extent an arbitrary one to delimit when looking at the emergence of the contemporary meaning of 'home'. Many of the processes of change in housing, domestic technology and family life which have played such a prominent part in shaping patterns of home life were under way long before the 1940s, so that post-war developments contain an important element of continuity with what was taking place before (Crow and Allan, 1989). Similarly the processes of change that have unfolded since 1945 are by no means exhausted of their potential to carry developments further, as, for example, the continuing growth of owner-occupation demonstrates. Yet while the post-war years do not

constitute a wholly self-contained historical entity, there is nevertheless some justification in focusing attention on what has happened
since the Second World War. In particular it is important to recognise
the ways in which changes in the earlier part of the period have
worked to shape subsequent events. To those emerging from the war
and the long years of depression which had preceded it, the post-war
world appeared to offer the opportunity of a new beginning in all
areas of life, with housing and home life being prominent among
them. In the assessment of this grand project of social reconstruction,
1945 stands as a starting point, and the ideals and material reality of
the time serve as a base line against which later developments in
home life can be compared.

Over the post-war period the ideal of home life which people have
striven after has proved to be somewhat elusive, not least because of
its tendency to run ahead of what is achievable in practice. While
there is nothing historically unique about this disjunction between
idealised versions of domestic life and the more mundane material
reality, the post-war years have been characterised by a remarkable
escalation of aspirations relating to the home and the allocation of an
equally remarkable amount of energy and resources into the project
of constructing home life. The main thrust of this chapter will be to
argue that although the material conditions in which people lead their
domestic lives have improved enormously since 1945, changes in the
way the home is organised have by no means always been those
anticipated. In general any domestic ideal has a tendency to shift over
time, reflecting the changing nature of the constraints and opportunities structuring the ways in which people actively engage in creating a
home. In particular it is important to stress that while the housing
situation makes up the most important element of the broad context
in which patterns of domestic life develop, the evolution of contemporary home life has been a far more complex process than simply
change in response to housing improvement.

POST-WAR RECONSTRUCTION

The improvement of housing and thereby of home life was given an
integral role in the plans for Britain's post-war reconstruction.
'Reconstruction' in this context meant far more than replacing the
housing stock destroyed or damaged by war-time bombing, extensive
though this was. The devastation of many older inner-city areas

which had previously been densely populated created an urgent need for re-housing, but it also offered an opportunity to bring about a dramatic improvement in the housing standards of the nation relative to those which had prevailed in the 1930s. Poor housing was associated with a number of social problems, in particular that of ill-health (Byrne *et al.*, 1986; Mackintosh, 1952), and it was felt that housing improvement would make a major contribution to the 'rebuilding' of family life (Aldridge, 1979), again understood as something other than a return to pre-war norms (Lewis, 1988). Post-war reconstruction in housing thus involved more than providing every household with a dwelling, although this was a highly ambitious objective in itself.

Alongside the quantitative goal of increasing the number of houses and flats built stood the more qualitative aim of bringing about the improvement of people's home life. This latter project was understood in a rather technical sense, involving 'a revolution in domestic architecture towards streamlined rational kitchens and a good number of bedrooms' (Riley, 1983, pp. 167–8). Improved conditions and facilities in the home were to play an important part in overcoming squalor, one of Beveridge's five giant evils, but they were also allocated a more positive role in the promotion of 'family life'. Against the background of concern over falling birthrates and the supposed decline of motherhood, greater attention was paid to the need for new homes to have sufficient space and to be conveniently organised for bringing up children. The 1944 Dudley Report made much of the benefits to be brought by housing officials consulting with women who, as housewives and mothers, were seen as primarily responsible for the modern home's smooth running (Boys *et al.*, 1984).

During the war, planners had looked forward to promoting new ways of domestic living, getting away from ideas of the home as a museum, a centre-piece of tradition, and anticipating the emergence of planned homes which would function as efficient, modern 'machines for living in' (Denby, 1941). Such expectations fed through into public consciousness, helping to make housing the most important issue of the 1945 General Election, at least from the electorate's point of view (Davies, 1984). The political significance of housing in the immediate post-war period has strong parallels with the situation that followed the First World War, when Lloyd George's promise to provide 'homes fit for heroes' led to much legislative innovation in order to stimulate activity in the building industry (Balchin, 1981).

However the limited success of these earlier experiments, together with the more urgent need for house building and the greater willingness of the government to follow an interventionist housing policy, meant that 'reconstruction' in the years after 1945 was planned quite differently, in terms of both its scale and its broader social objectives.

The dimensions of the housing shortage inherited by the Labour government in 1945 necessitated a building programme on an unprecedented scale. The Ministry of Reconstruction had already identified the primary objective in the field of housing as being 'to afford a separate dwelling for every family which desires to have one' (quoted in Cullingworth, 1979, p. 31), with the expectation that achieving this would eliminate overcrowding (Simon, 1986). This was an ambitious goal in the context of the prevailing conditions of excess demand for accommodation and a shortage of building materials. Put simply, what was being aimed at was the provision of 'homes for all', an objective akin to others inspired by the philosophy of the Beveridge Report (for example 'work for all' and 'health for all') and subject to the same tendency to underestimate the demand that such commitments were to reveal.

It is a measure of the extent of the problem that although the number of houses constructed in Great Britain reached over one million before the end of the Labour administration in 1951, this was still short of the target of 240 000 per year that had originally been set (Burnett, 1986), and a world away from Bevan's rhetorical electoral promise of 'five million homes in quick time' (quoted in Sked and Cook, 1983, p. 51). Although the war-time loss of 700 000 dwellings had been more than made up, because numbers of people marrying rose significantly during the later 1940s there remained in 1951 something in the region of three-quarters of a million more households than there were dwellings (Davies, 1984), in contrast to the pre-war surplus of dwellings. One reflection of this continuing housing shortage was that 'many couples had to begin married life in the home of one or other parent, more usually the wife's parents' (Marwick, 1982, p. 66), only later graduating to a home of their own.

In the immediate post-war years there was great pressure to maximise the number of dwellings built in order to meet the basic aspiration of every household for a home of its own, but, apart from the construction of some 157 000 prefabricated houses between 1945 and 1950, the government resisted attempts to compromise on quality in order to increase the total housing stock. Bevan, the Minister responsible in the Attlee government, justified this approach in 1946 on the grounds that 'while we shall be judged for a year or two by the *number* of houses we build, we shall be judged in ten years' time by the *type* of houses we build' (quoted in Malpass and Murie, 1982, p. 56, emphasis in original). Cutting standards he regarded as 'cruel', given the central part housing plays in people's lives, and he concluded: 'If we have to wait a little longer, that will be far better than doing ugly things now and regretting them for the rest of our lives' (quoted in Balchin, 1981, p. 109). In the light of electoral results to come in the 1950s this may well be seen as a political miscalculation, but Bevan believed that post-war reconstruction, at least as he envisaged it, would be undermined by giving in to pressures to place quantity before quality, or to relinquish governmental control over house building.

Council houses built in the later 1940s were more spacious and better equipped than those of the inter-war period, reflecting official concern with the way in which housing had previously been related to class. The government was keen to improve the lot of those people, mostly in low-income groups, who inhabited the worst housing conditions and justified this on the grounds of their needs being greater. However there was more to Bevan's approach than ensuring that housing for lower income groups was provided. If it was socially just to concentrate on the provision of housing to let for those in greatest need, Bevan felt it was also necessary to build housing of sufficient quality to avoid the emergence of single-class neighbourhoods, which he termed 'castrated communities', whereby 'colonies of low-income people' were segregated from 'the higher income groups living in their own colonies' (quoted in Murie, 1983, p. 55). Conservative thinking of the time also supported 'the ideology of home and community' (McDowell, 1983, p. 152) in which 'home' and 'community' stood as complementary rather than competing foci of people's attention, and in which the boundaries set up around the home were intended to secure privacy but not exclusivity.

Bevan's concern to promote 'mixed communities' was practised most explicitly in the pursuit of social balance in the New Towns, but he held it as a general principle that 'we don't want a country of East Ends and West Ends' (quoted in Sked and Cook, 1983, p. 51), and 'mixed development' incorporating a variety of house sizes was more widely adopted in building programmes in the late 1940s. The removal of the restriction that local authority housing was to be provided only for 'the working classes' effected in Bevan's 1949

Housing Act has to be seen against the background of inter-war trends towards residential segregation along class lines, and the desire to achieve a physical separation of home and workplace. With local authorities being responsible for 89 per cent of all the houses built between 1945 and 1951 (Balchin, 1981), Bevan's conception of 'reconstruction' in which public housing played the leading role was bound to have a major impact on ordinary people's domestic lives.

A further element in the 'housing drive' of the later 1940s was the improvement of conditions within the home. Higher standards of housing were viewed as being of particular importance in improving the position of women in the home. Consequently the local authority houses of the period were not only larger than they had been previously, they also had greater attention paid to how they were equipped, particularly in their kitchens and bathrooms (Burnett, 1986). Planning the home appeared to offer enormous potential for the improvement of everyday life, not least by allowing the latest developments in domestic technology to be taken advantage of (Denby, 1941), but this was all put into practice on the assumption that women's primary roles were those of housewife and mother (Boys *et al.*, 1984). The Beveridge Report 'located the woman firmly within the home' (Wilson, 1977, p. 141).

Beveridge's more radical suggestions of providing assistance (such as domestic help and nurseries) for the 'tired housewife' were not acted upon, partly on the basis of the argument that with the elimination of the drudgery of housework the home became a more pleasant place to be and home-making a respectable 'career' for a woman (Wilson, 1980). In this way, the approach to housing adopted in the 1945–51 period reinforced conventional 'nuclear family households' (Watson with Austerberry, 1986, p. 49). Developments in the following period worked much more vigorously to strengthen the synthesis of 'home' and 'family', while at the same time the links between 'home' and 'community' were perceptibly weakened.

THE GROWTH OF AFFLUENCE AND THE PUSH TOWARDS PRIVATISM

Against the background of the continuing housing shortage, promises to increase the number of new houses to 300 000 per year played an important part in securing the Conservatives' return to power in the General Election of 1951. The 1950s was to witness a significant shift in housing policy away from the programme of the immediate post-war years, and this was to have a marked effect on the nature of home life. At the level of political rhetoric, the 'housing drive' was replaced by a 'national crusade' in the words of the Housing Minister, Macmillan. In more concrete terms, the public sector building programme was modified, with these houses being built to less generous specifications, and then (after an initial increase to fulfil electoral promises) total local authority housing targets being reduced, in favour of the expansion of the private sector. The 1950s also saw owner-occupation encouraged and restrictions on private renting relaxed, and, towards the end of the decade, the shortfall of dwellings relative to households was finally eradicated (Central Statistical Office, 1985). It is also in this period that the modern domestic ideal of an affluent nuclear family living in a home of their own and enjoying the benefits of leisurely home life took shape, with emphasis placed on the privacy of the individual household rather than the wider community. Moreover this new, privatised lifestyle was presented as a universal opportunity rather than something open to only a privileged part of the population, as (for example) the bourgeois domestic ideal of the Victorians had been.

The shift in housing policy does not coincide precisely with the change of government in 1951, since many of the changes introduced by Macmillan were presaged under the Labour administration, while others (such as the expansion of private sector house building) took time to bring into effect. Macmillan's housing 'crusade' had its roots in Churchill's instruction to 'build the houses for the people', accompanied by the incentive that 'every humble home will bless your name if you succeed' (quoted in Sked and Cook, 1983, p. 119). With the target figure of 300 000 new houses per year achieved, the emphasis of housing policy switched to greater encouragement of private building for owner-occupation. This change, together with attempts to revive the private rented sector, left the public sector with a more restricted role than it had been allocated immediately after the war.

Just as the expansion of public sector housing had been perceived as the most appropriate policy to pursue in the years of 'reconstruction', so now owner-occupation fitted in with the changed politics of the period, which emphasised affluence rather than austerity, the individual family rather than the wider community, and middle-class rather than working-class values (Laing, 1986). According to government thinking of the mid-1950s, the housing shortage was in the process of being solved, and this was seen to open the way to allowing greater freedom of choice in housing for ordinary people. It was presumed that those who could afford to would want to become owner-occupiers, and between 1951 and 1961 owner-occupation rose from 29 per cent to 43 per cent of all households (Malpass and Murie, 1982), with increased building for home ownership and the sale of previously privately rented housing both contributing to this growth. Crucially, part of this growth incorporated working-class households (Boddy, 1980), allowing the idea to take shape that owner-occupation can be considered the ideal form of housing tenure, within the context of the development of what Macmillan (as Minister with responsibility for housing, and borrowing from Eden) called a 'property-owning democracy'.

While the increase in owner-occupation witnessed in the 1950s was dramatic in itself, it was taken by commentators of the time to be part of a much more general trend towards an affluent, home-centred lifestyle which could be enjoyed by everyone, owner-occupier and tenant alike. Home-based consumerism was taken to be central to this emergent lifestyle (McDowell, 1983), with women as home-centred wives and mothers playing a key role in the allocation of expenditure (Wilson, 1977), something advertising of the time shows (Marwick, 1982). Particular significance was attached to the widening ownership of consumer goods such as domestic electrical appliances (refrigerators, washing machines and vacuum cleaners) which reduced the drudgery of housework, and radios and televisions which catered for the growing amount of leisure time that could be spent together by family members (Hole and Attenburrow, 1970). Whereas before the war only about two-thirds of dwellings had electricity, by the 1950s it had more or less gained the status of a universal necessity. It was a period when

> assumptions about what was going on inside the home focused largely on the growth of possession of consumer durables. This in turn was dependent on connection to the electricity supply . . . the television aerial above symbolised the new way of life within. Television was . . . the defining symbolic object of affluence. (Laing, 1986, pp. 27–9)

Even among the less well-off social groups (identified collectively as manual and lower-grade clerical workers and old age pensioners) 76 per cent of households had a television set by 1961, and while the spread of other household appliances progressed less rapidly, the overall impression gained was one of affluent lifestyles filtering down the class structure (Hole and Attenburrow, 1970). These changes in home life were clearly central to the claims being made in Conservative ranks to the effect that the bulk of the British people had 'never had it so good', but they were to prove powerful too in affecting the perceptions of Labour politicians. By the early 1960s Crosland was writing that the changes reflected 'a basic human desire for choice, leisure, comfort, privacy and a more spacious family life' (quoted in Goldthorpe, 1988, p. 42), and although dissenting voices concerning the unmet housing needs of disadvantaged groups continued to be heard, comfortable privatised lifestyles had become established as a cultural norm.

Reports by sociologists of the time confirm that there was widely believed to be a transformation taking place in home life, made possible by the new housing conditions, the technology with which they were equipped, and the growth of leisure time. Several studies sought to illustrate this by comparing housing and home life in old, inner-city areas with physical conditions and patterns of sociability on the new, suburban estates to which people had moved, and which were taken to be more or less prototypical (Mogey, 1956; Young and Willmott, 1957; Willmott and Young, 1960). The latter houses were larger and better equipped, and had gardens. Their occupants referred to their new accommodation as being 'like heaven' (Mogey, 1956, p. 74), 'like paradise' (Young and Willmott, 1957, p. 103) compared to what they had been used to. Although it can be argued that these studies suffer collectively from a tendency to overplay this comparison by drawing on a stereotypical image of the traditional working-class community in which gregariousness is exaggerated, the fact remains that those involved in re-housing programmes frequently referred to a 'loss of community' and to the tendency of people to 'keep themselves to themselves' more than they had in the past.

As well as bringing the possibility of a more privatised lifestyle by freeing families from the need to share accommodation with others, the housing on the new estates also worked to produce more self-contained households as people were physically separated from their wider kin networks. In the extreme, home-centredness could be quite exclusive, as it was for Mr Stirling of 'Greenleigh', who stated: 'I'm only interested in my own little family. My wife and my two children – they're the people that I care about. My life down here is my home' (Young and Willmott, 1957, p. 123). Even in less absolute cases, however, the greater material comfort of the home, together with the growth of leisure time and the development of ideas of

family-centredness and companionate marriage, all worked to promote privatised lifestyles in which the home, particularly its furnishings
and upkeep, became an increasingly prominent element (Klein,
1965). This process Young and Willmott took to be one of the
diffusion of middle-class norms among the working class, with the
emphasis on sharing within marriage. As they wrote somewhat later,
but from within essentially the same perspective, 'the couple, and
their children, are very much centred on the home, especially when
the children are young. They can be so much together, and share so
much together, because they spend so much of their time together in
the same space' (Young and Willmott, 1975, p. 29). At the same
time as working-class 'embourgeoisement' was in process, improvements in domestic conditions and technology allowed those households which had previously employed servants to become more
self-contained as family units, a trend which also worked to undermine class differences in home life (Wilson, 1980).

While the modern domestic ideal was taking shape amid a general
mood of improvement, it was also becoming apparent that solving the
'housing problem' involved something more than overcoming the
absolute shortage of dwellings relative to households and the clearance of slums. By the end of the 1950s,

> it was clear that a new housing crisis was looming. In particular, much
> publicity was given to the growing problem of homelessness, the increasing
> scarcity of rented accommodation and the insecurity of tenants in London
> and other large cities. Behind the 'affluent society' still lay much private
> squalor in the housing conditions of lower-paid workers, immigrant
> groups, old people and others who had not been in a position to press their
> claims on national prosperity. (Burnett, 1986, pp. 286–7)

The housing problems of these marginalised groups were to play no
small part in the 'rediscovery of poverty' in the 1960s, but there was
already sufficient awareness of the need to consider the future
direction of housing policy for the government to appoint, in 1959, a
committee 'to consider the standards of design and equipment
applicable to family dwellings and other forms of accommodation
whether provided by local authorities or by private enterprise, and to
make recommendations' (Ministry of Housing and Local Government, 1961, p. iv). Published in 1961, the Parker–Morris Report,
Homes for Today and Tomorrow, signalled something of a new point
of departure in official thinking about housing and home life.

THE NATURALISATION OF OWNER-OCCUPIER

Against the background of the achievement of a surplus of dwellings over households and a concerted attack on slums, there appeared to be good grounds for thinking that the back of the housing problem had been broken and that the way was open for further steady improvement in the home life of the nation. Embodying the pervasive optimism of its time, the Parker–Morris Report gives the unmistakable impression that the problems of the future would be predominantly the problems of success, such as the problem of accommodating the rise in car ownership. The Report argued that in an era of prosperity it was a mistaken policy to encourage reductions in house sizes, as had taken place in the public sector in the 1950s. Thus, the Report contended: 'Homes are being built at the present time which not only are too small to provide adequately for family life but also are too small to hold the possessions in which so much of the new affluence is expressed' (Ministry of Housing and Local Government, 1961, p. 2).

What the Parker–Morris Report termed 'New Patterns of Living' arose out of high levels of house-building and the widespread ownership of consumer durables such as cars and televisions.

> All these changes are beginning to mean an easier, more varied and more enjoyable home life. Housewives now increasingly look to machinery to lighten their household tasks, and the family, and husbands in particular, now expect to help with much of the work that previously the housewife was left to do . . . These changes in the way that people want to live, the things which they own and use, and in their general level of prosperity, and perhaps also the greater informality of home life, make it timely to re-examine the kinds of homes that we ought to be building. (Ministry of Housing and Local Government, 1961, p. 2)

The Report argued that it was inappropriate to continue to build houses which social changes were making out-of-date. Rising standards since the Second World War had stimulated a growth in expectations at a rate with which new housing was failing to keep up.

In addition to recommending greater space and more adequate heating (including heating in bedrooms) to make housing more comfortable and convenient, *Homes for Today and Tomorrow* also noted the ability of occupants of new houses to resist architects' attempts to change their ways of living, citing the example of kitchens deliberately designed to be too small for people to eat their meals in which nevertheless continued to be used for this purpose. These factors, together with greater recognition of the diversity of people's needs and resources, make the Parker–Morris Report something of a milestone in the history of officially-approved housing standards. So, too, does the Report's emphasis on the tendency of people's expectations of their standard of housing to rise, with demands for quality replacing toleration of 'mere adequacy': 'An increasing proportion of people are coming to expect their home to do more than fulfil the basic requirements. It must be something of which they can be proud' (Ministry of Housing and Local Government, 1961, p. 3). A key assumption of the Report was that economic growth would continue, bringing a doubling of living standards in perhaps as short a space of time as 25 years, the additional resources allowing the further improvement of housing and home life to take place.

As the adoption of the Report's recommendations proceeded in the 1960s, several familiar problems of implementing housing improvement programmes were encountered. The most fundamental of these problems was that of cost, since the Parker–Morris specifications on dwelling size and fittings inevitably entailed greater expense. This problem was exacerbated by the imposition of expenditure ceilings on local authorities, and, as a result, the specifications became subject to a process of erosion, leading eventually to their abolition in 1981 (Malpass and Murie, 1982). In addition the Report's primary concern with dwellings' internal standards, and its highlighting of the need for variety in accommodation rather than fitting a diverse population into family-type houses, did little to discourage the growth of high-rise blocks of flats. These have subsequently proved unpopular with many tenants and been the subject of heavy criticism for the restrictions which they place on home life (Dunleavy, 1981; Coleman, 1985) but at the time they appeared to offer a solution to planners engaged in the difficult task of directing inner-city redevelopment.

The Parker–Morris Report had been concerned to consider housing from the point of view of people's requirements for a more spacious and comfortable home life, as the title of its second chapter, 'Homes for Family Needs', suggests. On the assumption of spreading affluence, people's housing needs were treated as being similar irrespective of whether they were in the public or private sector, but the issue of people's ability to pay more for housing built to higher standards continued to present problems. The predominant public perception came to be that raising housing standards universally would require substantial subsidisation of poorer households, and the association of council housing with subsidised housing grew more deeply entrenched as time went on, while the subsidisation of owner-occupiers received far less attention (Boddy, 1980; Burke, 1981). There had been a shift away from the philosophy of the later 1940s, when public housing was intended to be available for all people who preferred to rent, irrespective of their class, to the situation where from 1959 onwards local authorities were regarded as providers of housing only for those with 'special needs' such as the elderly, the poor, and those needing to be re-housed due to slum clearance (Murie, 1983). One effect of this association of the public sector with 'welfare housing' (Burke, 1981, p. 19) and dependence has been to strengthen the conceptual links between owner-occupation and independence and control.

If the 1950s was the decade in which owner-occupation was established as the most desirable housing tenure, the 1960s was the decade in which it became 'normal', politically at least if not yet statistically, and to this end further efforts were made to increase home-ownership among working-class people (Merrett with Gray, 1982). In contrast, the subsidised council house building which was entered into on a large scale was regarded as a short-term, exceptional phenomenon (Murie, 1983). By 1971 the White Paper *Fair Deal for Housing* was referring to the desire to become an owner-occupier as not only 'normal' but also something 'natural'. Home-ownership, it was suggested, 'satisfies a deep and natural desire on the part of the householder to have independent control of the house that shelters him [*sic*] and his family' (quoted in Boddy, 1980, pp. 19–20). A further White Paper, *Widening the Choice: the Next Step in Housing* (1973), put forward the claim that 'most people want to own their own home' (quoted in Boddy, 1980, p. 20), and by this stage owner-occupation was well-established as the ideal tenure type against which renting appeared problematic, even if the full thrust of the case against public housing was not to be felt until the 1980s (Cooper, 1985). The loss of support for public housing since the 1950s has been contributed to by its association with 'unpopular and high-cost forms of accommodation' (Dunleavy, 1981, p. 355), but this has only hastened the more general trend of opinion away from renting and towards what might be called the 'naturalisation' of owner-occupation.

Subsequent developments have worked to take these processes further. Whereas in the past 'a home of one's own' had been understood as not having to share accommodation with another household (Rosser and Harris, 1965), more recently the ideal has come to have a more precise sense, that of owner-occupation, and the choice and freedom from control that this is thought to bring (Saunders, 1984; Holme, 1985b; Pahl and Wallace, 1988). Getting married and 'setting up home' are taken to involve buying a house or flat, with renting or sharing property very much second-best options (Wallace, 1987; Mansfield and Collard, 1988). As the proportion of households which are owner-occupiers approaches two-thirds, houses are more literally people's 'own' than at any time previously, however much it is necessary to qualify this statement by reference to home-buyers' indebtedness or the scale of the discounts given to former council tenants exercising their 'right to buy' (Cooper, 1985).

It is not only through the expansion of owner-occupation that housing has become more literally people's 'own'. The growth in the opportunity for householders to engage in home improvement and thereby shape their physical domestic environment validates the belief that homes are what their inhabitants make them. Houses are places of work as well as of leisure (Pahl, 1984), and one of the principal forms of work undertaken in houses is the maintenance and improvement of the dwelling. Owner-occupation allows the benefits of such activity to be reaped, when for example it makes possible a move to a bigger, better house, and the significance of DIY in the domestic economy has undoubtedly grown since the period when studies gave it the status of a mere hobby (Klein, 1965).

The gradual extension over the post-war period of the precondi-tions of normal home life to the point at which they include owner-occupation can be accounted for in several ways. Clearly the naturalisation of owner-occupation has been encouraged by succes-sive governments, not least through policies which make buying 'a home of your own' the most economically rational course of action to follow for those who can afford it. In addition to making possible a greater degree of capital accumulation than is generally open to tenants, owner-occupation also ties in with other aspects of house-hold self-sufficiency (Pahl, 1984). Pahl argues further that home ownership appeals to the less tangible 'set of values concerned with homeliness, cosiness, domesticity and a belief that, if one can control just a small part of this large and threatening world, then one has achieved something worthwhile' (1984, p. 324).

In contrast to this the experience of tenants is often portrayed as being that of people subject to outside authority, at best paternalistic but at worst distant, authoritarian, and constraining (Coleman,

1985). The link between home-ownership and privatism is not a necessary one in that home-centred lifestyles are not enjoyed exclusively by owner-occupiers (Saunders and Williams, 1988), but the fact that tenants are answerable to a landlord places greater limits on their ability to achieve privatism than are faced by home-owners. The households of the 'middle mass' of society which Pahl describes as having over time grown 'more privatised, inward-looking, home-centred and autonomous' and 'consumption-oriented' (1984, pp. 319–20) are ideally home-owners.

PROGRESS AND REASSESSMENT

It is undoubtedly the case that housing conditions have improved enormously over the course of the post-war period. The observation of the 1977 Green Paper *Housing Policy* that 'We have more and better houses than ever before' (quoted in Liell, 1981, p. x) reflects no small achievement, whether what is being measured is numbers of dwellings built, types of dwellings, or some other indicator of housing improvement. It is also the case that a growing proportion of the population own their own homes, either outright or with mortgages. Inside these homes there has been a steady extension in the facilities taken to be standard, and in the domestic technology with which they are equipped. Central heating and telephones are among the more recent additions to the list of a dwelling's amenities considered normal rather than exceptional, and enjoyed by the majority of households (Allan, 1985). There appears to be a good deal of evidence to support the view (promulgated for example in the Parker–Morris Report) that home life is becoming easier. To the extent that difficulties remain, this may be interpreted as a sign of progress, confirming Bevan's view that 'the causes of housing problems are higher social standards' (quoted in Brown and Madge, 1982, p. 20). The Ministry of Housing and Local Government's 1953 prediction that 'There never will be an end to the improvements which we can make in our own homes if we are prepared to work and save for them.' (quoted in Watson with Austerberry, 1986, p. 50) is a more optimistic rephrasing of essentially the same point.

Yet the post-war record is not one of unambiguous progress in home life. In housing the size of dwellings in the public sector has fallen back from the levels of the 1940s, reductions which were not fully made good even by the adoption of Parker–Morris standards

(Short, 1982; Murie, 1983), while housing densities have at times increased, notably in the heyday of high-rise developments (Dunleavy, 1981). Private sector housing developments have also been subject to some erosion of their amenities, at least at the lower end of the market. Further, the achievement of a surplus of dwellings over households has not done away with the problem of homelessness, which has, rather, shown a tendency to increase since the 1950s (Burke, 1981). There are few signs that homeless people housed in temporary accommodation are sharing in the general improvement in domestic facilities (Watson with Austerberry, 1986; Bonnerjea and Lawton, 1987). The post-war government's objective of a decent and affordable home for all families, reiterated in the 1977 Green Paper, remains unfulfilled (Pascall, 1986, p. 133). By these indicators, post-war housing improvement has been some way short of universal.

Similarly there are grounds for re-examining more critically suggestions of general improvement in the technology with which homes are equipped and the revolution in domestic relations which was expected to accompany it. As Ungerson has noted there is a danger of being 'blinded . . . by shiny domestic technology' and overlooking the fact that 'housing generates housework' (1985, pp. 87–8), work which still has to be done. Although there are differences of opinion about the precise extent to which time spent on housework has decreased, it is clear that it is a much smaller change than is generally imagined to have followed the introduction of washing machines, vacuum cleaners and other 'labour-saving devices' (Vanek, 1980). In addition this work is still largely performed by women, even though it has become the norm for married women to engage in paid work outside the home (Pahl, 1984), a development considered by Campbell to be 'the single most significant change in the way we live' (1984, p. 40). On the evidence now available the early post-war predictions of homemaking and motherhood providing a satisfying career for women and of the home emerging as a site of growing equality between spouses through their sharing of both work and leisure appear to have been founded on questionable assumptions, although they have proved powerful influences on popular thinking.

Several things emerge when the development of home life over the post-war period is reconsidered. To begin with it is not surprising to discover that patterns of home life have turned out differently to those envisaged in the programmes of post-war reconstruction. To some extent this reflects the ambitiousness of goals such as the provision of homes with historically generous standards for all households, including those on the lowest incomes, but it also indicates a shift in perceptions about what constitutes ideal home life. Thus for example the idea of home-making representing a career for women and an alternative to their taking up paid work outside the home has progressively lost the power to convince. Even in the traditional working-class mining community studied by Dennis, Henriques and Slaughter in the 1950s there was a strong hint of dissatisfaction with women's restriction to the realm of home and family, conveyed in the comment that 'wives do not actively resent it' (1969, p. 203). Subsequent studies have shown a lower level of tolerance for the isolation and routine character of housework and child-care, as well as dissatisfaction with the loss of income that is entailed (Allan, 1985). In housing and home life as in other areas of society, post-war history is not simply an account of the failure to fulfil 'the high aspirations of 1945' (Marwick, 1982, p. 15). Although that is undoubtedly part of the story, the generation of further expectations and aspirations has also to be considered alongside it.

People's aspirations concerning their domestic lives are difficult to gauge with any accuracy, but some conclusions can be drawn from research that has been conducted. The war years undoubtedly saw an expansion of people's expectations in this area, and while the Mass Observation study *An Enquiry Into People's Homes* noted that 'most people are broadly satisfied with their homes' (1943, p. x), it also suggested extensive awareness of room for betterment. When consulted, 'large numbers of people come forward with a mass of practical, common-sense suggestions for improving the living conditions of their homes' (1943, p. ix). The satisfaction with existing conditions was clearly some way short of complete.

When it came, post-war reconstruction turned out to be double-edged, bringing not only improvement but also disappointment. Campbell's account of her personal experiences is in many ways typical of those of a whole generation:

> In 1950, my family, four of us, about to be five, living in one room, were re-housed on a new estate in a Cumbrian town. We got a house with three bedrooms, a bathroom, a separate sitting room and dining room, a kitchen big enough for a table and chairs . . . front and back garden, a coal house, inside lavatory *and* outside lavatory and wash house . . . And it was brand new . . . Happiness was an inside lavatory and built-in cupboards. Unhappiness was our cold bedrooms and condensation settling like dew . . . Our new houses were cold and uncomfortable . . . Like everything else, things were never as they seemed. (1984, p. 32, emphasis in original)

Relative to home conditions of overcrowding and inadequate facilities previously experienced, the new housing of the 1940s and 1950s can only have been an improvement for most of those who moved to it, but this did not mean that all of their expectations were met (Cornwell, 1984). The principal complaints voiced in studies conducted in the 1950s tended to relate to the 'loss of community' on the new estates more than to the housing conditions (Mogey, 1956; Young and Willmott, 1957), but both indicate that it was not found particularly easy to adjust to the new home-centred lifestyle.

Satisfaction with homes has to be understood relative to some point of comparison, the most obvious basis for comparison being between present and former homes. This simple but important observation underpins the recent argument that the favourable portrayal of high-rise living in studies such as Jephcott and Robinson's *Homes in High Flats* (1971) was bound to understate the problems with such accommodation since the tenants interviewed had moved there from Glasgow tenements little better than slums: 'Who, coming from such a harsh environment, could fail, *on the whole*, to prefer the cleaner, more spacious and more labour-saving modern flat?' (Coleman, 1985, p. 12, emphasis in original). Similarly the experience of being homeless inevitably leaves its mark on housing expectations, as Watson and Austerberry note: 'When questioned as to their ideal accommodation, women who have been living in institutions for a long time are inclined to set their sights very low' (1986, pp. 149–50). For those at the bottom of the housing market, most moves will be likely to bring some improvement.

Interestingly however Watson and Austerberry's respondents did not completely abandon more ambitious aspirations, even though there was an unbridgeable gap between these and the options realistically open to them. Holme's distinction between 'the immediate goal' and 'the distant ideal' (1985a, p. 144) is a helpful one here, since it suggests an alternative point of comparison by which satisfaction with home life can be judged, the 'ideal home'. Among Holme's young families in East London, some 'with varying degrees of pleasure, resignation or dejection, judged their present home the best they could hope for' while others 'reckoned it had everything they could want, even when set against their distant goal – their ideal home' (1985a, p. 144). People's aspirations to the domestic ideal are distinct from their more immediate expectations, but there are important links between the two, not least when rising long-term aspirations feed more short-term expectations, as has happened over the course of the post-war period.

The increase in expectations and aspirations relating to home life that has taken place since the Second World War is little short of remarkable. Housing standards are expected to be higher than those of the past, with facilities like central heating treated as 'normal', while owner-occupying households now outnumber tenants by a ratio approaching two to one. In terms of the technology with which homes are equipped, former 'luxuries' such as televisions and washing machines have become everyday items which are to be remarked upon only when they are absent. Partly in order to achieve a higher standard of living for the family, and partly in order to avoid experiencing confinement in full-time domesticity, it is now usual rather than exceptional for women to undertake paid work outside of the home. In all of these ways people's domestic situations and ideals have evolved dramatically in the short space of four decades.

There are signs that many of these changes which have worked to reshape home life, such as the expansion of owner-occupation and the growing sophistication of domestic technology, will continue. The precise course which the development of home life will take is, however, by no means easy to predict, and will depend on how certain matters, particularly those relating to power in and over the home, are resolved. Thus the changing relationships taking place in the wider society between women and men are bound to have an increasing impact on domestic organisation and domestic architecture (McDowell, 1983; Boys *et al.*, 1984; Austerberry and Watson, 1985). Similarly it is possible that control of the home may become a more prominent issue alongside the narrower question of home ownership (Campbell, 1984; Cooper, 1985). These and other issues serve to illustrate that a variety of processes are subsumed under the general term used to characterise post-war developments, 'the privatisation of home and family life' (Pahl, 1984; Saunders and Williams, 1988). The chapters that follow contain many pointers as to the shape of things to come.

Acknowledgement

I am grateful to Michael Hardey and Tony Rees for their comments on an earlier draft of this chapter.

3 Designing the Home: Domestic Architecture and Domestic Life

Marion Roberts

Modern architecture has often been criticised for not reflecting the needs and aspirations of ordinary people. These criticisms have not only come from local authority tenants but have been voiced by figures as far removed from 'ordinary' life as royalty.

It is the imagery of high-rise council housing which has come to epitomise the heartlessness of modern architecture. This is misleading since high-rise housing represented only 7 per cent of all council housing in 1981 (Dunleavy, 1981, p. 97). However the imagery is potent because it symbolises the divorce between professional, technical considerations and social realities. Dunleavy identified high-rise council housing as a 'technological fix', a ready-made solution to the problem of providing medium density housing in the inner city.

The word 'housing' itself is significant since it implies an anonymous mass, distinct from the friendly particularity of home. Yet whilst a home may be analysed separately from the notion of housing, to the person living in a house or flat the problems and pleasures which they experience are part of both home and housing. For example, the rent or mortgage might be high and might cause them financial strain as a result of government policies towards housing finance; yet they might feel great contentment and happiness with their family.

It is on this personal experience of home life which I want to focus this chapter. The reactions of a group of council tenants in the 1950s to their new council housing estate will be examined. These reactions were assessed from interviews which were carried out with a sample of tenants who had moved onto the estate when it first opened in the early 1950s. Although the estate was built before the era of high-rise housing, it would, on present day criteria, be expected to be unpopular. The estate consisted mainly of flats with no private gardens and a large amount of communal open space. Yet the

33

interviews with the tenants revealed their pride in their homes and in the estate.

The estate, which I shall call the Crescent, had been designed by the Architect's Department of the then London County Council, or LCC. (The LCC became the Greater London Council, which was abolished in 1986.) In the early 1950s the LCC Architect's Department was staffed by young progressive architects. They reinterpreted the ideals of the welfare state according to their own aesthetic system with a desire to design beautiful rented housing for all.

The architects, then, had progressive social intentions. Their interpretations of these intentions into a technical, aesthetic system had unforeseen social consequences. The type of estate which they designed looked attractive in a way which the tenants could identify with. However it reinforced the stresses and strains which women residents experienced in terms of keeping up a high standard of domestic work and child-care without appearing to expend effort in doing so. These stresses and strains manifested themselves in the social divisions perceived by the women tenants and in their own self-perceptions. These strains would have been experienced more by the wives on the estate than the husbands because of the women's responsibility for housework and child-care.

The tenants' experience of their housing was such that their self-perceptions of moving up through the social hierarchy were encouraged. However, in this process, divisions of gender were reinforced through the efforts which women had to make to maintain a beautiful home. These interactions of status and gender will be examined in the following passages.

The Crescent Estate was designed between 1950 and 1952 and built between 1952 and 1956. The first tenants started to move in from the end of 1953. Whilst the Crescent Estate is an example of modern architecture, it is not shocking or startling. It is built out of brick and there are no dwellings more than five floors above the ground. The estate was designed as 'mixed development', that is as a combination of flats, maisonettes and two-storey houses. The predominant dwelling type is flats: there are 579 flats and maisonettes and 32 houses. The site was developed at a density of 100 persons per acre and there are approximately 1800 people accommodated on the estate.

The estate was built on the edge of an area of North London which had been developed as an upper-middle class suburb in the early nineteenth century. This nineteenth century suburb, although it consisted of some four roads, was distinctive, comprising large houses with spacious gardens. The Crescent was built partly on the site of three houses which were demolished to make way for it. The road pattern of the nineteenth century development was incorporated into the 1950s scheme and existing mature trees which had been in the back gardens of the demolished houses were retained.

A minority of the dwellings on the estate have gardens. The flats are arranged mainly in five-storey 'T' shaped blocks set out at different angles to each other. None of the flats has any private outdoor space apart from a balcony. The estate is set in a rolling parkland of closely clipped lawns with shrubs, bushes and flowerbeds. Individual blocks of flats are approached from the road by winding, picturesque footpaths. The five-storey flats are entered by a communal staircase and lift at the centre of each block. These give onto open access balconies leading to each flat's front door. The three-storey blocks of flats have an internal communal staircase and internal corridors leading to front doors.

According to current design theory, such as Coleman's (1985), the estate would have been likely to have caused problems because there was a large proportion of undefined semi-public open space, a lack of private space and, for many of the dwellings, a long distance from the front door to the street. Were the Crescent to be proposed as a development today, it would be predicted to be a failure because of its design. That it was not is due, I shall argue, to the attitudes of its designers, estate managers and most importantly to its first tenants. Housing estates are considered to be successful if they are neat and orderly, inside and out; if there is an absence of dirt, litter and graffiti and if the tenants appear to be happy with their lot. In the subsequent passages it will be demonstrated that the Crescent was successful within those criteria.

I have stressed the word 'success' because although the estate was successful in that the tenants enjoyed living there, the nature of that success could be questioned. I shall suggest that in the struggle to have a beautiful home, both husbands and wives worked hard. Women however appeared to bear more of the burden since they had to combine child-care and housework with waged work and, moreover, to suppress outward signs of doing domestic work. Maintaining an attractive home enabled the tenants' perceptions of their status position to increase so that they could feel superior; but this increase was achieved at the expense of women combining three jobs.

In the same way that technical and social issues were intertwined in terms of the estate's success so were, I shall argue, categories of status and gender. It was through gender divisions that men, in having a 'nice' home, were able to rise through the status hierarchy. Women then as now play the major role in making and maintaining a home and thereby ensuring their family's status position.

THE ARCHITECTS' VIEW

The LCC Architect's Department underwent a renaissance in the 1950s. The Housing Division of the Department had attracted progressive young architects when it was formed in 1950, and many of the newly appointed staff were energetic and idealistic. They believed in Beveridge's vision of the welfare state and were excited about their part in designing for it. In 1949 the stipulation that council housing should only be provided for the working classes was removed by that year's Housing Act. Some of the younger LCC architects saw themselves as providing houses not for an inferior class of people, but for all. One man, the architect for the Crescent Estate, summed up his attitudes as follows:

> It would not be housing for the poor and it would not be housing for the underprivileged. It would simply be housing on a rental basis. And we saw it as anybody moving into those houses. And if I say that I suppose one had a middle-class idea of this it wasn't designed for the middle classes, we thought it would be nice to have privileges which maybe we had enjoyed and others hadn't which would be universally available to everyone. We saw it as a dream.[1]

Although this architect's views might be dismissed as unrealistic now, they were tenable when they were first expressed. In 1951 the majority of property (69 per cent) was rented – 52 per cent from private landlords and 17 per cent from local authorities. Only 31 per cent was owner-occupied (Murie, 1983, p. 72). At this time a municipal landlord need not have meant either having different tenancy arrangements or living in a different type of dwelling to the majority of households.

Given the social idealism of the staff in the LCC Architect's Department and their enthusiasm, it was not surprising that they should have attempted to break new ground in their design work. They were aided in this task by Council Members and the Housing Department who favoured the idea of building estates which appeared to be 'mixed communities'.

The notion that council housing estates should be modelled on the physical appearance of a rural village and, through the visual image of community, be transformed into a 'community' had been current since 1918. The first design manual for council housing, the Tudor Walters Report, was based on Garden City ideas first promoted by Ebenezer Howard (Swenarton, 1981, p. 5–26; 88–114). Raymond Unwin, who in all senses was the main architect of the Tudor Walters Report in 1918, had published his ideas on low-cost housing as early as 1901. He thought that estates should have the appearance of an organic community, a rural village. He suggested that this, together with a 'definitely organised life of mutual relations, respect or service' would ensure an harmonious unity to what would otherwise only be a collection of buildings (Parker and Unwin, 1901, pp. 92–7).

However the notion that a rural village is an ideal place to live may be questioned. Whilst an 'aesthetic blurring' may be induced by a picture of a village and the peace and repose it evokes (Davidoff, L'Esperance and Newby, 1976, p. 163), the harsh realities of rural life are concealed by this idealised image. For example Darley, in her book on model villages, explained how some agrarian landowners, to further their prestige, built large country mansions, removed existing settlements from their land and rebuilt them in a picturesque setting some distance away (Darley, 1975, pp. 2–5). The subjugation of the tenantry was such that they had no opportunity to complain about this callous behaviour. Williams has also commented on this aspect of the agrarian revolution whereby landowners manipulated the landscape to present rolling vistas from which any signs of agricultural production, such as barns, animals or farm labourers were removed (Williams, 1975, p. 129). Thus the 'natural', picturesque village with its feudal relations with the local squire was a man-made creation based on cruelty and oppression.

From Elizabethan times, there were two sorts of village, the 'open' and the 'closed'. People were free to move in and out of the open villages. Closed villages however were subject to the close control of the local landowner, aesthetically and socially. Housing conditions were generally better in closed villages and they tended to look more picturesque because of the tight control over development. Given the paternalistic manner in which council housing had been provided before the Second World War, it seems fitting that it should have been modelled on the 'closed' model village.

In their new schemes for council housing, the LCC architects jumped over the park gates, as it were. Estates were landscaped in the manner of aristocratic parks with closely clipped rolling lawns, carefully arranged views and well-disposed trees and shrubs. The architects were aided by the sites chosen – the Crescent, as has already been mentioned, was situated partly in the gardens of some nineteenth century houses. The famous Alton estates at Roehampton were set in grounds which had been landscaped by Paxton himself.

Just as in the park of the country house any suggestion of agricultural production was suppressed, in these new LCC estates visual signs of domestic production were also organised or eliminated. Great care was taken that disorderly features such as washing should be hidden from general view. Brick-built stores were provided for tenants' prams and other items. Gardens were not provided around the flat blocks because, as another LCC architect commented later, gardens 'conflict with the desire to provide public open space and to open up landscape views. The backyard kind of garden, with clothes posts and rabbit hutches is untidy by its very nature' (Cleeve Barr, 1958, pp. 36–7). On the Crescent the flat blocks were approached by winding paths, just as in landscaped parks the roads were hidden behind trees. Children's play was confined to a single play area. Washing, as on all LCC estates, was prohibited from being hung out above balcony level.

The visual metaphor of the landscaped park draws on the vocabulary of a class superior to the rural peasantry housed in the village. The architect of the Crescent Estate saw the use of this visual imagery as a product of the architects' own class backgrounds and as a desire to create a peaceful and harmonious scene.

> I think the nature of the middle classes is a sort of *nouveau* situation, which is often a pleasant one . . . if you're brought up with a garden with flowers in it, your parents liked those flowers and that garden, and there was, sort of, you know, the click of the cricket bat and the cooing of the wood pigeons and things like that. There was that sort of idea which everybody thought was so nice. Particularly, it always related to maybe Oxbridge particularly because quite a lot of those students had been to Oxbridge . . . and there were lawns with marvellous buildings set in lawns, and gardens.[2]

In designing these new post-war estates the architects were able to combine skilfully new configurations of dwellings in schemes which drew on older, more traditional forms of landscape design. Rather than transcending class, this re-ordering of old and new elements was, as is suggested above, evocative of a middle-class way of life in its visual order and harmony.

THE TENANTS' RESPONSE

This visual imagery was appreciated by the first tenants I interviewed. These interviews were conducted in 1982.[3] They were all with tenants who had moved onto the estate when it first opened and had stayed there. I took care to approach tenants from different contacts – through a community centre, a day centre and simply by knocking on doors. The interviews were semi-structured and lasted on average one and a half hours.

From a sample of 15 extended interviews only one person disliked the estate and some resorted to hyperbole in their expressions of enjoyment: 'Well, to me, there's no estate that compares with this estate.' 'You could travel the whole of London and you wouldn't find a flat like this.' Much of the pleasure which they found in the appearance of the estate came from its layout and design. In particular the quantity of greenery implied a suggestion that the estate was not a council estate, but privately owned or rented. One woman said:

> I've always had thought that this estate in its layout equates very well with a private estate. The layout of this I cannot fault.
> [*Marion:* How do you see it being like a private estate?]
> In the way that we're not all concrete are we? I mean whichever way I look out of my flat, that way I look on a square, with green and tree, that way I look on a park, that way I look on another square as you can see. Now in not many council estates can you do that.

Although only three of the tenants alluded to comparisons with a private estate, eight valued the greenery highly. One woman suggested that it had made her happy:

> This to me, the grass and the trees, and the . . . appearance of country. I don't think I would have been as happy on an estate without all the grass, all the trees, you know what I mean? . . . It really has been that advantage. In Hoxton it was just bricks and bricks . . . that isn't the reason I moved from Hoxton but I'm thinking, had I stayed there I wouldn't have been so happy with the atmosphere and the environment as I am now. Makes a lot of difference.

Of the tenants who valued the greenery, four suggested that the landscaping itself contributed to the unique character of the estate, and hence to its superiority, not only over other LCC estates, but in the whole of London: 'You couldn't ask for a better layout, with windows all around. Wherever you are you can see greenery.' 'Yes, it was, it was one of the nicest estates I've ever seen in London. It is and was, and whoever planned it, they left all the lovely trees and scenery they could and they left it there.' Three of the tenants attributed their appreciation of the Crescent to its layout. Comparisons were made with the alienating appearance of pre-war inner-city council flats:

> So really, we always say we're just proud of it around here . . . I think it's the way the estate is laid out that give people a pride in it. It must be something with how the place is being built, you get rows and rows of barrack-like blocks, I don't think people take so much pride in it.

DIVISIONS BETWEEN WOMEN

The pride of the tenants I interviewed did not rest only in the appearance of the estate. It was also vested in the tenants themselves and in the attitudes they had towards keeping up appearances. Although one woman did state tolerantly: 'We were all very nice people here, keeping the place nice', there were differences expressed between two groups of tenants. These differences did not disturb the general impression which I had formed that the tenants were decent respectable people who lived on a decent respectable estate; rather they refined it.

The division could be summarised as being between those who saw themselves as ordinary working-class people living on a nice estate and those who felt themselves to be superior, living on one of the best estates in London. These divisions were mainly defined by women; one man who I asked about it replied:

> [*Marion:* Did you think that the other people who lived on the estate, who'd moved onto it at the same time as you, were people like you?]
> Well, it's hard to say because there were lots of them that you didn't know. Took a long time to be honest, there were one or two that put on airs and graces which you'd find out afterwards was only affected. I'd say we were all more or less from the same sort of level, I would say. Just ordinary hard-working people. (*Laughs*)
> [*Marion:* The people who put on airs and graces, how did they, you know, exhibit that?]
> Well, mainly, it was second-hand conversations I had from other people. Because, you see, you'd get more from women on that than from a man. And I would only get it from my wife, talk to her or listen to her conversation with her and some other neighbour that happened to be within earshot.

WOMEN'S RESPONSIBILITIES

It was in women's responsibilities for housework, home-making and child-care that the differences between tenants were made most manifest. Stacey has categorised members of the working class into 'rough', 'ordinary' and 'respectable'. In Stacey's definition 'rough-ness' could be characterised by a failure to be 'clean and decent' and to remain within the law (Stacey, 1960, p. 153). Although two of the tenants I interviewed referred to other people urinating in the lifts and otherwise being indecent or disorderly, none of the tenants I interviewed or who were specifically referred to came in the category of 'rough'. The differences came within degrees of respectability. I shall argue, in my discussion of these divisions, that an extra burden rested on women's shoulders in maintaining appearances.

Just as in the landscaped park, 'pleasing prospects' were main-tained by the suppression of agricultural production, so on the Crescent Estate visual harmony was maintained by hiding signs of domestic work. The hanging out of washing provided an example of this kind of design and management intervention. LCC policy was not to allow the hanging out of washing above balcony rail level on estates. In response to a Council Member's question, officers had replied: 'Tenants are constantly asked not to display washing on balconies but in spite of this some clothing is hung on balconies to dry or air. Every effort is made to prevent it.' Some sections of the Architect's Department disagreed with this rule, however. Cleeve Barr, the Head of the Research Section, was later to comment:

> In the author's view flat dwellers suffer a great many restrictions as a result of not having a backyard or garden and to deny them this facility is to stress formal appearances too far. A south-facing balcony is a very sensible place for clothes-drying. How many such critics, if the scene were on the Continent, would not be delighted to take colour photographs of a picturesque scene of balconies covered with red blankets or streaming shirts. (Cleeve Barr, 1958, p. 93)

The architect who designed the Crescent agreed with the main-stream of official opinion and thought that washing hung out on balconies would spoil the appearance of the estate. It seems that some of the tenants I interviewed had similar views. One remarked: 'They allow you to hang washing out there as long as you don't have it over the balcony rail.' And her friend commented: 'We wouldn't put it up high would we? Like one or two people I noticed do now, but we wouldn't. It looks slummy, doesn't it?' The second of these speakers,

Mrs Dennis, had brought up six boys in a three-bedroomed flat with
no garden. She denied that the rule had caused her any inconveni-
ence. 'There were eight of us, when I had my children at home, and
I've always done my washing, haven't I? I've had no problems.'

By contrast, Mrs Webster, who defined herself as 'not house-
proud', had found the convention irksome. She commented:

> We got a cupboard in the kitchen where you can dry, but I've never used
> it, never. Nobody does. Turns your washing yellow. And look at the gas it
> takes. On sunny days we have them out here, on the balcony, but when we
> first moved here you wasn't supposed to do it, you know. 'Cos we were
> here for six months and I'd already got my washing hung on a Tuesday,
> hung out and they fetched three inspectors round. One of them turned
> round, he said that's not the way to dry your washing he said, you've got
> them cupboards.

Nevertheless Mrs Webster did not totally oppose the rule, in
keeping with her overall sense of respectability. She added: 'But the
only thing I don't like is hanging it out Sundays. I don't think they
should hang it out Sundays, but they do. Most of them do, so. Well,
they never used to years ago, but they do everything now, don't
they?'

Whilst Mrs Webster may have flouted convention over the issue of
washing, she had strong views on children playing. Again, making
disparaging comparison with present day practice, she remarked:
'Well, half the mothers go out to work now, don't they, leave the kids
to roam about and do anything. I was always at home when my kids
came out of school and that, and always had their dinner ready for
them.' Mrs Quick, who told me that the tenants had all been selected
for the estate and that she thought that was good, also thought that
children should not play freely outside: 'I sort of didn't let the
children play in the street, they went to Scouts and Guides and went
to Church on Sundays.' One woman regarded the control of children
as an indicator of the estate's superiority: 'This is one of the best
estates in London, I don't know if you've been to any other estate,
this is the best estate in London. We didn't have children running in
and out of the laundry.' The notion that children should not be
allowed freely outside was supported informally by the caretaker.

> 'Course the original caretaker was quite strict, he used to come with his
> little dog, and chase the children off the grass. And the dog got to know
> what his duty was and the dog would chase them off as well! It was rather
> funny 'cos the dog could run faster than the caretaker.

The strain which this restriction imposed upon different mothers varied according to their circumstances and to their desire to control who their children played with. Mrs Leary, who had six children and worked full-time, sent her children out to play unsupervised: 'They were alright. They played. And then there was the park, it's so near you know.' For other women, it was not so easy. Mrs Taylor, who had two daughters, was concerned about sexual harassment: 'The other danger is the not very nice men you get sometimes, with children. The danger that, apart from crossing the road, you get these men that are not very nice, even adults, teenagers and that.'

For one respondent, the question of child-care and play placed a heavy burden upon her. Not only was Mrs Ivel concerned with what her children were doing, but also with whom. When her children were young Mrs Ivel worked at home, part-time, for a local accountant.

> But going back to children in flats, the thing that I found very difficult to cope with was the question of children and play. Now I used to make a point of rushing around to do all my work in the morning, then in the afternoon I'd take them through to the shops . . . or else I'd take them over the park to play. So that means it puts a terrific strain on the woman that she's got to get all her work done in the morning to get her kids out of the flat in the afternoon you see. Well once they start school they want to mix with their peers you see, but I thought well, I don't really like them going out to play so I used to have kids in to play in my place because I'd rather be looking after other people's children and know that my own were alright than sending my own out to play but it came to a point where you just had to let your own children go out to play and it used to worry me, it used to worry me sick. So if I let them out to play, once every quarter of an hour, and I'm up on the third floor, I'd be rushing down to look at them, to see if they're alright . . . you were under a terrific amount of stress and strain the whole time. There's no doubt about that. No doubt about it.

The wish to supervise children's play closely was a complex combination of a desire to keep the appearance of the estate orderly and a concern for their welfare. The desire to keep up appearances also manifested itself in wanting to have a handsomely fitted out flat. The rents for the Crescent, in common with other post-war LCC properties, were high compared to other council flats and some privately rented properties. This placed a burden on tenants with earnings at, or below, the average working-class wage. Two-thirds of the women I interviewed had waged employment as well as responsibilities for housework and child-care. Whilst I did not ask them specifically why they worked, money is the most obvious reason for taking up employment.

One woman commented on how people's pride in the estate had devolved into pride in their flats.

> But I've got friends on the estate that you could go in, and you could eat your food off of their – I mean if they had that parquet, they've mostly got fitted carpets – you could eat your food off of it . . . which I think to me, just reflects the whole attitude of people when they did move in here. You know they were all so thrilled with it, they all came here with hardly any furniture, and of course over the years as the children got bigger and they got out to work so of course now they've all got lovely homes.

The LCC only provided the shell of a home, walls, bare concrete floor, kitchen fittings and sanitary appliances. The remainder – furniture, carpets, curtains and domestic appliances – had to be supplied by the tenants themselves. The furniture and fittings required to fit out a three-bedroomed flat is greater than that required for two rooms in a slum. This increased the financial pressure on tenants.

GENDER DIVISIONS

The financial pressure applied across the household, to both husbands and wives. The time at which it must have been greatest was when there were young children, as this man records:

> I used to work long hours, and see, the funny thing is, I assumed that like when I got married, that in a way your life carried on much the same. You go out and enjoy yourself, but it isn't that way, obviously, your money's got to be channelled into different areas, especially when there's children, it really puts the kibosh on it. So I sort of really had my working life, in those early days I was on night work, I used to work seven nights a week: really it was work and bed.

Whereas men's lives may have been split between home and work, women's lives were more complicated and involved juggling the competing demands of housework, looking after children or other dependants and waged employment. For Mrs Quick, this meant that she had to work part-time:

> I only ever worked part-time after I was married, first of all I didn't want to leave the children. I always wanted to be home when they came back from school, so I worked locally, yes I worked locally, and then when Mum came to live with us I didn't want to leave Mum. So it's part-time all the time.

In the 1950s the demands upon women to be 'good' wives and mothers at the expense of waged employment were greater than they are today. Consequently there was a defensiveness amongst the women I interviewed about their problems in combining their triple responsibilities. For example, Mrs Harris, who had two part-time jobs – one of which involved leaving home at 5.30 in the morning – and who, despite having a very 'domesticated' husband, did the shopping, cleaning and cooking apart from Sunday lunch which her husband cooked, said that she had 'no problems'. However she did admit that she fell asleep whenever she went to the cinema! Similarly, Mrs Leary, who had five children when she moved onto the estate and a full-time job as a cleaner on the railways, had no complaints.

The way in which these women managed was by having elaborate and well-organised household routines. Mrs Harris described her routine to me:

> Actually I had two jobs because I used to get up and do office cleaning in the morning, so I used to be up and out at 5.30 in the morning, and then I went straight on to [the second job] till about four o'clock . . .
> [*Marion:* How about shopping?]
> Well I used to do that in my lunch hour you know. Being at Park Lane I used to take a bus and go down to Edgware Road, along the, you know, Church Street Market, is it? Yes, I think it's Church Street Market and because I wasn't tied to time, as soon as I was finished, sometimes I was back for one, other times I was back, getting my teas [Mrs Harris was a tea lady in this job], I used to do all my shopping and take it home. That was no problem, really.

When she got home, Mrs Harris did a little housework every night and cooked a meal.

HOUSING, STATUS AND GENDER

Thus the tenants' perceptions of their status position was dependent on the layout and design of the estate, the management practices of the local authority and the activities of the women tenants in home-making and child-care. Each contributed to the other: the pride which the tenants felt in the layout of the estate meant that they wished to 'keep it up'; the LCC enforced, in at least one case, an orderly external appearance. The judgements which the women tenants made on each other helped to maintain their high standards of housekeeping. In this way technical and social influences were intertwined. It would be impossible to attribute the 'success' of the estate to one causal factor.

However the 'success' of the estate was hard-earned, by the women and the men. The women had to combine housework, waged work and child-care, all the while attempting to suppress any visual signs of domestic work such as washing, noisy children playing, and clutter and mess. By inference, the men had to work long hours. Thus the gain in housing standards and in increased status was not without cost in time, stress and work.

Moreover gender divisions were supported by the higher standards to which the tenants aspired. Whilst it might have been possible for role reversal on an individual basis to have been achieved, no services were offered by the council, apart from laundries, which could have lightened the burden of housework and child-care. Furthermore high rents increased the pressure on higher wage earning members of the household, that is men, to remain in waged work. It would have been difficult for households dependent on a single low wage to have afforded these council flats when they were first opened.

THEN AND NOW

On the Crescent, the most common complaints about the estate now which were made to me during the interviews were about the decline in the standards of caretaking. As one woman put it: 'But when we came here it was quite nice, we had a nice caretaker and everything. He kept the estate lovely but now it's going to rack and ruin.' Although this complaint was voiced by virtually all the tenants I interviewed, the estate did not look to be a 'problem' estate. There was a minor amount of litter and no graffiti. Another tenant commented that there was something 'missing' about the estate, that it was not as it used to be.

Further comments, some of which bordered on racism, were made about the number of black families who had moved on to the estate. During the 1950s only white households had been selected to live on the Crescent. One further change was the presence of children. With a change of caretaker, children now played on the grass and were visible and audible. The decline in caretaking services and the changing population of council tenants was not particular to the Crescent but symptomatic of more general changes in local authority housing.

Housing has changed since the 1950s in that now approximately two-thirds of households are owner-occupiers. Council housing, since the advent of the 1977 Homeless Persons Act and the 1980 Housing Act, is increasingly becoming residualised. This is because tenants who can afford to become owner-occupiers have strong financial incentives to do so, leaving local authority housing increasingly to those relying on state benefits. Since councils were given statutory responsibilities for housing certain categories of homeless people, three-quarters of all single-parent families now live in council housing. This means that the 'respectable' attitudes of the tenants housed in the 1950s are harder to maintain. Similarly a reduction in council maintenance staff and government funds to carry out essential repairs has meant that estates do not look like their private counterparts. There is no doubt that the architectural and constructional experiments of the 1960s have also damaged the image of council housing. System building, with its expanses of raw streaky concrete and its deficiencies such as condensation and dampness, has meant that its inhabitants' aspirations to upward mobility were limited from the start.

However for the households living in single-family owner-occupied houses similar stresses and strains apply as in the 1950s. Housing costs are high for many people, particularly since the boom in house prices during the late 1980s. Pressures to keep a comfortable, peaceful home are still present. There have been no interventions to relieve women's 'double burden', apart from access to a wider range of jobs. Child-care facilities have not increased and shopping has become less localised with the advent of the supermarket. As the other chapters in this book demonstrate, men are not undertaking a significantly wider range of domestic chores. Problems within domestic architecture and domestic life remain unresolved.

Notes

1. Interview with 'Beak' Adams, the job architect for the Crescent Estate, by the author on 3 July, 1984 at his office.
2. As in note 1.
3. The interviews were carried out as part of research for a PhD which was funded by the Science and Engineering Research Council.

4 The Making of Mother: The Role of the Kitchen in the Home
Jennifer Craik

INTRODUCTION: MOTHER IN THE KITCHEN

'Generally people, and women in particular, remember their childhood kitchens more clearly than any other spaces in their lives' (Greenbaum, 1981, p. 61). Memories of the kitchen are memories of gatherings around the kitchen table, of the smells of cooking, and of the sounds of chatter and laughter. Yet many kitchens today lack a central table or perpetual occupants. The kitchen is still significant but perhaps not in the way that it was. The argument of this chapter is that the kitchen may be seen as the panopticon of the modern home, as the control centre of domestic space from which all can be seen and to which all defers. It is the site and source of domestic power, and yet, like Bentham's ideal prison, it is constrained by its very internalisation and institutionalisation. The kitchen has become the double-edged sword of domesticity, at once the metaphor for family life and the sign of domestic isolation.

The kitchen has been rationalised by architects and designers into a standard set of facilities and appliances which can be arranged in a standardised choice of floor plans. These plans aim to produce an efficient 'work triangle' which minimises walking and the activities of kitchen chores. This emphasis stems from the partial application of principles of scientific management to the kitchen, the tenets of which have long been taken for granted. While those physical plans have been accepted, the social dimension of scientific management in the kitchen has been contested. Efficient design and household appliances have not reduced the amount of time spent on housework. Housewives have not acquired vast amounts of leisure time. Housework is not significantly more pleasant to do. Indeed the experience of many indicates that housewives have become more isolated and more desperate as these changes have occurred. Participation in the workforce frequently produces a multiplication of demands rather than a resolution to domestic drudgery.

There is now a considerable literature addressing these consequences with an emphasis which stresses the disenfranchisement of women from public spaces with the development of the private family home. Her role has changed from manager to servicer or caretaker, from a profession to menial drudgery. The answer is still seen to lie in her liberation from the kitchen, by escaping into the workforce and allocating chores among family members. The analysis suggested in this chapter adopts a slightly different argument. Rather than the home merely constituting the marginalisation of women the process of constructing the 'feminine' privatised domestic sphere was the lynchpin of the success of public economic life. Mary Pattison's influential book, *The Principles of Domestic Management*, published in 1915, likened the family to a 'small democratic government, and the house was the nation that it administered' (quoted by Handlin, 1973, p. 52). This Hobbesian-like metaphor emphasised the centrality of the properly-functioning family to the public sphere. The choice of the three sections in the book – Personal, Practical and Political – reflects a continuum between public and domestic life in which the housewife played the key role: 'Through the efficient care of the home the wife would develop her own sense of purpose, and at the same time the nation would rest on a firm foundation' (Handlin, 1973, p. 52).

Efficiency characterises the practical domain but the house was also the site of instilling appropriate attitudes to work, to the law and to moral virtues, such that 'better homes will give us better government and better politics better homes' (Handlin, 1973, p. 53). This political dimension is an important aspect of these developments which is frequently overlooked in studies of housework that emphasise the rhetoric of housework alone.

The importance of the social and political power of the home ran through many of the early household manuals and not just those of utopian feminists (Hayden, 1981) but the most successful manuals in terms of sales and reprints were the most conservative ones, of which Isabella Beeton's is perhaps the best known. These manuals concentrated on recipes and etiquette gradually eliminating the concern with managerial aspects and the reform of appliances.[1] During this period women were entering the workforce in increasingly large numbers producing a range of effects including contact with new ideas, the development of a specific group of consumers, and less time for housework.

Calls for the reform of housework have persisted through this century, albeit from varying perspectives, but all have stressed the reclassification of housework from managerial skills to menial chores, a shift that has eroded the social and political power of the home from an active to a symbolic role. It has meant a significant loss of power for women in the home. While they mostly still do the bulk of housework, they have lost the professional management component. The illusion of mother's parole has disguised the construction of her panopticon.

The idea of a panopticon involves both the exercise of power from the all-seeing vantage point of the kitchen as well as the assumption of duties and directions as occupant of that position. Shifts in the specialisation of the kitchen as domestic space along with changes in attitudes towards, and activities of, women during this century have decreased the power and increased the duties of the housewife or home-maker. Unwittingly freedoms for women in the workforce and public space, as well as consumerism, have contributed to the decline of domestic power. The kitchen is still the powerhouse of the modern home but its forms of power and the sites over which it is exercised have varied. The role of the housewife in the kitchen has become redolent with ambivalence and the hollow exercise of power.

THE DEVELOPMENT OF THE KITCHEN

'It can never be said that the atmosphere of a kitchen is an element in which a refined and intellectual woman ought to live; though the department itself is one which no sensible woman would think it a degradation to overlook' (Mrs Ellis, *Wives of England*, cited by Oakley, 1976, p. 52.) The kitchen has always been the site of controversy because it is able to articulate household functions and relationships within the home and beyond. Mrs Ellis's ideal of the separation of a lady from the kitchen was eroded with the emergence of Victorian notions of hygiene and order. The lady of the house became the mistress, manager and housewife as the nineteenth century progressed. These social changes were reflected in the physical relocation and redesign of the kitchen. Mrs Beeton saw these changes in terms of efficiency and management, giving the following guidelines for a well-designed kitchen:

1. Convenience of distribution in its parts, with largeness of dimension.
2. Excellence of light, height of ceiling, and good ventilation. 3. Easiness

of access, without passing through the house. 4. Sufficiently remote from the primary apartments of the house, that the members, visitors or guests of the family, may not perceive the odour incident to cooking, or hear the noise of culinary operations. 5. Plenty of fuel and water, which with the scullery, pantry and storeroom, should be so near it, as to offer the smallest possible trouble in reaching them. (Beeton, 1861, p. 25)

Here kitchen functions are seen as separate from the house and its activities. This ideal was best achieved by the differentiation of household tasks and persons to perform them, with the mistress of the house occupying a supervisory role, which Mrs Beeton compared to the commander of an army (Beeton, 1861, p. 1), and within a large household, hierarchical supervision among the staff: 'Running the house was broken down into minutely specified spheres of action: cook cleans back passage and steps, housemaid cleans front steps, hall and landing only, parlour maid is responsible for dining room and drawing room' (Davidoff, 1976, p. 136). The size of the house and household determined the number of staff and degree of specialisation of duties. This however functioned as an ideal. In practice duties frequently overlapped, especially as the availability of staff declined. Moreover the mistress herself probably did more work than she admitted (Davidoff, 1976, p. 139).

The decline in domestic labour was not simply due to competing sources of employment. The 'servant problem' also referred to the domestic politics that arose from having strangers living in the house – affairs and unwanted pregnancies were common between male owners and female staff. At the time when women were increasingly defining their role as mistress of the house, along with economic pressures and the tendency towards new, smaller houses, the mainte-nance of strictly professional and hierarchical relations within house-holds seems to have become very strained. This was especially so when the staff was reduced to one maid. Handlin has argued that emerging concepts of domestic efficiency and household appliances conveniently solved many a housewife's dilemma.

Servants rarely wore a uniform, the outward sign of rank, and awkward attempts to treat 'Bridget' as a member of the family were often made. Despite these gestures of equality, the relationship was always full of friction, so the efficient care of the home provided a welcomed solution to this perplexing dilemma. (Handlin, 1973, p. 51)

This trend had several impacts. First, the housewife became not only mistress of the household, but of all its productive activities. These extra responsibilities solved the problem of potentially disruptive outsiders in the home but created considerable duties for the mistress. Technological developments, household manuals, magazine advice, and advertising campaigns were therefore readily devoured in order to come to terms with this new state of affairs[2]. Some of the more arduous duties were handled by day staff who came in to cook, clean and tidy. This provided work for poorer women yet enabled them to run homes of their own, which live-in employment had not. This contact ensured that the homes of employers became ideal 'models' of domesticity to which working women aspired and approximated in their own homes. This process may have contributed significantly to the growth of the idea of the 'mass market' and of women as a specialised, uniform consumer group.

By the 1920s the modern kitchen had emerged. Its features were praised in terms of Taylorist principles of scientific management whereby the management of the house and the production of its services were seen akin to factory work, the object of rational principles and technological developments (Handlin, 1973)[3]. As such, the housewife was cast as a 'professional' who needed specialist skills and working conditions:

> The kitchen was the centre of the 'professional' housewife's world, replacing the parlour as the focus of domestic guides and women's magazines. They variously described it as 'laboratory clean', 'tightly constructed' like a ship's galley, and 'rationally planned', comparing its organisation to that of an army barracks or a hospital. (Wright, 1975, p. 4).

This professionalisation of the housewife was part of a wider philosophy about her role as the powerhouse of the economy in which families were seen as the building blocks of the nation.

TECHNOLOGY AND DOMESTICITY

The specialisation of the kitchen has also been related to technological developments in the form of 'labour-saving' devices for housework. Yet it is now well documented that new devices have not reduced the amount of time spent on housework but have merely re-allocated duties elsewhere and created new tasks (Ravetz, 1965; Handlin, 1973; Wright, 1975; Davidoff, 1976; Oakley, 1976; Bose, 1979; Allport, 1983; R. Cowan, 1985). Ruth Cowan has compared studies which show that time spent on housework (around 60 hours per week) has in fact increased, irrespective of class. Indeed, the greater the access to labour-saving technology, the more hours spent on housework (R. Cowan, 1985, pp. 190–1). The only factor significantly to reduce the time spent on housework is a woman's involvement in the workforce, though generally this means that she still does the same jobs but in less time.

Various authors have examined technology in terms of the rhetoric with which it has been promoted, incorporating additional roles for the housewife: as aids to child-rearing and as the objects of consumerism. Attention to these duties coincided with the 'dirt war' when the purification of the home environment became all important as the guarantor of social purity. This war on dirt came to concern order: 'nineteenth-century cleanliness really had more to do with tidying and polishing – sparkling glasses, gleaming silver, brass, copper and polished wood – than our notions of dirt control. Tidiness was seen to be as much a moral as a physical attribute' (Davidoff, 1976, p. 129). Consequently 'housework' came to include moral and social techniques and trainings as much as housework itself. Given the multiplication of tasks, attention turned to reducing physical labour. Because increasing amounts of time were devoted to home maintenance housewives welcomed inventions such as the icebox (and later electric refrigerator), the steam iron, the gas (then electric) cooker, vacuum cleaners, electricity and electric gadgets, and washing machines. Although designed and promoted around notions of efficiency, other factors determined their marketability, such as the interests of manufacturers and the advertising strategies of promotion.

Equally, the new technology was sold in terms of the housewife's ideal of femininity in which the appliance became the sign of, and a means to, perfect family life. Yet as Murcott (1983) has observed, the concept of housewife and house-management gradually narrowed to the role of 'wife' and 'mother', which was metaphorically signalled by the practice of *cooking*. Beeton's dominant attention to cooking was perhaps a forerunner of this. Irrespective of who actually occupies the role of cook, the activity is still denoted as the primary element of house-making. 'Being cook is presented as being wife and mother, the main components of housewife – in a cookbook for the 'liberated' and another for men as much as any other' (Murcott, 1983, p. 35) Murcott suggests that Beeton's 1861 morality persists in cookbook emphases on cooking as work, on knowing the right techniques, on economy and labour-saving, and on the Protestant Ethic (a term which is constantly evoked in the cookbooks which Murcott studied). Cooking has become the over-arching sign of the home: 'technology

has to be seen as altering nothing . . . The homeworker is worse off –
but she is still the cook and still bound to the machines in the kitchen'
(Murcott, 1983, p. 37). The centrality of cooking is reflected in the
idea of the work triangle as the organising principle of kitchen space,
that is, around the preparation of food (see, for example, Gilbreth,
1930).

This century has witnessed the consoldiation of the kitchen into a
pivotal role in the house linking with other living spaces (by half walls
or open plan) and with direct views of other areas. While that shift
has usually been related to technological and social changes, at least
one commentator has linked it to the development of suffrage and
democratic forms of political activity. The following description
characterises an historic Sydney house in terms of such shifts:

> The plan of 'Purulia' is the plan of a maidless flat . . . Maids, the mistress
> said, were vanishing . . . now the kitchen is the most used and, commonly,
> the least pleasant room in a house . . . the kitchen becomes more and more
> a family room and the seat of universal chores.
>
> A study of the history of the kitchen . . . throws clear light on the
> progress of humanity towards equality . . . Briefly told, the kitchen began
> its advance from beneath a detached roof at the rear of the house. First it
> entered a wing facing a courtyard; then it moved slowly along the wing side
> by side with the struggle for political freedom. By the time all men were
> equal at the poll the kitchen was separated from the parlour only by a
> narrow servery.
>
> At 'Purulia' the kitchen adjoins the living room and the front door.
> There is nothing to distinguish it from other rooms save the utensils of its
> usefulness. It is, perhaps, the pleasantest room of the house for it is where
> the most useful work is done. Yet the sight of this kitchen does not incline
> me to think that equality is any nearer. I believe equality is an illusion.
> (Hardy Wilson, 1919, p. 15)

THE SPATIAL POLITICS OF THE KITCHEN

Changes in the role of the kitchen during this century relate to several
factors including women's involvement in the workforce, notions of
scientific management, efficiency and cleanliness, the changing constitution of families and households, and the growth of a consumer-
based society. From the 1900s to the 1930s the kitchen remained a
large room that dominated domestic life despite gradually being
augmented by domestic appliances: 'The home was to be the bastion
of family life, the kitchen its command centre, and the woman its
sergeant. The large wooden table remained literally at the centre of

women's activities.' (Greenbaum, 1981, p. 59). As the kitchen became more specialised, however, its functions and social role became
more isolated, with the trend towards the 'cooking kitchen' that
banished other activities to other places, including general socialising
and family activities[4]. As the kitchen was redefined as an area for the
preparation of food, it could be built 'much smaller than was formerly
the case when it was used as a combined sitting-room, laundry and
general workshop' (Greenbaum, 1981, p. 61).

Kitchen duties were articulated in terms of management principles
as well as in terms of the image of the housewife, an emergent
category associated with consumerism. Women were to be taught the
techniques of home management. Advice emphasised correct ways of
doing things as well as self-improvement, hygiene and professionalism in household tasks. The coming of electricity was regarded as the
ultimate answer to housework, facilitating the use of labour-saving
appliances in order to concentrate on management, child-rearing,
friends and shopping. These ideals were advocated everywhere; for
example, in a 1935 competition by *Architectural Forum* to design
'The House of Modern Living' for the mythical 'Bliss' family:

> In all the published schemes the kitchen was designed as a separate space
> closed off from the rest of the house. The designers seem to have made the
> assumption that Mrs Bliss would work in isolation. In the grand prize
> winner's solution, there was a laundry and a small planning desk incorpo-
> rated into the kitchen, reinforcing the idea of the housewife as the 'captain'
> of the domestic ship. (Barkin, 1981, p. 62)

The emphasis on training women to become competent and
efficient housewives was underscored by the centrality of domestic
economics and domestic science courses in the education of women in
which the goal was the achievement of satisfaction through caring and
managing. Thus earlier notions of household management shrank
from a concern with negotiating the space between family and public
life to centring on the 'inner glow' of being wanted within the home.
That re-definition of the professionalism of housework was reinforced by the trend towards smaller kitchens with mass produced
'efficient' units. The kitchen became synonymous with efficient food
preparation in a 'work-saving "U"- or "L"-shape, complete with
built-in cabinets and, possibly, just possibly, a few extra feet for a
small dinette table' (Greenbaum, 1981, p. 60).

The kitchen became the main focus of labour-saving principles, as
celebrated in Lilian Gilbreth's seminal article showing how to reduce
the work in making a cake from 50 to 24 steps by the imposition of a

'work circle' to reduce the amount of walking (Gilbreth, 1930; Denby, 1941). The activity of eating was banished to the formal dining room although informal snacks were possible in the new mini-kitchen.

This idea of the kitchen was consolidated in the 1940s and 1950s aided by the impact of Hollywood images of domesticity and by the post-war encouragement for women to return to their homes:

> Plans for the new post-war (1944) kitchen most captured the imagination of women. Billed as 'the modern American kitchen', it appeared in women's magazines, in literature of the gas and electricity companies, on countless newsreels and in publicity designed to excite and inspire women for their post-war role. (Allport, 1983, p. 68)

The new kitchen emphasised efficiency and modernity, two prime signs of 'the modern woman' who was taken as epitomising the post-war world. The design of such kitchens emphasised labour-saving organisation of space and use of appliances, as well as standardising the essential furniture and fittings of this re-conceptualised domestic space through mass production. Allport characterises the Australian Commonwealth Housing Commission's standards for the post-war kitchen as follows:

> The modern kitchen aimed to release the housewife from the uninteresting routine of domestic work by making the home more convenient to run and easing the preparation of meals. It envisaged a sink, stove, refrigerator and cupboards all built into one fitting so that the housewife could move from one appliance to another with a minimum of steps. Ovens and washtroughs were raised to a height sufficient to eliminate frequent back-breaking bending, and unnecessary walking would be saved by built-in dining alcoves for informal family meals. (Allport 1983, p. 68)

The impact of the specialisation of domestic spaces and duties meant that women could be very isolated in their dream home, a situation that was acknowledged in some ideal home schemes:

> . . . workers and children have a surfeit of communal life during the day. Not so the woman. While, therefore, the living room should face west or south on to garden or balcony, with the utmost obtainable privacy from being overlooked or overheard by others, the kitchen, the workshop, should look onto the street, so that the woman can join, however indirectly, in the life of the neighbourhood. In the afternoon, if the home has been well arranged and equipped, she will have time and energy to meet her friends and join in some communal activities. (Denby, 1941, p. 23)

This advice has not been followed. Almost without exception, kitchens are located at the back of the house, although they now look on to a landscaped back garden. In other ways however the isolation of the kitchen has been resisted by physically remodelling the kitchen to increase its size and, by taking down walls, to link with other spaces: 'An entity called the "island", long the darling of home design magazines, came of age. The centre of gravity shifted. People no longer sat around the kitchen table; they stood around the island or peninsula counter' (Greenbaum, 1981, p. 61).

These changes have re-populated the kitchen away from mother's fierce control to variable occupants with diverse purposes and rights. In many respects the last bastion of the housewife's control has been lost through these changes and though this may accord with the involvement of women outside the home there is still a lingering desire for the perfect kitchen as the lynchpin of the home. As an analyst of women's writing noted, women

> seem inevitably to exist in the 'private sphere' – the home. It is ironic since many women left home for a new country (America) and worked outside the home. They all seem to have a dream for a better life that is translated into a physical space: a white kitchen, a new bedroom set, a living room for company. (Bauer Maglin, 1981, p. 43)

In short the kitchen has become the metaphor for family life, not just in terms of specialised function but in terms of articulating domestic patterns in general. The kitchen is now a specialised room for food preparation as well as the key social space in a house. As such it is designed to organise and integrate with other spaces in the home and with other occupants. The social usage of the house has involved a two-way process of influence: the house is normalised by the family, while the family is normalised by the house (MacArthur, 1984). Aspects of family life influence the house through the availability and terms of mortgages which include the pressure to keep the house saleable, as well as forms of home improvement, some of which increase re-sale value – though individual eccentricities in taste have to be moderated in the light of re-sale potential. For example an ensuite bathroom increases the value of a house, but not a bidet; a jacuzzi does but not a swimming pool; light fittings but not a wallpaper feature; colonial restoration – cast iron, lattice, opened verandahs – but not 'Greek' modernisations – stucco, columns, arches. The house becomes a sign of family life which is spelt out in decisions concerning its design, usage, interior decor and renovations.

On the other hand, the house imposes possibilities and constraints upon its occupants through economic factors and patterns of home-ownership. Factors like the size and location of a house, size of garden, detached or not, etc., are all directly associated with economic status and credit worthiness. It reflects conditions of ownership (owner-occupier, rental or capital-gain), patterns of marriage and divorce, and practices of child-rearing. The house thus constructs the parameters of family behaviour: through provision of space and access, economic imperatives enjoin moral conventions.

Key to these patterns of usage is the role of the kitchen, less as the physical site of social activity than as the structural framework in which relationships with other spaces are determined. By the physical arrangements and stylistic decor the 'essence' of family life is articulated in a set of choices, priorities, activities and taste. It is in this sense that the kitchen works as a metaphor.

STYLING THE MODERN HOME

The modern kitchen relies as much on its style as it does on its appliances. The creation of interior design has become an obsession with home-buyers, home-makers and decorators, making important the way in which the 'everydayness' of a house is articulated through the choice of furniture and furnishings as well as the choreography of their arrangement (Hess, 1981, p. 30). Interior design and decor aims to reduce the isolation of the home-maker and to articulate the characteristics of a particular family life by combining function with style. This is made explicit in advice for home renovators:

> Your first step in your quest for a better kitchen is a search for style. . . . First impressions of kitchens and the way you recall them later are usually colour-related. . . . But remember that efficiency is paramount in the kitchen and never let the style override the need for order, speed and ease. (*Better Homes and Gardens*, 1987, p. 9)

Even the achievement of an ergonomically-sound, energy-efficient kitchen is the outcome of family life: 'Analyse your domestic life and the way you feel a kitchen should be used. Achieving the perfect kitchen depends on recognising and responding to your own family's priorities.' The kitchen should be based on a 'work triangle' between food storage, the sink and the stove, ideally following 'the sequence of food preparation from one appliance to another' (*Better Homes and Gardens*, 1987, p. 20). As indicated earlier these can be organised in a U-shape, L-shape, galley, single line or island, as determined by the basic shape of the kitchen, by passageways and adjoining rooms, and with the aim of minimising walking. Other key considerations include the choice of 'labour-saving appliances', the opening direction of refrigerator and oven doors, the location of small electrical appliances, and the choice of flooring and benchtops. As already suggested, the functional fittings of the kitchen have been standardised while the overall design trend has been towards open plan which 'facilitates the activities of a bustling household and has a streamlined appeal that always looks good'. The aim is to 'ensure an easy flow between kitchen, living and dining areas and the garden beyond' (*Better Homes and Gardens*, 1987, p. 24).

Function and lifestyle come together in the creation of a 'mood' for the kitchen, created by choice of finishes, colours, bric-a-brac, furniture and furnishings. The kitchen constitutes 'a psychological focal point of family life as well as a physical one' (T. Cowan, 1985, p. 10). Kitchen 'styles' include farm nostalgia, colonial, minimalist, traditional, contemporary minimalism, *trompe l'oeil*, Japanese, *primitif*, and high-tech (T. Cowan, 1985, pp. 103–4). The selection of a style is intended to 'create the atmosphere that will help to raise hopes and aspirations beyond the kitchen' (T. Cowan, 1985, p. 105), thus the kitchen is seen as reflecting and shaping the specifics of family life.

Such decorating styles tend to fall into four broad categories – modern, traditional, oriental, country – denoting, respectively, adventure and ambition; family, ritual, security; simplicity, sophistication, aestheticism; homespun qualities, the natural (Murdoch, 1986, p. 90). Such styles combine the 'reflection' of personality with the 'projection' of a public image. These tend to play on nostalgia for past periods, project future utopias or construct an ideal image of family life. Style and fashion overdetermine use and tradition. Interior design has replaced household management as the focus of domestic ideology.

Central to changes in domestic organisation has been the idea of personality or character that has accompanied the birth of individuality and the training of social persons. This has ted into patterns of usage and ways of denoting that usage, in terms of what is now called 'interior design'. Rooms have become more numerous and more specialised. Their decoration and organisation has been allotted to the woman of the house. Her tastes are especially evident in the layout and decor of the kitchen; father's vision is largely confined to the decor of his (*sic*) den or study. The living room makes a more formal statement about the family unit. The dining room either reiterates that formality or reflects an image of entertaining, often incorporated with a family room, a space of multiple forms for 'actual' day-to-day living. With any luck, the children can be contained away from these signs of family life in a TV or games room. The bedroom has also become the site of concerted stylistic endeavours. Since the 1950s each child ideally has her/his own bedroom, decorated to denote her/his interests, passions and temperament. Parents share a bedroom decorated according to the woman's choice. This is most clearly evident in the choice of soft furnishings – curtains, bedding and lighting. As one article offering an explanation of different decorating styles put it:

> You may prefer different colours in different rooms of your home, which may reflect the fact that you see yourself differently according to what each room symbolises in your life. The living room and dining room, for most women, represent how they want to be seen publicly, so the colours you choose for those rooms presumably reflect how you want others to perceive you. The colour you have in your bathroom reflects your romantic and sexual dispostion. The bathroom symbolises how you feel about your body. (Murdoch, 1986, p. 91)

Another trend which reflects changes in family life can be seen in the development of the bathroom, which has involved a move from outdoors to indoors as the idea of the bathroom as a specialised room has developed. Early housing had an outside toilet and a movable tub for bathing. This was later attached to a shed or scullery, often a laundry as well. Baths on legs and crude showers developed. Crudity was the keyword. Ablutions were an unfortunate necessity. Things have changed. Now the bathroom is to be enjoyed. It is the site of democratic access and for the enjoyment of each occupant. Privacy is central. This accounts for the fashion for en suite bathrooms for the parents, providing a special measure of privacy and often special glamour decor – a 'reward' for their parental duties.

Bathrooms exhibit a growing number of facilities from the basic toilet, washbasin, shower, bath to bidets, jacuzzis, spas, etc. A special decor and design has developed to accompany sunken or raised features: slate flooring, wooden panelling, 'feature' tiles, bathroom furnishings. Exoticism is currently emphasised and it is reinforced by the 'vegetation' of the bathroom. Once anathema to notions of hygiene, it is now almost mandatory to fill the bathroom with plants, as exotic as possible: 'ideal' bathrroms open onto a special courtyard of *tropicana exotica*. The bathroom has become the site for the indulgence of private pleasures and for exorcising those obsessions with the body.

THE MAKING OF MOTHER

These trends index the changing role of the housewife from professional manager to caretaker, responsible for overseeing and regulating this diversity and fluidity. Housewives have lost the domestics, the daughters and other relatives to help in the tasks of providing meals, washing clothes and cleaning the house. But they are still primarily responsible for carrying out such duties or seeing that they are done. By constructing the kitchen as the panopticon of the modern home a housewife can fulfil these duties while overseeing everyone else. To this end the kitchen is located centrally with views and access both inside and out:

> A mother could watch her children outside through the picture window or inside, with the popular open-floor plan. This visibility was based on a new premise of zoned planning in the home. The 'activity area' of living room, dining area, and kitchen had few walls, providing as much space and togetherness as possible. (Wright, 1981, p. 254)

The use of so-called kitchen or 'cafe' curtains underlines this role, restricting vision at the top and bottom of the window, thereby focusing the field of vision on a structured glimpse of the world outside. This world of work has its pleasures, for example in the placement of a television set in the kitchen:

> The television has invaded the kitchen. . . . Judging from the percentage of commercials that are about food, drink, nutrition, cleansers, shiny floors, and spotless glasses, a visitor from a strange planet might draw the conclusion that television was invented for the kitchen! (T. Cowan, 1985, p. 86)[5]

Even the garden reflects the reconsituted role of mother. In Australia the idea of the garden has shifted away from the ordered, sparse English-style garden of European shrubs and flowers, which functions *to be* visible, as an index of the formal house, and towards a secret garden filled with native and exotic plants, studded with annuals of mother's choice, and landscaped with water and garden features – and all visible from the kitchen. A bushland is created as controlled disorder, variety, surprise; like wisteria, wandering everywhere but ultimately bounded by the garden fence. For mother, it functions as the metaphor of her secret life.

CONCLUSION

This chapter has argued that the place of the kitchen in domestic architecture has changed from reflecting the public status of the family by signs of formality to making visible and institutionalising the dominant role of women in family life. But even here it has changed from reflecting significant managerial power for women and become just a sign of motherhood and femininity. The house has become redolent with 'feminine' characteristics and forms of organisation. Women are constructed as the primary do-ers in family life for which they may organise the 'look' of their domestic space. Such minutiae have become the nub of domestic decision-making such that these details of theme, style and lifestyle organise the family agenda.

Interestingly these changes have been represented by architects as merely providing greater privacy for the family, by shielding it from the street, etc. Yet 'housebound' women have been effectively cut off from the outside world by architectural designs which locate the woman in the kitchen at the back of the house so that her whole life is oriented around the kitchen. The consolation prize for this enforced solitude is her choice of interior decor and the provision of 'views' from the kitchen – styled interiors and landscaped exteriors.

To participate in the outside world, mother must leave this sanctuary, usually by car, and travel to where 'public' life occurs, often to the shops, now elevated to large-scale shopping centres and shopping towns which provide another contained environment plus special events for mother. Other frequent activities include sport, aerobics, trips to the school to drop off/pick up children, and having coffee with other 'girls'. In short there is a radical split between the lives of women as the centre (pivot) of home life and as the periphery (margin) of social (outside) life. Domestic life is repeatedly defined in terms of social spaces, patterns of access and codes of behaviour. Women have become the apparent winners in this trend if measured in terms of their visibility inside the house. The reality of women's lot within the house has increasingly and insistently become one of multiple, simultaneous demands. These conflicts are exacerbated by involvement in the workforce since work and home involve contradictory statuses and demands.

Traditionally, in terms of domestic 'power', women in the home have considerable clout to determine household decisions including routines, furniture and furnishings, consumer patterns and financial allocations, as well as often near total responsibility for child rearing. Many of these areas of decision-making are no longer the sole province of women. On the other hand men frequently perform many tasks which are often not recognised as housekeeping activities, such as painting, home maintenance, gardening, lawn-mowing, renovations, and car maintenance. While not everyday 'drudgery', these activities entail considerable skills and energies. Yet little attention is paid to men's activities around the house. It is a limited set of kitchen-oriented tasks which conventionally make up definitions of 'housework' and domestic power. Women have come to define themselves in terms of their home environments and household tasks at least as strongly as external criteria, such as employment. Thus a recent article entitled 'How to get your man to help in the house' advised that the first step was to give up control of the house and 'to accept another person's standards. . . . You may think that would be okay with you – but most women identify with their homes and don't find it easy to relinquish their control' (Lee, 1988, p. 125). It suggested that women 'think that doing household tasks is the way to show love. [Women] volunteer their own servitude' (1988, p. 125). It is this construction of domestic space as a self-contained powerhouse that is at the base of domestic politics.

Moreover much of what has been made visible about the home has been from the vantage point of those not within the assumed tradition of family life – feminists, widows, widowers, bachelors (male and female), single-parent families, shared houses, etc. *Actual* household demographics and therefore usage mean that the ideals of 'Mum', 'Dad' and 'family' are often irrelevant. It is the constant *promotion* of such ideals that needs to be displaced rather than the actualities of household usage.

In short, household management as a powerful 'profession' has become a set of chores that anyone can do, but against a backdrop that promotes the ideal of mother in her domestic bliss. It is this distinction that needs to be addressed since it is this illusion that produces the rhetoric of domesticity and threatens to consume actual occupants of the home. As one woman remarked: 'I *love* this house, but I think of it as my beautiful prison.' Like Cinderella's coach, mother's panopticon is in constant danger of turning into a pumpkin.

Notes

1. Ravetz argues that Beeton was highly selective in her use of material from Webster's *Encyclopedia*, devoting 90 per cent of her book to recipes and menus at the expense of material concerned with its supposed subject of 'household management' (1968, p. 446).

2. An important aspect of this argument is the recognition of different cultural inflections in the development of the kitchen as an index of political and social forces in different countries. For example the British context needs to be read in terms of the Victorian age, in particular the aspiration towards middle-class respectability denoted by possessions, efficiency, cleanliness and leisure (Beeton, 1861; Davidoff, 1976; Darrow, 1979). In the pursuit of these ideals, manuals constituted guidebooks which were desperately needed and sought in order to come to terms with new social situations and political change. In contrast, manuals in France played a part in very quick transformations that accompanied post-revolutionary conditions. Darrow (1979, p. 42) argues that women consciously and actively adopted roles of domesticity to assist in constructing new forms of lobbying power through family status and trainings. These entailed moral, political and class reasons that were explicitly tied to the new French state. In America the role of the home and of housewives was crucial to the establishment of self-sustaining societies that suited the pioneering, frontier conditions but connected with European homelands. The notion of home in America stressed efficiency over the British concern with respectability, while acting as a catalyst of national purpose and unity. In this context revolutionary manuals played an important role. The German uptake of American ideas adapted those principles of scientific management to socialist programmes of women's and architectural reforms.

3. The re-design of the kitchen varied with the form of the house, a factor determined by class and available housing stock. Working-class houses frequently had no kitchen – perhaps only a fire downstairs in the scullery or out the back. Some houses had an open grate which functioned as a cooking fire and source of heat generally. Despite such variations a shift towards a specialised kitchen (or area) can be noted along with a set of specialised functions denoted as kitchen tasks. The research for this chapter derived from a study of the Queenslander, a form of housing typical of Northern Australia until the 1930s. This wooden house on stilts features a verandah (at least eight foot wide) on at least one side; on more expensive houses the verandah extended all round. Changes in the location and function of the kitchen are particularly clear in such houses, and many of the points made here relate to that architecture and social context.

4. Bullock (n.d.) on the development of the kitchen in Germany.

5. Even so, the location of a television set in the kitchen was a contentious issue in the 1950s. Indeed Spigel argues that there was a taboo on women watching television, stemming from its perceived role

as a distraction from housework that would threaten 'to reveal her most slovenly housekeeping to the observer' (1986, p. 13). Symptomatically furniture associated with the television, especially chairs for viewing (that is, reclining easy chairs), were designed for men and children; women feature in advertisements as actively assisting 'in the viewing comforts of others' (Spigel, 1986, p. 11) and usually doing domestic chores while watching.

5 Gender and the Construction of Home Life
Pauline Hunt

In England for cultural, and possibly climatic, reasons most inter-personal relationships take place behind closed doors. Domestic life is not readily available for investigation. What really goes on in most people's homes remains a mystery, an intriguing and frustrating mystery:

> There is hardly a garden in England which is not surrounded by wall or hedge or railing, the obscurer the better . . . There is hardly a window in any family house which is not curtained effectively to obscure the view of the inquisitive passer-by. And as a consequence there is no play or book or film so successful as that which deals with the intimacies of family life, which, except in one family – his or her own – are a complete mystery to the ordinary man or woman. (Spring Rice, 1981, p. 16)

As a consequence the would-be investigator is at a loss even to devise pertinent questions. Some years ago in an attempt to grapple with this situation I supplied five professional middle-class house-holds and five manual working-class households with instimatic cameras. I requested them to photograph aspects of their home environment that they particularly valued. The first round of inter-views were based on these photographs, which had the merit that the subjects of the research formulated the initial agenda. They, not I, decided the topics of conversation. At a later stage I took some photographs myself and conducted interviews along more systematic and orthodox lines. Much of what follows draws on the experiences of these ten households.

GENDER EXPECTATIONS AND CORE-CONCERNS

Men and women confront different social expectations and realities in the performance of their role as husband or wife. It is still the prevailing expectation that men will provide the main financial contribution to their family; and in practice this expectation becomes a moral requirement that the individual man may experience painfully if circumstances, such as unemployment, prevent its fulfilment. Furthermore his self-definition and conception are usually directly related to his occupation and to his ability to provide financial support to his family.

Social expectations for married women, especially mothers, centre on their domestic contribution. They are expected to exercise home-making skills and nurture their young. Husbands may well 'help' with this, but the main responsibility resides with the person being helped. Furthermore even when her financial contribution equals, surpasses or replaces that of her husband, her self-definition and conception usually remain anchored in her domestic role.

This different social perspective for men and women permeates domestic practice. Several men in my enquiry worked regularly in the garden. They did so by choice. The separation of their socially obligatory work from their domestic life had the effect of highlighting the home as an arena of freedom wherein work is transformed into play. By this token Oakley may be more justified than Edgell (1980, pp. 10–11) thinks in excluding male-associated tasks, such as household repairs and gardening, from her definition of housework.

Since the man's obligatory work takes place elsewhere, much of the work he does in the home expresses his preferences. This is the social basis of the observation made by Barbara Pym through the thoughts of Miss Lathbury in *Excellent Women*:

> Surely wives shouldn't be too busy to cook for their husbands? I thought in astonishment . . . But perhaps Rockingham with his love of Victoriana also enjoyed cooking, for I had observed that men did not usually do things unless they liked doing them. (1980, pp. 10–11)

Repair and maintenance jobs may confront men as a chore, but in contrast to the woman's daily round of repetitive domestic work they tend to be one-off or irregular jobs. When his wife is absent or ill he may take on some of 'her' work load, yet the responsibility remains hers, for almost any work a male breadwinner does at home is beyond the call of duty, that is beyond the requirements of his social role. No social compulsion is involved.

DOMESTIC COERCION

For most breadwinners paid work is the direct opposite of home life.

His toil in industry is rarely experienced as productive leisure, primarily because his paid work seems to be as unavoidable for him as his wife's domestic work seems to be unavoidable for her.

The unavoidability of the breadwinner's paid work is not simply an economic matter; it is experienced as a duty because his standing in the eyes of his family, and the community, is conventionally measured in terms of his ability to provide his family with economic security. The home-maker's domestic work is similarly experienced by her as an inescapable duty. At first glance a houseworker, especially a full-time houseworker, would seem to be largely free of social pressure in the performance of her highly privatised job. The main influence on her performance would seem to come from the recipients of her labours – her own family members. Certainly a large part of her job is geared to the accommodation of her family's needs and desires. Yet the wider community makes itself felt, and not only through the pressure of expectations exerted upon her by neighbours, her husband's kin and work associates, and the parents of her children's school friends and their adult associates. There is also a more general pressure resulting from her perception of her domestic role in society, which tends to be reinforced through cultural images and messages relating to domestic practice. This is explored by Josephine King and Mary Stott in *Is This Your Life?* (1977).

The wishes of her own family constrain the houseworker's freedom to set her own standards. The most frequently encountered family preference concerns a desire for a relaxed attitude towards order and spruceness. Sometimes this is seen in terms of masculine authority:

> *Mr Scott:* Have you ever been in a home where you have a house proud woman? Where the husband, and usually they are little men, you know hen-pecked, they sit on a chair and they daren't move . . . in case the wife gets on to them, either about not sitting properly, or putting the paper down. Things like that. It wouldn't do me. There would be more bothers than enough if she started that. But there are houses like that. I know quite a lot.

This sounds as though Mrs Scott has to conform or else. Yet Mrs Scott, like the other women I talked with, genuinely felt that it was undesirable that family members should constantly feel the need to be on their best behaviour. This would contradict the basic notion of what being at home meant. In the main, houseworkers would rather tidy up disorder than establish the kind of regime that would inhibit disorder being created in the first place.

This was the message of the interviews. It was not the message of the photographs, which illustrated the houseworkers' concern with the second, the publicly oriented, source of constraint. Most of the women respondents went out of their way to clean and tidy before taking, or permitting others to take, photographs of their home. Similarly some of the homes were put in order for my visits. So the homes in the photographs, and as I saw them, appeared to be particularly well-kept.

The contradiction between the visual and verbal sources of information point in my view to a contradiction between family (private) norms, and what are seen to be the social (public) norms which define the houseworker's job. She wants her home to be seen (publicly scrutinised) as clean and tidy, and at the same time she wants it to be experienced (privately appreciated) as free and easy. The houseworker's practice tries to reconcile these contradictory objectives. When family members are home she does not veto their disorder-creating behaviour but she constantly re-establishes order since, as Mrs Carter said: 'You never know who may come.' If someone should call and see the disorder, she has no doubt which family member will be held to have fallen short of her duty.

In the privacy of her own home she is sensitive to potential public scrutiny. Since she decides how to translate this sensitivity into domestic practice the standards she sets seem to be of her own making. It is as though she makes a rod for her own back. If the work gets her down she seems to have only herself to blame. The impression that her duties are self-imposed results from the privatised nature of domestic work. In fact the houseworker's duties in the home are a socially ascribed role which bind her in the same way as her husband is bound by his labour market duties.

SERVICES PROVIDED

The home-maker's skills are directed towards others – towards meeting the needs of family members. This means that when the recipients of her labour are away from home, at work or at school, the home may be far from homely. In winter it may be cold if the homeworker is economising on fuel bills. Wet washing may be around, furniture may be out of place while cleaning is in process, hot meals are unlikely to be cooked 'just' for the houseworker on her own either now or in the past (Roberts, 1984, p. 112). A transformation occurs when the recipients of her labour return; the house is warm, welcoming and in order, and a hot meal will shortly be served. This transformation may be taken for granted or expected. (Dennis *et al.*, 1969).

Thus much of the work of providing home comforts remains hidden from the recipients of those comforts. This is less true if the homeworker is employed full-time outside the home, in which case the weekend, far from presenting an opportunity to relax, represents an opportunity to catch up on domestic chores. Even for the full-time houseworker the family's presence at weekends leads to an increase in some chores, notably cooking and tidying.

A full-time houseworker is likely to organise her home to fit in with her husband's work timetable, and her children's school routines. If she does take on a paid job she will try to ensure that it is compatible with the externally imposed timetables of family members. She will, in other words, seek a job that fits in with her domestic duties (Adams and Laurikietis, 1976). The hallmark of a houseworker's relationship to her husband and children is her availability. She puts herself at their disposal. Her time is tailored to their needs. This is why, as Oakley has said, the image of someone waiting epitomises the social situation of a housewife and mother (Oakley, 1979, p. 11). She waits for her husband's arrival to serve the meal, she waits on the family at table, she waits by the swings and at the school gate, she waits for the baby to fall asleep. And all this waiting expresses subordination, for it is those with most power who command the time of others (Frankenberg, 1986).

Class factors will enter into this picture, in relation for example to child-rearing practices:

A woman wants to be a good mother and aims at giving herself to her children selflessly, providing them with concentrated attention, generous care, a lively mind quick to offer stimulus of an appropriate kind, perfectly balanced and delicious meals, unlimited time, and unstinted love. . . But the constructive play turns into a litter of cardboard boxes all over the kitchen, tacky flour and water paste in the coconut matting, and finger paints on the curtains. The carefully prepared food is rejected with noises of disgust from the older child and is simply expelled from the baby's mouth as a great glob of goo. (Kitzinger, 1978, p. 43)

The working-class mother is likely to be saved this frustrating lack of co-operation since her investment of time is unlikely to take the form of planning for and consciously extending the range of her offspring's experiences. The time she devotes to her children is best expressed by the phrase 'being on call'. She puts herself at their disposal.

Class differences are also observable at mealtimes. James Little-john found for example that upper-class housewives control the distribution of food, whereas the working-class wife 'performs a servant-like role during the meal' (1963, pp. 127–9). She manages to consume her food in between the interruptions required in order to meet her family's requirements.

SELF-IDENTITY

The houseworker's occupation is so geared to meeting the needs of her family that the identification of her own needs, separate from theirs, becomes blurred. This is apparent in relation to the use of domestic space. Children and husbands usually have a territory of their own within the home. Children have their own rooms, or, if they share a room, their own part of a room; their own desk or cupboard. Husbands may have a shed or garage to work or relax in, a hobbies room in the house, or the garden may be seen as their particular domain. Now that the days of handbag-carrying women have largely drawn to a close, houseworkers rarely have a clearly marked-out personal territory – although for some the dressing-table may be a non-transportable handbag equivalent. The kitchen is frequently seen as the woman's room and yet, particularly if meals are consumed in the kitchen, it remains a family room which is not comparable to the husband's den.

Why is it desirable to have personal territory? Two obvious answers spring to mind: in order to have a place where it is possible to engage in personal activities relatively undisturbed; and a place where personal possessions may be stored. Neither of these obvious answers was obvious to the houseworkers I talked with. Most of them interpreted questions about the need to have a place to be on their own as questions about feeling depressed. Then the response was in terms of going into the bedroom for a good cry, or taking a long hot bath. Frequently they found questions about personal territory baffling: 'I'm on my own a lot here in the daytime when the children are at school'.

Similarly few houseworkers had personal items of property – clothing and jewellery apart – distinct from general household goods. The strong identification between the houseworker as a person and her home is reflected in the type of gifts she receives. Household items, or items that will be enjoyed collectively in a family setting, are frequently seen as appropriate gifts for the housewife. Ornaments, rugs, table-ware, domestic utensils, pot plants, etc. would almost always be given as gifts to the woman of the house – not the man. For him it is more appropriate to give gifts that he will enjoy consuming individually, or that fit in with his particular interests, tobacco, drink, an item of sports equipment, or a book, for example. As a result the need for personal territory seems remote to many houseworkers:

Pauline: Do you ever feel the need to have somewhere to put your own things?
Mrs Holland: These are my own things. (*Her hand sweeps round indicating all the furnishings in the house.*)
Pauline: And you don't feel the need for a room like Peter's [Mr Holland's]?
Mrs Holland: No. Like Peter has got his own personal things, not private, but things he's had before and since he's been married, upstairs. I haven't. Like this is my room, the house sort of thing.

In this situation the objects that houseworkers cherish most are 'signs of ties that bind the family together'. (Csikszentmihalyi and Rochberg-Halton, 1981). A china cabinet often expresses close ties between the home-maker and her family, and is valued by her precisely for this reason – *Mrs Scott:* 'I like the whole thing, because that cabinet it's got something from everyone in the family, plus friends and relations, that has'.

The lack of personal territory and property, and the lack of a felt need for such, is expressive of the extent to which the houseworker's self-identity becomes submerged in the job of caring for others. She may remain fairly contented with her lot so long as the cared-for others constitute an appreciative audience for her labours. Yet the arrival of children often brings about a polarisation of gender roles within the household, and the interests and lifestyle of the husband and wife begin to diverge. Over time such divergence can lead the breadwinner to regard the home-maker's efforts with indifference. In these circumstances when the offspring leave home the homeworker is left without an audience, and the meaning goes out of the home-making task.

Csikszentmihalyi and Rochberg-Halton noted the importance of the husband's interest in domestic matters.

In those families where the husband expressed positive affect towards the home, 73 per cent of the wives also did; in those where the husband was neutral, only 46 per cent of the wives were positive; and of the ten families without husbands, in only one did the wife have a positive view of the home. (1981, p. 133)

Occasionally the houseworker may relish the scope for unilateral control that her husband's indifference affords her: *Mrs Poskier:* 'I run the home. If I say no, it's no!' Yet Mrs Poskier's home-making skills were not without an audience, for her teenage children were still living at home at the time of the interviews. When they leave to establish homes of their own, her domestic management skills may well be experienced as less satisfying and more meaningless. Then, like Mrs Scott, most of her satisfaction may come from visiting her children in their own homes. Yet this is an inadequate substitute in a world of nuclear families where homes are seen as the domain of the married couple, and where they operate as separate establishments (Shorter, 1979). Since Mrs Scott is not the focal point of her children's households, and her own house lacks an appreciative audience, she comes close to being emotionally homeless.

DOMESTIC AUTONOMY

Despite confronting the houseworker as a social necessity home-making contains emotional rewards and fulfilments. Planning is a central feature of the job. Home-makers spend a lot of time planning meals and ensuring that favourite items appear on the menu. They store up treats for the children, and activities for them to do on a rainy day. They organise the switch from summer to winter clothing; putting away and bringing out items as the season requires, and they check that each family member has a suitable range of clothes and footware.

These organising activities reach a peak as special occasions approach. Houseworkers anticipate the holiday needs of each family member. Birthday festivities are painstakingly prepared, and purchases and preparations for Christmas begin months before Advent, even a whole year before if the houseworker is a member of a Christmas club. All this is work, but work tinged with a joyful anticipation of the pleasure that will be the result. When circumstances, like the Miners' Strike of 1984, make it difficult for a 'good Christmas' to be provided for the children great anguish is felt; although in the case of the Miners' Strike organised women were able to provide gifts and festivities on a collective basis (Beaton, 1985, pp. 249–52).

Within the limits imposed by the breadwinner's control of domestic finances (Hunt, 1978), home-makers can exercise consumption choices over the clothing styles of family members and the leisure facilities of the home. Increasingly toys come complete with manufactured lifestyles in the form of comics, TV programmes, clothing and clothing accessories, lunch boxes and bags, duvets and stationery items all bearing the relevant logo. In this all-round sense manufacturers create the image of a 'My Little Pony', a 'He Man', a 'Care Bear' or a 'Postman Pat' child. And the home-maker in her capacity as an organiser of consumption can collect items of the style on offer.

Decisions concerning the purchase of food items give the home-maker further influence over family members. Also in her relationship with her children she has the power to make them happy or otherwise. Her position of influence may well find expression in her aesthetic preferences. So, for example, Mrs Holland values a framed print of a crying boy. There are several versions of crying boy pictures on sale in High Street shops and market stalls. Mrs Holland's picture, like most of them, shows a boy with tears on his cheeks set against a plain indeterminate background. His clothes do not give a precise clue as to either date or place. His head is lit from above, and his hands reach out inviting comfort; an invitation Mrs Holland responds to: 'I always want to pick up the child and love it because it's crying.'

Given the gender division of labour that characterises our society it is usually the mother who would comfort a child, and the possession of the ability to comfort is a source of pleasure. In other relationships one's intervention does not have such a direct or intense effect. Indeed many of the circumstances surrounding Mrs Holland's life are quite outside her control. The power of mothering is an isolated and confined power but Mrs Holland can relive it every time she looks at this picture.

It does not seem all that surprising that this ability directly to influence the lives of family members should be jealously guarded, although in 1939 Margery Spring Rice did find it surprising:

> Indeed a curious phenomenon in the position of women is that those who most need some measure of freedom from the restrictions of family duties, are often the first to resist the legislation which might give it to them. They are passionately jealous of any usurpation or delegation of their own authority.
>
> Examples of this are provided in the great difficulty which occurs in persuading women to go into hospital for their confinements. Although trained home helps can be provided to look after father and children the mother shows an inherent disinclination to entrust her home even temporarily to the care of someone else. (Spring Rice, 1981, p. 14).

Although the home-maker can experience great pleasure in the caring role she exercises in relation to her own family,·the privatised nature of the household can mean that caring stops there. If she and other family members turn their concern and protectiveness inwards towards their own household, this may represent a simultaneous turning away from the welfare of the wider community, as Barrett and McIntosh (1982) have argued. Conversely though, Csikszent-mihalyi and Rochberg-Halton have found that it is the recipients of the loving care of family-oriented women who become most involved in community activities (1981, pp. 146–55).

DOMESTIC ARTISTIC EXPRESSION

The arrangement of domestic furnishings and the style of the home represent a form of artistic expression created by the homeworker. If several young children are at home, or when a mother attempts to combine paid work with running a home, the effort to keep the house in order can be experienced as a desperate struggle against dirt and chaos, rather than as the creative process of renewal described by Bachelard (1969, pp. 68–9):

> A house that shines from the care it receives appears to have been rebuilt from the inside; it is as though it were new inside. In the intimate harmony of walls and furniture, it may be said that we become conscious of a house that is built by women, since men only know how to build a house from the outside, and they know little or nothing of the wax civilisation. . . And what a great life it would be if, every morning, every object in the house could be made anew by our hands, could 'issue', from our hands.

Yet as soon as the pressure of keeping household mess in check eases, the creative process of home-making comes to the fore. Bachelard's 'wax civilisation' may be more applicable to professional middle-class homes containing furniture that will mellow rather than become shoddy with age. Even so, in working-class homes the composition of the home, the colour scheme, the arrangement and selection of ornaments and furnishings, the use of light and shade and space combine to express the artistic skills of the home-maker. Most of the interviews I conducted took place in settings bulging with visual evidence of the home-maker's deep aesthetic involvement in the domestic environment.

Jean E. Hess (1981) in her study of domestic interiors in Northern New Mexico found a well established set of aesthetic practices and values. The women believe that the 'neutral' furnishings (couches, curtains, etc.) should always match. Women carefully plan the purchase of these larger items, leaving little to chance. Against the background of an emphasised color scheme, touches of brighter color are scattered. . . 'Brightness' is a word recurring often. . . But an article is 'bright' and 'shining' only if it is clean. Women devote as much time as possible to dusting, sweeping and straightening their homes. . . Women often purchase or make decorations in twos or threes so that they can be arranged symmetrically. . . The balancing and clustering of objects seem to help control clutter, imposing order on potential chaos . . . doilies and cloths serve to mediate between objects, protecting one object (a table or cabinet) from another (a plant or lamp). The theme of mediation or protection is in turn elaborated into a theme of covering. Lacework may cover whole shelves, small rugs or serapes cover furniture which is already upholstered, and a large carpet is protected by smaller ones, placed where people are most apt to walk. (1981, pp. 31–2)

I have found similar aesthetic practices employed in the creation of working-class homes, which were characterised by ornamentation, warm textures and sometimes warm bright colours. The emphasis on warmth extended to clothing and food. The working-class definition of a main meal continued to be a hot substantial dish. The provision of this, and a warm house to welcome incoming family members, constituted the core of the houseworker's home-making duty.

There was also a preference for modern and new materials, so that the environment and its contents were changed every few years, involving much redecorating and the purchase of new furniture and furnishings. I found that curtains and cushion covers were likely to be changed even more frequently. There was a readiness to use artificial materials which resembled, but did not masquerade as, their non-artificial equivalent. Thus plastic flowers and wallpaper resembling stones or wood were frequently encountered in working-class homes. There was a tendency to cover and decorate, so that lavatory seats and stands were often surrounded by fluffy mats; flowerpots and paper-handkerchief boxes were covered in decorative material; frills or bobbles were often added to lampshades or curtains.

CONTRASTING CLASS CULTURES

In an afterword to Hess's article on domestic interiors in New Mexico the editors suggest that the care and skill employed in the creation of such environments should be studied as a form of process art (Hess, 1981, p. 32). I think this is clearly so, but would add that cultural and especially class factors should be taken into account in the study of domestic process art. In my own enquiry I found that professional homes exhibit opposite traits from those identified above. The basic decor and furnishings were not frequently changed. There was a preference for furniture that would age well, and could therefore be kept for long periods, and possibly be handed on to future generations. I found a preference for plain and subdued colours, unadorned surfaces, simplicity of design and uncluttered space. Synthetic materials, particularly plastic products, were abhorred when used as substitute materials; thus plastic combs were acceptable but not plastic vases or flowers.

I think that when households are short of money this contrasting aesthetic approach is accentuated. For example, if a household of students from professional homes could not afford the kind of picture frame they wanted, which would probably be plain wood or metal, they would be far more likely to display their pictures unframed than to buy a cheap substitute frame. If 'nice' ashtrays could not be afforded tin-cans may be provided, or as Anna Coote reported, a carved wooden spoon stuck in a bottle may serve as an ornament (*The Guardian*, 19 May 1977). Such improvisations have clearly cost nothing. They demonstrate an unwillingness to purchase cheap but 'nasty' substitutes for expensive goods, and by so doing they commemorate the good taste of the owner who, it seems, prefers to go without rather than to buy something which is not worth having.

Poor working-class households are much more likely to resort to cheaper versions of the desired product. The difference between what they purchase and what they wanted will not be primarily one of design and colour but of the material from which the product is made. So, for example, both prosperous and poor working-class homes may favour ornate gold picture frames, but in the former households the frames will be painted carved wood, and in the latter they will be moulded plastic that has been spray painted.

When cheaper substitute materials are employed in working-class homes this is rarely with an intention to fool anyone. Such households are not trying to appear to be other than they are. The substitutes merely enable household members to approach the effect they desired at a price they can afford. Furthermore, since in all probability the furnishings and decor will be changed within a few years, it makes little sense to use very costly materials.

I think that when trying to understand the basis of such class-related aesthetic preferences it is useful to ask from what the groups in question are trying to distance themselves. In the case of manual workers the first answer is obviously cold weather. The work of many working-class men takes place either out of doors or in cold uncomfortable circumstances, and warmth as expressed in texture, colour, covering, heat and food will continue to be prized so long as this is the case.

Secondly, economic want, and the more remote prospect of homelessness and destitution, continue to cast a shadow of insecurity over working-class lives. Although the stark and austere image of the workhouse, and the powerlessness inflicted upon inmates, is now a relic of the past, emotionally it symbolises the quality of life from which working-class people distance themselves when they make their homes. The right to be free of restrictions within the privacy of the home, the velvet-embossed wallpaper, the thick pile carpet, the up-to-date furnishings, the radiant fire (albeit a gas or an electric fire with an open grate facade), the substantial steak-and-kidney pie in the oven, the decorative ornaments and bright colours combine to clothe and protect, and to demonstrate that one is protected, from the cold winters of want, and the power of external authorities. The use of such blanketing as an insurance policy against destitution, that can be stripped off layer by layer in times of hardship is graphically illustrated by Hogarth in *A Harlot's Progress*, and tellingly described by Elizabeth Gaskell in *Mary Barton*.

It is usual in works of sociology to see the upper social ranks as setting cultural trends which are emulated by the ranks below them. Young and Willmott's study *The Symmetrical Family* (1975) may serve as an example of this approach. But if one is less concerned with fashion and more concerned with identifying cultural ideologies, it may be wiser to look in the other direction and ask from what or whom are people trying to distance themselves. When this perspective is applied to professional middle-class groups it can be seen that the trend setter, in inverted form, is the working-class. Professional middle-class decor is the opposite of working-class decor because the former are concerned to distinguish themselves from the latter. This is why consumer-durables long since rejected by the working class in favour of the protective aura surrounding modern goods are sometimes reclaimed by the professional middle class. Not only have such objects, given their age, acquired a scarcity value, they also represent objects that no longer grace working-class homes.

OWNERSHIP

I looked at the photograph Mr Carter had taken of his wife outside their house. Through her efforts their house was experienced as a home. That was her achievement. The house was also her place of confinement. In the photograph she is shown outside the house but within its jurisdiction. That represented her life situation. She is turned towards her husband who is taking the photograph. Her gaze is downwards. Subjectively she was totally within the situation. Mr Carter has photographed his wife leaning on the gate he had stripped down ready to paint. She is at the entrance of the house he has paid for. She stands in front of the car he uses everyday to drive to and from work, in order to earn the money to support himself and his family in their home. That was his achievement.

As owners and consumers they had secured a degree of control over their lives; they could make choices. Of course through its privatised nature this form of self-expression is very limited, especially so for the home-maker who has few other means of self-expression available to her. 'It is unfair that she should receive feedback to her own self mainly from the restricted circle of the family, whereas her husband and children, fortified by her attention, can turn to the wider arena of public life to reap rewards and confirmation of their skills.' (Csikszentmihalyi and Rochberg-Halton, 1981, p. 168.) The editors of Hess's article on domestic interiors feel the same way:

> The home was our only kingdom. . . If we want our energy and strength to go into other channels, we have to work at a transitional solution which may deprive us of a personal world altogether . . . we have to cope with our deep-seated, deeply instilled sense of responsibility. That means finding a more creative way of love and collaboration, of educating our children, or caring for a house, and we have to convince those we love that there are other ways of accomplishing these things. (Hess, 1981, p. 33)

Families have a huge emotional stake in the status quo, and unless the 'more creative way' is clearly defined and looks achievable little is likely to change. In working-class homes in particular the domestic interior expresses being on the receiving end of a mother's love. While the emotional rewards for the mother herself are limited to the feedback she gets from her own family, she was in the past a recipient of the caring environment created by her own mother. Thus the emotional roots of the home she creates reach back into her own childhood. Perhaps this enables her to relive her childhood in a way that is not so readily available to most men. This may in part explain

why amongst adult ex-victims of child abuse men are under-
represented. As Beatrix Campbell (1988, p. 18) has commented:

> Retrospective surveys suggest that people reorganise their memory: what
> seems to be the case is that men forget. So the pattern that we have based
> on these retrospective disclosures shows an almost minimal proportion of
> boy children being abused. Now if the current work on child abuse is right,
> then that's not accurate and a much higher proportion of boys are being
> abused.

Commitment to the status quo is fuelled by the fact that within the
confines of private ownership the houseworker and her family can
give expression to their lives, relatively free of interference. As Stuart
Hall (1984, p. 19) has said, 'At least you aren't required to tug your
forelock and look "deserving" as you approach the till.' As an owner
and consumer within the jealously guarded privacy of the home one is
largely free from the potentially damaging scrutiny of external
authorities. Too often for working-class people the receipt of benefits
and allowance has been tied to a paternalistic inspection of, and
intrusion into, the household's domestic practice. Small wonder that
there has been a tendency to keep the world at bay behind hedges,
gates and curtains. The ability to decide one's own practice within the
hard-won privacy of the home was emphasised by the housewives
interviewed by Oakley: 'many used this phrase "you're your own
boss" to describe the housewife's feelings of being in control' (1974,
p. 42).

In modern capitalist society property ownership confers the right to
be in control. Anthony D. King in his study of *The Bungalow* (1984)
quotes a study of old people's homes in Britain (Peace, 1982) which
concluded that it was not the design of facilities to which residents
objected but the fact that they did not have exclusive (property)
rights over their use. As property owners people can exercise a
direct, if marginalised, control over their lives. The margins of this
control can be widened by redefining the rights of owners and users
on a community-wide basis, as in the community architecture movement (Knevitt and Wates, 1987).

And the margins of control within the cherished territory of the
private household can be re-defined. One household that I studied
was based on an outstandingly egalitarian relationship. It was a
two-woman household. The ownership of personal property, notably
books and records, was strictly delineated. Each had her own private
space within the house, and the organisation, arrangement and use of
joint space was extensively discussed between them:

Delia: I quite often come across Pat reading, and I quite often say 'Do you mind if I sit and either half chatter to you or just be around while you are reading?' I mean we actually ask each other, and she will say.'yes' or 'no'.

In most other households the presence of family members in communal rooms passed without comment. Indeed it seems to be usual for little or no thought to be given to the way adult family members interact with one another and utilise the home environment. When thought is given it tends to be after the event, when someone is displeased by the way things have worked out. By and large established patterns of behaviour between adult family members are taken for granted; that is to say a large chunk of domestic practice confronts the individual as part of the given world. By contrast Pat and Delia exercise considerable control over their environment. Almost all changes and forms of association are consciously explored with a view to arriving at a mutually acceptable practice. They are both aware that their consciously evolved domestic practice is the outgrowth of their political involvement; and in turn their creation of a cherished domestic territory strengthens their capacity to be involved in community politics.

Inequalities between men and women, and between adults and children, characterise most households; inequalities concerning access to financial resources; inequalities in the use of space; in the use of time; in the development of personal interests and pursuits. These inequalities create barriers to the conscious use of the home as a means of extending control over the domestic environment. The rights of property owners and users are not individual rights in any but single-person households. In so far as egalitarian domestic practices can be evolved a basis for collective control of the household is thereby created that may well have an impact on the practice of family members in the wider community.

Note

I am grateful for a grant from SSRC which made this research possible.

6 Privatised Families and their Homes
Fiona Devine

INTRODUCTION: THE TRADITIONAL WORKING CLASS

It has been widely argued that life for the so-called 'traditional' working class was dominated by both paid and unpaid work to achieve a basic standard of living. Men worked long hours performing strenuous and sometimes dangerous work in occupations such as mining and fishing and in heavy manufacturing industries such as steel production (Walker, 1950; Horobin, 1957; Tunstall, 1962; Dennis et al., 1969). Yet, despite the harshness of their work, their shared experiences engendered a strong sense of solidarity amongst workers. They valued the companionship of workmates and sought their company in their leisure time too. Traditional working-class men, it was argued, belonged to an occupational community and their lifestyles took a communal form (Zwieg, 1961; Lockwood, 1966; Dennis et al., 1969).

Similarly women worked long hours undertaking physically hard unpaid work in poor housing conditions (Slater and Woodside, 1951; Spring Rice, 1981; Gittens, 1982). Women's lives were dominated by the heavy burden of raising comparatively large families and catering for the needs of their husbands. The major part of the day was spent on domestic tasks which secured the continued existence of the household. Despite the 'almost unredeemed drabness' (Spring Rice, 1981, p. 94) of their daily lives women also found some compensation in the company of other women who shared the same circumstances as themselves. Although their free time was less tangible than their husbands', they enjoyed the companionship of other women when they had a free moment (Mogey, 1956; Young and Willmott, 1957; Kerr, 1958).

In sum, men and women led very separate lives from each other because paid and unpaid work played a large part in structuring their lifestyles. Men spent most of the day outside the home while women's lives were mainly confined to the domestic sphere. They came across different groups of people in the course of work and formed strong

82

attachments with these people. They enjoyed the companionship of these attachments in their leisure time too which meant that little time was spent with spouses in the home. The local community and not the home occupied the central position in people's lives.

THE PRIVATISED WORKING CLASS

However commentators in the late 1950s and early 1960s argued that members of the working class no longer led a communal existence whereby men's and women's lives were dominated by paid and unpaid work to sustain a meagre existence (Laing, 1986). Instead, it was alleged that a 'new' affluent working class had emerged whose members led a more privatised home- and family-centred lifestyle, keeping work and non-work relations separate. Work, therefore, did not structure the whole of people's being. Men and women no longer sought or needed the company of those around them as consolation for the harshness of their lives. Instead they sought better standards of domestic comfort for the household.

The movement of both men and women 'into' the home was noted although greater attention was paid to the growing importance of the home in men's lives. Men no longer wished to spend their free time in the pub discussing work with workmates when they could be relaxing in the comfort of their homes (Zwieg, 1961, p. 6). Their leisure time was kept quite separate from their work concerns and workmates. The home was a much more attractive venue in which they could relax and escape from paid work. Furthermore they helped their wives with domestic duties which allowed women to enjoy more free time so that their lives were not so dominated by domestic chores.

Women's lives also became more privatised as they enjoyed a better equipped home and the company of their husbands. It was noted that residential mobility and the search for better housing often meant that women could not sustain frequent contact with kin and long-standing neighbours. However, despite any initial loneliness which they might have felt, they still enjoyed better standards of domestic comfort in the home (Mogey, 1956; Young and Willmott, 1957). In sum, the importance of the local community was declining and people attached much more importance to their home lives and the company of their immediate family.

It was Goldthorpe and his colleagues, however, who developed and used the concept of privatism most fully in their attempts to explain changing working-class lifestyles. They argued that new consumption aspirations generated an instrumental orientation to work. The search for the 'economic pay-off' from work had important implications for a worker's non-work life and that of his family. The study of affluent workers in Luton found, for example, that families had moved away from long-standing companions in their previous community in search of highly-paid manual work. In their new locale they did not have the companionship of kin and established neighbours and workmates in close proximity. Instead they were forced to rely on the companionship of the immediate family in the home. Yet this privatised existence was not unwanted as 'primacy was clearly given to the material well-being, the social cohesiveness and the autonomy of the conjugal family over against the demands or attractions of wider kinship and community ties' (Goldthorpe *et al.*, 1969, p. 108).

Thus Goldthorpe and his colleagues shared a similar account of changing working-class lifestyles with the British embourgeoisement theorists. In particular they emphasised the importance of new consumer aspirations as the catalyst for change from communal to privatised lifestyles. However, unlike Young and Willmott and other commentators of that time, they continued to stress the structuring influence of paid work on lifestyles. While the British embourgeoisement theorists neglected paid work altogether, Goldthorpe and his colleagues highlighted the implications of the conditions of work and orientations to work on people's non-work lives. As well as geographical mobility, they found that communal sociability was restricted by shift work and overtime. Leisure time was also curtailed if a wife was employed. Hence the demands of paid and unpaid work shaped the pattern of people's lives outside employment, leaving little scope for extensive sociability outside the home (Goldthorpe *et al.*, 1969, pp. 101–3).

PRIVATISM RECONSIDERED

It is only recently that commentators have reconsidered the nature of people's daily lives and the extent to which they may be described as communal or privatised. A new consensus has emerged which suggests that members of the working class have long led a privatised existence rather than a communal one. That is, extensive communal solidarity amongst the traditional working class was probably exaggerated. The 'new' causal account has identified a wider range of factors facilitating the emergence of home- and family-centred lifestyles. Privatism is seen as not just the result of rising consumption aspirations but also as deriving from more far-reaching processes such as the changing nature of work, standards of living and politics. Many of the new accounts locate privatism in the nineteenth century, both for the working class and the middle class (Thompson, 1975; Daunton, 1983; Davidoff and Hall, 1987; Marshall *et al.*, 1987; Williams, 1987).

Daunton (1983), for example, documents the changing definitions of 'public' and 'private' which emerged as a result of housing developments in the late nineteenth century. As the overcrowding problem was tackled, the home became a more private world exclusive to one family. Homes tended to be more separate and self-contained from others close by, so that people did not come across each other so frequently as they went about their daily lives. At the same time space outside the home became more public and open in comparison to the secluded alleyways which had existed between tenement blocks so vividly described by Dickens in *Bleak House*. Daunton went on to note that the extension of gas and electricity into the home, better sanitary conditions, higher wages and the gradual emergence of markets of domestic goods contributed to a home- and family-centred existence. In a similar vein Roberts (1973) highlighted the importance of cheap transport which allowed the working class to escape to better housing in the suburbs of towns. They were no longer forced to live in crowded houses in close proximity to their place of work.

The confinement of women to the home also emerged over the course of the nineteenth century. As the factory system emerged, children were excluded from paid work by protective legislation and women were also forced out of paid employment to care for increasingly dependent, rather than economically independent, children (Land, 1980). Since they were excluded from paid employment outside the home, women were increasingly associated with domestic work and child-care. A strict division of labour was created, initially by the middle class, later by the working class, whereby women were confined to the private sphere of the home and family while men lived in the public world of employment, leisure and politics (Davidoff, L'Esperance and Newby, 1976; Williams, 1987).

Thus the prosperity which was enjoyed after the Second World War merely confirmed an already existing trend towards home- and family-centredness amongst the middle and working classes. The slum clearance and move to better housing described by Mogey (1956) and Young and Willmott (1957) may well have allowed a greater proportion of the working class to enjoy higher standards of domestic comfort than had previously been the case. Working time continued to decline as hours decreased, the 'weekend' became a more distinct part of the week (Young and Willmott, 1957) and holiday entitlements increased. Finally the post-war period witnessed the expansion of markets of domestic appliances and forms of entertainment which could be enjoyed in the home (Gershuny, 1983, p. 58).

Thus the emergence of home- and family-centred lifestyles is no longer associated simply with rising consumer aspirations or increased geographical mobility amongst the working class as both proponents of the embourgeoisement thesis and its critics alleged. Yet while current accounts of changes in the nature of people's daily lives offer a more sophisticated analysis of changing lifestyles, problems still exist. In particular, specific detail about the dynamics of the processes involved has been lost in the rather sweeping historical accounts of changing lifestyles. It is assumed that the impact of all of these changes has been the same: to contribute to greater home- and family-centredness.

Moreover the re-interpretation of history still relies on the distinction between communal and privatised lifestyles. It has merely backdated the period when communal solidarity was said to decline to the end of the nineteenth century rather than the post-war period. The different lifestyles are still held to be opposites with mutually exclusive properties. Thus, despite renewed interest in lifestyles, the extent to which people's lives may be accurately described as privatised has not been explored in any depth. Privatism has emerged as an uncontested concept.

RESEARCH INTO PRIVATISM

Against this background a piece of qualitative research was conducted to explore the substantive content and meaning of home- and family-centred lifestyles. Interviews were conducted with 30 married couples who were resident in Luton and where the husband worked at the Vauxhall car plant[1]. The interviewees were aged between 21 and 67. Four couples had no children, six couples had children aged under five while 12 couples had children aged between five and 16. Seven couples had children aged 16 and over who were still living at home while three couples had children who lived away from home. The sample, therefore, comprised a group of people who occupied different positions in the family life-cycle. While all of the men in the sample worked on a full-time basis, the economic activity rates of the women varied. Eight women were economically inactive[2], 12 women were employed part-time and 12 were employed on a full-time basis.

Luton, of course, was the town chosen by Goldthorpe and his colleagues for the study of affluent workers. In that study home- and family-centred lifestyles were found amongst a sample of geographically mobile workers and their families who had moved to Luton in search of highly-paid manual work. The three main employers of the town, Vauxhall, Laporte and Skefko employed large workforces and attracted many people from outside the town to work at the plants (Goldthorpe *et al.*, 1968, pp. 3–4).

Although Goldthorpe and his colleagues interviewed a sample of people who were new residents in Luton they claimed that the respondents were 'prototypical' of the new working class (Goldthorpe *et al.*, 1968, pp. 175–6). They stressed, in particular, the desire to lead home- and family-centred lives and noted the impact of in-migration on the local community. The Luton team expected privatism to become more prevalent amongst the working class. These claims have remained unsubstantiated. What we do not know from the study is the extent to which people who have not been residentially mobile or who have lived in an area for a relatively long period of time lead privatised lifestyles. Moreover tightly structured questionnaires were used in the survey by Goldthorpe and his colleagues so that the interviewees' thoughts and feelings about their daily lives were not explored in any depth. Consequently arguments about the desire for privatised lifestyles were the product of rather general impressions gained from these interviews. By returning to Luton and conducting a 're-study' of the *Affluent Worker* series these issues could be addressed.

In the present study husbands and wives were interviewed separately[3]. The interviews, which took a discursive form, focused on patterns of sociability with the family, neighbours and friends in the locale or 'community' and with workmates. The interviewees were also asked about the organisation and completion of domestic work and the nature of their free time. Finally, the interviewees were questioned about their consumer aspirations and their social and political attitudes. While attitudes to the home were not the central concern of the research the data does provide some interesting insights to the place of the home in people's lives and the meanings they attach to it.

Emphasis will be placed on the way in which people's changing working lives and life-cycle position influence the extent to which their existences are home-centred. This of course is not constant. The form and nature of home-centredness and the meaning which people attribute to the home does change with their circumstances. The paid and unpaid work necessary to secure people's material existence are amongst the most important factors here. For example the location of their work clearly influences the degree to which people's lives revolve around the immediate family in the home. Equally the work roles which men and women play in sustaining family life differ and vary across the family-cycle. Consequently in what follows, the extent to which people's lives are home-centred will be analysed in the context of their various work tasks and their family-cycle position.

ESTABLISHING THE HOME

Two couples in the sample were in the early stage of the family-cycle but all of the women had been employed for different lengths of time after marrying and before the arrival of children. Marriage in itself had not been a bar to employment as it was in the past (Walby, 1986). Husbands and wives worked full-time in paid employment and spent most of the day from the home. This, of course, implies that young married women spend more time away from the home than was the case in the past. They are no longer immediately confined to the home by marriage and the imminent arrival of children.

Securing a well-equipped and comfortable home for themselves and their children was and had been an important dimension of the 'projects' of all the couples in the sample. The younger members of the sample were keen to establish their homes by buying the 'basic' needs of daily life such as cookers, fridges, beds and other pieces of furniture which are now taken for granted in most people's homes. Domestic appliances such as washing machines, vacuum cleaners, microwave ovens and other pieces of kitchen equipment were sought to lighten the domestic burdens of cooking, washing and cleaning and help create the clean, bright, efficient and modern homes the interviewees wanted[4].

The most costly items of a well-equipped and comfortable home could be bought when husbands and wives both worked full-time. It was deemed more useful to have the home established before children arrived since they generated much of the work that needed to be done around the home anyway. Domestic appliances would be there to use when child-care and domestic demands are particularly high. As Kim Dodd suggested:

> I would like to start a family now despite being young and only married for a short time as I like children. We can't afford it though especially with moving. we're moving to a bigger house which we'll need if we're going to start a family. We're moving before I give up my job for children. We can afford to move now.

In contrast to Goldthorpe and his colleagues' findings (1969, pp. 127–9), it was not considered rational to coincide child rearing with the peak earnings of the husband in the early years of marriage. The potential earnings of wives were more important. It should be noted, however, that the more costly items of furniture were expected and would have to last a good many years when family finances were tighter. Consumption on items for the home was not unfettered by financial constraints.

Those without heavy financial commitments could also enjoy establishing a home according to their own tastes and style. Bridget and Stephen Underwood had been married for five months and they were busily involved in creating the home which they wanted. As Bridget Underwood described:

> With just getting married we are buying furniture and getting sorted out. There's lots of things I want to do. One week we might do something like put glass in all the new doors inside the house. Now I want to knock out that wall. We will have to re-decorate everything but it depends how the money goes.

The early stages of the family-cycle, then, are devoted to establishing a home which has the latest domestic appliances and which is decorated according to the tastes of its inhabitants. How, in fact, do young couples use their homes and how far are their lives outside employment home-centred?

We have already observed that young men and women are engaged in paid employment for most of the day and that they are away from the home for that period. When paid work has finished for the day men and women return home to eat, relax and sleep. Like others, they must perform domestic chores. As other writers have noted (for

example, Hunt, 1980), this stage of the family-cycle is associated with
the most egalitarian domestic division of labour. This is primarily the
case because the actual burden of domestic tasks is low. It was
expected that husbands and wives jointly undertook domestic chores
and by doing so completed them in a shorter period of time. Stephen
and Bridget Underwood both worked as production operators at the
Vauxhall car plant and he suggested: 'You couldn't have me and
Bridget coming in from work and me sitting there while she is doing
all the cooking. It wouldn't agree with me and it wouldn't agree with
Bridget.' It was unacceptable, therefore, to allow one partner to
undertake the household duties alone when both of them had spent
the day at work. Paid work outside the home was tiring and couples
sought to limit the burden of domestic duties in their so-called
non-work lives. The equitable division of domestic work broke down,
however, when there was more tangible free time from work. At
weekends the young women undertook the more time-consuming
domestic chores alone while their husbands enjoyed leisure pursuits.

Young couples and indeed all of those who were economically
active outside the home were tired when they had completed a day's
work. The impact of paid work on people's energies seems to have
been overlooked in the literature on lifestyles and yet it is a major
influence on the nature of people's leisure. Thus the interviewees did
see the home as a haven where they could relax after a day's work
and this applied to both the men and women who worked outside the
home. Irene Cass, who worked full-time as a sewing machinist,
described some of these feelings:

> With work I am standing all day and it is very tiring. When I come in I
> don't want to move. I feel exhausted. I'm entitled to relax. I sit down with
> a cup of tea and a fag [cigarette]. Sometimes I just go to bed after a meal if
> I feel like it.

The home, then, stood in contrast to the workplace, being
comfortable, clean and free from the noise and grime of the factory.
Couples relaxed there in the evenings enjoying activities like watching television, knitting, reading the daily newspapers and gardening
which did not require huge amounts of time and energy. Given that
paid work does sap people's energies it is not surprising that they
should wish to remain in the comfort of the home and enjoy hobbies
in that immediate context.

Equally though, people are not confined to the home, and when
there is more tangible free time they do enjoy leisure outside the
home. Men frequently participate in leisure activities, and particular-

ly sport, which take them away from the home for different periods. Such activities are often enjoyed with parents, siblings, workmates and old school friends. While women are more confined to the home with domestic chores they still visit their parents, siblings and friends. Thus while young couples without child-care responsibilities spend a lot of time in the home, they also enjoy 'outside' leisure activities and the company of other people. Their lives were far from privatised even though much of their everyday routines revolved around sustaining the home. There was no positive desire to limit sociability with others or to lead a particularly home-centred lifestyle in the search for higher standards of living as the Luton team argued. Instead paid and unpaid work structures the nature of people's day-to-day existence.

THE FAMILY AND THE HOME

The arrival of children changes the nature of people's lifestyles considerably and this is especially the case for women. Their lives become more home-centred as they leave formal employment to care for young children, for their work is now firmly located in the home. Moreover the unending nature of this work and the fact that it is performed in the home has implications for their free time which also tends to become more home-centred. Thus major shifts occur in the significance of the home for these women. Men's lives, on the other hand, are less structured by child-care and for them the meaning of the home is little altered.

Four women in the sample were raising young children at home full-time. They expressed strong views on the need to leave paid work and stay at home to care for their children. They assumed that they would leave the labour market and they stressed their sole responsibility for the well-being of their children. Lisa Smith, who cared for an 18-month-old daughter, summed up these sentiments clearly: 'I think if you have children you should look after them. I think it is nice as they grow up to know who their mum is and not have baby-sitters every day or go from this person to that person.' The women had clearly looked forward to the birth of children and accepted the change in their daily lives. They looked forward to staying at home caring for their children and completing domestic tasks. These attitudes should, of course, be placed in the context of limited child-care facilities in Britain which rob women of a genuine choice about the organisation of child-care and paid work outside the home (Dex, 1987).

At this stage of the family-cycle the women spent most of the day at home actively involved in child-care and domestic work. At the same time and by virtue of being at home rather than out at work, the women took on the bulk of other domestic chores. It was felt that a wife should perform household tasks during the day because she was 'free' to do so. They undertook domestic duties which they had shared more with their husbands in the earlier years of marriage. It meant that men could return home from paid work and enjoy their leisure with fewer domestic intrusions into their free time. Reflecting on the move from some sharing to a greater responsibility for housework falling on her shoulders after the birth of her daughter, Lisa Smith said:

> When I worked full-time, we did the housework together; washing up at the end of the day and day-to-day clearing up. I used to say to him that once I was at home he wouldn't have to do any of that any more which he doesn't now. Now I'm at home all day I do all of it. Matthew doesn't do anything but he does take over the baby when he comes home from work.

The associations of work lying outside the home are very clear.

Thus the bulk of the women's days were filled with child-care and domestic responsibilities. This is not to suggest that women do not have any free time at all as some studies of housework have implied (Oakley, 1976). The women were keen to complete the bulk of their domestic tasks in the morning. They sought to be as efficient as possible so that 'slack' periods in the afternoons could be spent with their children. Undoubtedly the women derived a great deal of pleasure from their children when they could give time to playing with them and entertaining them. As Rita Aziz, with a young son, described it: 'These days I am mostly with my son playing with him. Since he came along my leisure time is playing with him.' These findings confirm the time budget analysis conducted by Gershuny and Jones (1987, p. 30) for the period 1961 to 1984 which found that domestic work has become less time-consuming but that more time is now devoted to child-care. Other activities which the women regarded as their leisure included watching television, dress-making and knitting. These latter activities embody an element of domestic work as Hobson (1978) has noted, but this does not necessarily mean that women do not enjoy them.

Nevertheless, as other studies have suggested (Gavron, 1968;

Hobson, 1978; Holme, 1985a), women experience considerable isolation when they remain at home all day. The initial excitement of leaving paid employment to have children and to care for them at home recedes as daily life becomes more mundane. The women in the sample felt isolated from other working people and emphasised the sheet boredom of remaining at home and catering for their children all the time. While the company of children was enjoyed they were also a 'handful' and were obviously a different type of company to adults.

Yet the most important factor contributing to women's isolation in the individual home has been neglected. That is, women experience a greater degree of isolation than in the past when they are rearing young children because there are very few women who are in the locality during the day with whom they can spend their free time. Their mothers, sisters and friends are almost invariably employed, and even when they are on hand, they still have domestic duties to attend to. Alone, women with young children spend more time in the home, as few other social or leisure arenas are available to them. In general, women with young children do not undertake many leisure pursuits outside the home.

Of course, this is not to suggest that these women are completely isolated. Other women in the same circumstances as themselves may be met when, for example, they use local facilities such as clinics, schools and the corner shop. They can visit other young mothers in their homes and while away a few hours talking and playing with their children. Weather permitting, they can go with other women for walks and visit the local parks to entertain their children. Most women caring full-time for young children though are dependent on a small number of other women for company and shared leisure activities. Their lives reflect the way in which rearing children is predominantly based on the home.

Thus while the length of time which women spend out of the labour market is shortening (Martin and Roberts, 1984), the time spent outside formal employment is more home-centred than in the past since other women are not available for companionship. Women caring for children on a full-time basis experience a period of short but intense home-centredness. It is not surprising, then, that one of the reasons women look forward to returning to paid employment when their children are less dependent is to 'escape' from the isolation and boredom which results from staying at home all day. While the women themselves might not describe their homes as 'prisons', the way in which their home-centred lives are isolated from others is a source of dissatisfaction and unhappiness. As Jane Bennett, who had come to know one woman in a similar situation to herself, still felt:

> I hate staying at home all day. It drives me up the wall. I'm looking forward to going back to work. I miss the company more than anything. You tend to lose touch when you pack up work. You say you'll keep in touch but you never do.

Men's lifestyles do not alter to such a radical extent as their wives' with the arrival of children. They continue to work full-time and are away from the home for the majority of the day. They still return home drained of energy even if the work is not itself physically or mentally tiring. As a Vauxhall worker, Peter Ibbotson, noted, paid work 'is tiring from just being there'.

As has been suggested, the domestic division of labour does change with the arrival of children. Men are no longer engaged in the same sorts of domestic activities: that is, many of the husbands took over the care of children and they were very keen to do so. This allowed their wives to continue their domestic tasks without interruption. Such domestic routines have, of course, been noted elsewhere (Hunt, 1980; Backett, 1982). However this is not to suggest that men opt out of domestic work completely during this stage of the family-cycle. Given that there is more domestic work and child-care to be done, men are drawn into the domestic routine. As a consequence much of their free time is filled with activities located in the home.

The male interviewees were keen to stress that they did 'help' their wives in the evening although unlike in other studies, for example Edgell (1980), few of the men claimed an equal role in the domestic division of labour. It was important to husbands that they relaxed together with their wives. As Robert Edwards, whose wife cared for two daughters at home, suggested:

> If I come in and Rachel hasn't finished I muck in. There's no set pattern. I always try to say to her that when I finish work you should finish work. If we're going to sit down for the evening we should all sit down. I think it's wrong that one should be slogging away and the other one is sitting down. You're supposed to be a family so you should help each other.

The home then is not a place where people pursue a range of activities independently of each other, but a communal place where members of the household are expected to participate in its central activities. Inhabitants of a home are supposed to socialise with each other and co-ordinate their interests and concerns. Personal space, where a member of a family can be alone or engage in activities on their own, is not necessarily given very high priority, as Hunt (this volume) also found. This picture of home life is not, of course, all that different from the image of the home in traditional working-class life described by Hoggart (1957), if his more romantic assessments are omitted.

In the evenings men spent time watching the television, reading the daily newspapers, gardening or undertaking some DIY. In this respect too their activities were, for the most part, home-centred. They were pursuits which allowed them to 'potter' without demanding considerable amounts of time and energy. They could do so in the immediate vicinity of the home which also meant they could complete an activity and relax almost immediately if they so decided. This is a similar picture of daily life to that found by Pahl (1984) in his study of household work strategies in the Isle of Sheppey although the extent of DIY activities is not so great.

At this juncture it is important to consider the way in which the home is a 'haven' from the world of work for men especially but also for women. All of the men in the sample worked at the Vauxhall car plant. The factory was noisy; workers were under constant pressure to work quickly; and grime and dirt were features of car production. Workers looked forward to returning home where they could relax away from the 'bustle' of the factory. The home was associated with a slower pace, quietness and comfort. The comfort of the home was a high priority for all the members of the sample, for it is in comfort that people can relax from paid work and be free from annoyances. Comfort was defined as having nice furniture and fittings in the home, enjoying modern domestic facilities like central heating and washing machines to relax in warmth and reduce domestic work. In a comfortable home people could genuinely relax and 'feel' at ease. Reflecting on his plans and aspirations over his life Leslie Kent suggested: 'I've seen people spend money on things and yet their home is not comfortable and their family is not comfortable. Now to me that's all important. The family is the thing and their comfort and your own is important.' The attainment of a comfortable home, therefore, is the means by which people can enjoy real relaxation and rest.

However, when men have more free time from work at the weekends, they continue to enjoy individual leisure pursuits. While women continue to undertake domestic work or facilitate their

children's leisure (Deem, 1986), men are still able to leave the home
for sporting or other leisure activities. A drink at the end of the week
was 'legitimately' enjoyed by men as a way of escaping from the
mundane routines of work and home. As Matthew Smith suggested:

> At the weekends I might go to the club with my brother-in-law and his
> father. I know lots of people there as I used to go there before I was
> married. I also used to go with Lisa. She doesn't usually go out now. She
> doesn't believe in baby-sitters when the baby is so small. I give my time
> and attention to my wife and child all week so the Saturday evening is my
> free time.

Thus it is still the case that women are confined to the home as they
raise children while men enjoy leisure pursuits outside it. In this
respect at least, life for the privatised worker and his family is not all
that different from traditional working-class lifestyles.

FAMILY, WORK AND THE HOME

The experience of isolation in the home for women with young
children is shorter now that more women return to employment, and
do so sooner, after the birth of their children (Martin and Roberts,
1984). While women have always worked to sustain the material
well-being of the family, the increasing participation of married
women in the labour market since the Second World War has taken
them outside the home. That is, the separation of home and paid
work which emerged at the end of the nineteenth century has had an
important impact on women's working lives too. In this respect,
women's lives are less home-centred (or at least less confined to the
immediate locale in which they live) than they have been in the past.
On the other hand, the increasing rate of economic activity amongst
married women has led to some having more home-centred leisure.
This results from their continued responsibility for domestic and
child-care tasks when they finish their paid work. Arrangements do
not return to the more equitable domestic division of labour evident
amongst young couples before the arrival of children (Hunt, 1980).
While the 'double burden' of work on women's lives (Pollert, 1981;
Yeandle, 1984) has been widely recognised, the impact on lifestyles
as a whole has not been fully explored.

Since the Second World War married women in Britain have
tended to return to employment on a part-time rather than a full-time
basis so that paid work can be fitted in with child-care and domestic

responsibilities (Dex, 1987). Indeed many women can return to paid work part-time only with the help of family and friends who will look after their young children. Interestingly the return to part-time work after the birth of children is far more prevalent in Britain than in the United States and a number of European countries (Dex and Shaw, 1986). Against this background, 12 women in the sample were employed on a part-time basis and 12 women were employed full-time.

The return to paid employment outside the home means that women are less free to structure their time according to their own wishes. Obviously this does vary according to the number of hours for which a woman is employed. When paid work is completed they must return home to resume domestic tasks and child-care. There are fewer opportunities to enjoy the company of other women in the locale. The company of fellow workers is enjoyed occasionally but a greater degree of organisation is necessary for this to happen since they are not immediately to hand. Women are also tired from their varied work tasks and the home is once again the most immediate site of leisure.

Those women who were employed part-time valued the free time between different work tasks where they could relax at home. Again the immediacy of the home is important. Catherine Hayes had four children at school and worked part-time as a home help. She described how:

> I finish work at half-past one and I spend the afternoon cleaning and preparing the dinner. I don't have that much free time. I have half an hour before the children come in from school when I have a cigarette and relax.

Free time was enjoyed between a range of tasks which had to be completed. Given that leisure time is in short supply women do relax in the home where they do not have to engage in particularly active pursuits and where they might enjoy some peace from the demands of others.

Being alone in the home is a form of relaxation to women whose lives are largely full catering for the needs of others. They can structure their own time within constraints and undertake activities which they enjoy. As Barbara Wright explained:

> I like to know that I can come away [from work] at two and have the rest of the afternoon to myself. I know in advance what I'm doing. That time between my job and my family coming home is the part of the day I can have to myself. It gives me a little time to think and maybe do a little something on my own.

Those women in the sample who were employed part-time and who had a little time to themselves did not undertake a wide range of activities in this free time. Like their husbands, they 'pottered' around the home doing domestic-related activities. What was important was the ability to structure their own time and have some control over the pace of their lives. The women could do this when they were alone at home. Again this illustrates the way in which people can control their lives more at home although the ability to do this varies for men and women according to the family roles which they play.

Women who are employed full-time find their time is accounted for to an even greater extent. They are away from the home for a large part of the day and they must complete domestic chores before they can relax. It is not surprising to find these women enjoying home-centred leisure since the home is a haven of rest for them as well. Furthermore, their weekend activities are constrained by domestic commitments and the desire to relax without too much effort. Anita Palmer, who was employed as a full-time production operator at the Vauxhall car plant, worked the opposite shift to her husband so that one parent was always with their young son. She noted:

> I've got no hobbies away from the family. I would love to but I haven't got the time. My idea of weekends now is to be with Neil and my son. I don't see much of them in the week so that is my pleasure to be with my family.

Like men, women find themselves sapped of energy after both paid and unpaid work. They would like to have the time to enjoy a more extensive range of activities. However the routine of daily life which revolves around sustaining the household dominates their lives. It leaves time only for passive forms of relaxation in the home. As Brenda Richards, who worked as a secretary for a security firm, explained:

> Work is tiring. I do word-processing now which is tiring on the eyes. The company has taken on a lot of work and, therefore, it is very busy. People are demanding work ready from me all the time. It's a bit hectic. I don't want to do anything when I get in. I watch television, read and do some knitting. In the summer I do gardening. I very rarely go out in the week. I'm very boring really.

Of course the advent of television and radio has encouraged people to relax in this manner in the home (Gershuny, 1983).

Women's return to the labour market also has consequences for the nature of men's lives as women can often return to paid work only with the assistance of their husbands or other sources of help such as the wider family. It means that men cannot provide help only intermittently but they must become involved with caring for their children in a more systematic fashion. Martin Farrell; who had two children and whose wife was employed full-time, illustrated the work involved: 'When I finish nights I come in and get the children's breakfast and send them off to school. Then I cook the dinner before I go off to work. When the wife is working then of course you've go to do it.' This implies that both women and men devote considerable amounts of time to sustaining the daily existence of the household and the well-being of its members.

Even when hours of work do correspond for husbands and wives, the men in the sample were keen to stress the need to help. Margaret Kent worked at home sewing for a local clothing factory and her husband Leslie felt: 'When you see that your wife has to work very hard it just isn't fair with her having to do the washing up and then do the sewing. Helping comes through necessity more than anything else really.' This is not to suggest that the domestic division of labour is fundamentally changed when women return to paid work as the different responsibilities of men and women are maintained. Nonetheless the return of married women to paid work does mean that more of their husbands' free time revolves around domestic tasks in the home. Thus men and women both develop routines in which the home is central.

CONCLUSION

In sum the data suggest that men and women do lead home- and family-centred lifestyles as the Luton team alleged. Goldthorpe and his colleagues rightly pointed out that people's day-to-day existence does revolve around sustaining the individual household. Work, both paid and unpaid, fills a substantial proportion of any day and structures the form and nature of leisure. People are 'exhausted' at the end of the day and seek only to relax. They do not have the time or inclination to undertake active leisure pursuits outside the home; the home remains the site where husbands and wives unwind.

People's lives are dominated by their material existence. There was little evidence to suggest that people positively desire to exclude others from their lives and to live a home- and family-centred existence. Indeed, the interviewees did enjoy the company of family, neighbours, workmates and friends. Households were not as individualised and self-contained as Goldthorpe and his colleagues envisaged. However people enjoyed the company of others only where the daily routine allowed. The work involved in sustaining the household does mean that the family in the home occupies its own time and space. Where free time corresponds with the free time of others, social contact will be enjoyed. This implies that while families are not confined to the company of each other in the home they do not partake in the kind of extensive socialising found in the tradition-al working-class community by Young and Willmott (1957) and Dennis *et al.* (1969).

The impact of wives' increased participation in employment on the nature of people's lives has been noted. This was, of course, not considered by the Luton team. The home is also a haven from the outside world for those women who are engaged in paid employment. Like their husbands they are tired from work and want to relax at home when domestic chores have been completed. The home is enjoyed as a site which is quite distinct from paid work. However the home does take on a different meaning when women leave paid employment to care for children full-time. They find there are limited opportunities to enjoy leisure pursuits outside the home, especially since most people are at work. The period of economic inactivity is extremely home-centred for women. Given their experiences of boredom and isolation it is not surprising that they wish to return to paid employment when their children are less dependent. At the same time the return to paid employment means that even more effort is devoted to sustaining the material existence of the home. Women might enter the public world of paid work but their leisure remains home-centred.

The centrality of the home in people's lives and the importance which they attach to a comfortable and well-equipped home has been emphasised in this account of the interviewees' lifestyles. However their attitudes towards the home vary across the family-cycle. Men and women perceive and use the home differently, and this reflects their different family and work roles. The dynamic nature of people's home lives should not be underplayed.

This exploration of the nature of home-centredness also highlights some of the problems of drawing a strict distinction between public and private worlds which the concept of privatism entails. The family in the home is not completely isolated from the public world, although it occupies its own time and space. This implies that sociologists must continue to search for a more sophisticated understanding of the way in which people's home and family lives weave and mesh with the lives of others and come to constitute the social world.

Notes

1. Unlike the *Affluent Worker* study, the sample which I generated did not have tightly defined boundaries. As the aim of the research was to explore the nature of people's lives in greater detail, a wide range of respondents was sought. Similarities and differences in lifestyle could then be explored within the sample.
2. Although eight women in the sample were economically inactive, their reasons for 'inactivity' were different. Five women were raising young children while one woman had not worked in the labour market since the birth of her children, the youngest of whom was 17. Finally two women were retired from formal employment.
3. The final sample consisted of 30 couples and two women. The latter's husbands declined to be interviewed but interviews were conducted with the two wives.
4. Whether domestic appliances reduce the amount of time which women spend on domestic chores, as distinct from altering the form of labour involved, remains a source of controversy within sociology (Bose, 1979).

7 Reconstructing the Public and the Private: The Home and Marriage in Later Life

Jennifer Mason

This chapter is based on research into the lives of a group of long-married couples. Investigating the significance of the home itself was not a central feature of the research design, yet as the data began to accumulate it became clear that the home was a major focus of the couples' married lives. In this chapter I will discuss aspects of this centrality of home, and show the ways in which the meaning and experience of home are negotiated by husbands and wives, within certain constraints, in a process embedded in gender relations.

THE SIGNIFICANCE OF THE HOME IN LATER LIFE

It is fairly easy to establish in broad terms why the home has a central relevance for older married couples. Sociologically there are a number of indicators of this based on changes in public and private boundaries in later life. Most obvious are life course transitions such as retirement, and departure of children (where applicable) from the parental home. In the population as a whole, 60 per cent of people aged between 60 and 75 live in two-person households, compared with 23 per cent of those aged between 16 and 59 (OPCS, 1984, p. 19). People aged over 45 are also distinctive in terms of housing tenure. For example, 91 per cent of outright owner-occupiers, and 69 per cent of council tenants are aged over 45, yet there are fewer mortgagees (32 per cent between 45 and 64, only 1 per cent over 65), and those whose housing comes with a job (30 per cent between 45 and 64, 7 per cent over 65) (OPCS, 1984). This indicates a kind of distilling or settling of housing tenure patterns, and life course data show that for owner-occupiers in particular there tends to be a transition in later life from mortgage to non-mortgage ownership (Mason, 1987a, pp. 59–98).

These transitions, amongst other things, mean that the nature of home and privacy within it, as well as the boundaries between home and the public world are undergoing transformation and are likely to be open to renegotiation.

Because of its experiential and sociological centrality, the home provides a medium for further analysis as well as being of interest in its own right. For example, focusing on the home allows us to address questions relating to public and private domains which have been shown to be conceptually vital to the understanding of gender relations (Elshtain, 1981; Stacey, 1981; Imray and Middleton, 1983; Siltanen and Stanworth, 1984; Pateman, 1987) yet which tend to lead into a perpetual relativism when addressed head on. The problem is that public and private domains do not sit neatly at either end of a continuum, but are constantly intersecting and articulating with each other on a number of different levels.

This means that it is both inadequate and inappropriate to suggest a straightforward, descriptive content for either public or private spheres. The concepts public and private can refer for example to physical locations, experiential realities, symbolic meanings, rule-governed boundaries and interpersonal relationships. In sociology, 'public' can be and has been used as a shorthand term for: paid work, productive work, workplace, men, institutions, political, outside, unfamiliar. 'Private' correspondingly can denote: unpaid work, domestic work, home, women, familiar. But what is sociologically compelling about these apparent dualities is the way they intersect and operate in social and power relations.

A full and rounded conception of the home should embody the experiential arena within which these intersections and articulations take place, supplying a valuable analytical arena for the sociologist. This involves understanding the home as material, that is as a location; as spatial, that is as regions within a location; as temporal, that is as constituted and reconstituted over time, even at different times of the day; as 'metaphysical' (see Higgins, this volume), or pertaining to ideologies and values; as social, that is as groups of people and the relationships between them.

These dimensions of home occur in various combinations and do not necessarily occur all at once. Each represents a dimension of interaction (rather than a resource or property, for example) through which home is constituted, and the dimensions are not independent of one another. Constituting the meaning of home in everyday life means sorting out where and what it is on each of these dimensions, and analysing the meaning of home can therefore tell us much about the dimensions as well as the home. What is more, I want to show that this everyday sorting out is a contentious practice, and involves gender and power relations. The home, what it is, what it means, and how it is experienced, does not just happen, or get structurally determined, but is the product of negotiations by people who operate within certain constraints. Looking sociologically at the home can therefore also help us to understand processes of negotiation in their structural context.

The research on which this chapter is based involved a qualitative study of the married lives of 18 couples, where both spouses were aged between 50 and 70. All respondents had been married for at least 15 years (most for over 30 years) (Mason, 1987a). The interviewees were drawn from a range of social class backgrounds. Couples were interviewed jointly, and then on a separate occasion each spouse was interviewed individually, in semi-structured tape-recorded interviews which took place in their own homes. The interview setting was conducive to talk about home. Interviews usually took place in the lounge or 'front room', although sometimes in the individual interviews the kitchen or dining room was used because the other room was occupied by the spouse and occasionally other family members. I was often spontaneously shown around other 'public' regions of homes (see Allan, this volume) like kitchens, lounges, dining rooms, gardens, but only on one occasion given the 'whole tour'. The combination of joint and individual interviews elicited data on divergences between couple and individual presentations or versions, as well as areas of tension or consensus. An analysis of these differences has informed what follows.

RECONSTITUTING THE MEMBERSHIP OF THE HOME

The membership of my interviewees' homes was undergoing change, most obviously because of the departure of children, although membership of a home is not straightforwardly about where one's address is. I shall consider two main sets of potential members: kin, and friends or neighbours.

Kinship and membership of the home

Most of my data in this area concern adult and dependent children, so it is in the main the filial relationship I shall consider here. Seventeen of the couples had children, not all of whom had left the parental home. Five of the couples currently had (mainly adult) children living in their households, but all of these couples also had adult children who had left from between two and 16 years ago. In two of the cases, adult children had returned to the parental household after absences.

Behind these patterns were some important themes and contradictions. One of the central themes, and one which is familiar within the sociology of kinship, was the general view that whether or not adult children were still living in the parental home, it would always remain their home. In a typical statement, one of the women told me 'This is always their home. They will always have a home here'. No-one contradicted this, even where the home in question was not the one the children had grown up or lived in, and as mentioned some had put the norm into practice by having children back as temporary residents. On the face of it, this normative view of the couples' home being the family home looks rather like findings from kinship and community studies of the 1950s and 1960s. These have informed a tendency within sociology to assume that if home is important for older couples it is because of times past, and family brought up there. A classic statement of this comes from Townsend's 1950s study of working-class elderly people in Bethnal Green:

> Home was the old armchair by the hearth, the creaky bedstead, the polished lino with its faded pattern, the sideboard with its picture gallery, and the lavatory with its broken latch reached through the rain. It embodied a thousand memories and held promise of a thousand contentments. It was an extension of personality. To the married children it was also the reminder of their history and achievements – this the chair scorched by a sparkler on Guy Fawkes night, this the wallpaper where you looked for animal shapes, that the doormat which had to be lifted at the corner if the door was to be shut. 'We always go over *home* to see Mum on Sundays', said a married daughter. Part of what the children felt for their parents was what they felt for the parental home. It was not only the place where associations with the past and long usage provided comfort and security in old age. It was a symbol of family unity and tradition. (Townsend, 1963, pp. 38–9, emphasis in original)

Townsend's study was of course conducted in previous social, historical and economic conditions, and social changes clearly have some relevance. It is now generally much less likely that parents will be living in the same house they have lived in all their lives, or a house that has been in the family for several generations as was the case in his study population. Furthermore, the demographic possibility of a 'post-parental' phase of married life, namely a period after the departure of children and before death when husbands and wives are likely to be living alone together, has only really opened up since the mid-twentieth century for most of the population (Anderson, 1985). Changes like these actually provide the necessary conditions for 'home' for older people to be much more about *building for* a family stage based on them as couples, rather than *repairing* or *salvaging* bits of stages where home was based on a wider kin group.

Yet the importance of 'a home of one's own' for facilitating and symbolising the independence of 'the couple' *vis-à-vis* wider kin in this sense, is usually discussed in relation to younger rather than older people, as one of the status transitions on the way to adulthood (Leonard, 1980; Wallace, 1987; Mansfield and Collard, 1988). Mansfield and Collard's study of young newlyweds shows that: 'Material ownership of a home demonstrates adult status, but more importantly it provides privacy and a personal domain in which to exercise the newly-aquired autonomy of adulthood' (Mansfield and Collard, 1988, p. 55). Whether owned or rented, setting up a 'proper' home away from the parental home helps to establish some kind of independence, and provides a public expression of the legitimacy of the couple's relationship.

There were two factors in my study group which go some way towards contradicting the 'couple home as family home' scenario provided by Townsend, and which indicate parallels of a sort with the 'home as a building block in the couple relationship' image of Mansfield and Collard. The first point relates most directly to the couples' ideas about the appropriate route to adulthood for their children. Against the 'this is always their home' notion was another norm: everyone accepted that the proper thing for children to do was to set up their own homes; the children should want to do this, and the parents should encourage them and facilitate their independence. Some of the interviewees were clearly happier than others about this, but all assumed that adult children's homes should and would be elsewhere. Thus although it appeared that all of the interviewees would have been willing to have their children return to the parental home, the possibility or actuality of this was always presented as a temporary and less than ideal arrangement, as one woman with this experience put it: 'just while he finds his feet again'. Other people explicitly recognised the relevance of normative timetables in respect of children leaving home, for example by talking about children who had left too early, stayed too long, being about the age when they should be making a way for themselves, and so on. All were acknowledging that children would, and should leave the parental home permanently at a certain stage, and in a proper way.

The second point indicating that the home was really to be more a couple home than a family home is more directly related to the married couples themselves, and their need for independence from their children and other kin. This centred on the newly-perceived appropriateness of excluding relatives from daily life at home. This was less to do with maintaining independence in the face of increasing frailty, and more about reasserting autonomy following its compromise during child rearing. As one of the women put it:

Margaret: I think really the great difference is to do with the children leaving home. When they've gone you've got the place to yourselves and you haven't got the hassle of teenagers and over living around in the place and wanting to be at the sink when you want to be there and having their friends in and out, you know, four people fitting in together. Four or more people, whereas when they've gone there's just the two of you and life becomes much easier. You know, within the house because there's only two people in it instead of four. . . Coming in, girls coming in late at night and not being able to sleep because they're not back yet and all this sort of thing. You haven't got any of that now . . . it's much more relaxing.

Another couple, Evie and Pete, explained it like this:

Pete: To be quite honest, although we like company, *you* don't [*to Evie*] like company, because they disarrange your house.
Evie: No, dear, I wouldn't say that at all.
Pete: In a way [*laughs*] I'm only, you know, I'm only being fair, just think, when the kids come home, they're not untidy or anything like that but, naturally they shift here, they shift the cushions, they'll sit there and that, and they've only been here five minutes and it looks as though a bomb's hit it. It's only because they've disarranged something. I think you get possessive, I think that's the word. Well *I* do at least.
Evie: No it isn't, it's selfish, it's um being on your own for so long, having the house tidy that's it, it's being selfish//
Pete: You do you get selfish, and you get possessive, this is the point. And when they go back you think 'phew'!
Evie: Yes, you think 'ooh it's lovely and tidy again'.
Pete: That's right, and it's only as I say perhaps a few cushions been shifted or, or a newspaper lying about when, when it's not normally if you know what I mean. It's not what *we* would normally do.
Evie: It would be nice if you was in sort of a big house or mansion where you could let them have a wing or something [*all laugh*].

What came out of all the interviews very clearly was that home was important as an expression of the relationship between the couple. This was sometimes presented as qualitatively good, and sometimes as bad or rife with irritations. As one husband said:

> *Bill:* Everything is so different, changed in fact. Shall we say a period of 15 years, nearly 20 years, you've had a family round you and so on and so forth, and you suddenly unload. Therefore, you two, the two people who are left, then suddenly will probably find they have to make adjustments again. I mean you're then much more conscious of each other, there aren't the children there to, you know, widen the circle, if you see what I mean, and so irritations are just between the two of you, if there are any irritations.

At other points in his interview Bill stated very clearly that he felt it appropriate and right that the children had left home. The common denominator in his account and the accounts of other interviewees was the centrality in everyday life of 'the married couple at home'.

There is, of course, a tension between the focus on couple-homebuilding on the one hand, and on always maintaining the 'family home' for children on the other. For example, in all cases, children living elsewhere nevertheless held, and generally exercised, greater freedom of access to their parents' home than parents did to those of their children. This was demonstrated in, for example, their having front door keys, dropping by unannounced, behaving like a resident and not a guest, 'helping themselves', putting the TV on, answering the phone, and generally having access to the 'private' regions within the home. Some of the parents resented this, some positively liked and encouraged it, others thought it natural and unworthy of comment, but none prevented it. Yet conversely, by their accounts none of the parents exercised this free and resident-like access to their children's homes, although some expressed more satisfaction than others in the way they were made to feel 'at home' or otherwise once they got there. Of course, if one were to interview the children themselves there might be a lack of consensus over the extent to which parents maintained this strategy of non-interference.

The main point is that on the one hand, insofar as homes are groups of people, these children were always part of the family home, albeit their status was more like honorary or associate members. On the other hand the issue of how far it was possible, desirable, or legitimate to exclude children from the physical location of the home was clearly an element in a negotiating process whereby the home was being reconstructed both materially and ideologically as the locus of the older married couple. Reconstruction related to norms about dependence and independence of children as well as to the interviewees' own couple-centredness. The contradictions and ambiguities encountered in these negotiations may well be a result of social and historical change as well as life course transitions. In other words, couples such as these may be in the position of reconstructing not only their own everyday lives at home, but also of re-writing the rules about family and home in later life.

My data on other kin members' relationship to the couple's home were much less complete. On the whole I observed 'exceptions' being made to allow other kin membership, for example elderly parents, and in one case a sister. Where possible this was negotiated on a temporary basis, and did not constitute 'real' or even honorary membership in the sense that it was presented as 'taking in X to our home', rather than 'letting Y come back home'.

Friends and neighbours

The data I generated on the inclusion or exclusion of friends and neighbours from the home is more sketchy, but there are some discernible patterns. Unsurprisingly, most people talked about maintaining a friendly distance from neighbours (see Allan, this volume), and some had felt that the rules governing this distance had needed underlining in 'retirement'. For example, one man told me that:

> *Tom:* I just nod and say 'hello, nice weather', and that. I don't want them forever jumping over the garden fence. I don't like that, always in and out of each other's houses. Don't get me wrong, we're friendly. But now I'm at home in the day . . . well, you might never get rid of them.

It seems unlikely of course that neighbours would want to do this, since they are likely to have similar ideas about maintaining boundaries, but the use of the stereotype serves to underline who is excluded. Some people had relationships involving minimal levels of support with neighbours like, for example, taking each other's washing in, but were keen to establish the reasons why this did not contravene the boundaries. On the whole people spoke either of having less, or about the same, contact with their neighbours than in the past, the chief difference being in underscoring the rules of distance. Certainly there was no move towards including neighbours within the boundary of the home.

Much the same was true of friends. Although some of the interviewees (mainly middle class) had entertained friends in their homes fairly regularly in the past, and some continued to do so, others said that they were a bit more 'choosy' now. One woman, for instance, told me that:

> *Shirley:* One of the things I think perhaps happens as you get older, you learn tolerance, but you also become more intolerant . . . I'm certainly more intolerant of spending my time, which is very precious, um, in friendships that aren't really friendships but they've become habits. So I tend to keep those friends who aren't really friends at a distance, whereas I didn't use to when I was younger. I'm much more selective about who comes here now.

In summary, what was tending to happen was a reconstitution of the everyday membership of the home into the married couple only. Children became honorary, and sometimes most honoured, members although co-residence was ideally on a temporary basis only.

RECONSTRUCTING THE HOME

Aside from changing home membership, other life transitions lay behind a reconstruction of the meaning and experience of the couples' homes. The main implications of these transitions were for the relationship between husbands and wives, and the centrality of home to that relationship. I am going to draw out two important transitions and their effects here: retirement and ageing.

Retirement and the home

First of all, both the men and the women, but especially the men, were beginning to spend more time at home than they had in the past. At the same time home was becoming more important and valued as the lynchpin both of daily life, and of the stage of family life popularly called 'retirement'. Indeed, these changes were being played out in relation to retirement from paid employment, a transition which can be located initially at the social-structural level.

However, retirement is not a uniform transition, and neither does it straightforwardly produce a standardised 'being at home' life stage. People negotiate their way through the ending of paid work in various ways. They negotiate with other people, and they negotiate around structural and normative constraints. This processual aspect is one of the reasons why scholars aiming to study 'people in retirement' run into problems of definition: what criteria should be used to ascertain whether or not retirement has occurred? If retirement is defined as 'the ending of work', this merely raises the question of 'when does work end?' But when *does* work end? To assess that we need to know what kind of work: paid, unpaid, full-time, part-time, 'main life jobs' (Parker, 1980, p. 36). Yet people move in and out of different kinds of work, and do not always simply do one sort at a time. The concept of 'main life job' may be a particularly unhelpful one for understanding women's experience of paid work and its ending (Szinovacz, 1982; Martin and Roberts, 1984). And for those who wish to study 'households in retirement' these definitional problems are further compounded: whose work-ending is to be taken as the marker?

The original aim of my study was to examine some of these negotiations and transitions rather than to study 'couples in retirement', so I had not tried to standardise the various employment and work statuses of my interviewees by editing out of the sample people who did not appear to be 'retired'. Interviewees' employment statuses were as varied as, for example, a (voluntarily) redundant accountant/company secretary now working in casual part-time un-skilled manual employment; a previously full-time hospital social worker now working part-time in similar work but on a consultancy-tutor basis; a part-time cleaner now 'retired' although he had left his job voluntarily and was officially unemployed. Although in five of the 18 cases it could be said that both spouses were in some senses 'retired', none of these cases conformed to the stereotypical image of the transition: that is, both spouses reaching retirement age and retiring formally. Ill-health, voluntary and involuntary redundancy, voluntarily leaving a paid job, were all components of the equation. In five other cases neither spouse had retired, but nevertheless each of these couples had witnessed some form of employment transition for at least one of the partners in recent years like, for example, a reduction in paid working hours, a change of job or employer. In each of the remaining eight couples, one spouse had 'retired', or at least finished paid work permanently.

Therefore despite a great deal of variation, every couple had witnessed some form of later life work transition for one or both spouses. Everyone interviewed said that retirement was important and relevant to them both individually and as a couple, and it was clearly on everyone's agenda for consideration. It is this everyday discourse of retirement, and its relationship to home, which is significant here and, in particular, the ways in which the husbands and wives were negotiating retirement and deciding, as part of that process, what *counted* as retirement.

This issue is thrown into relief when considering the bearing wives' and husbands' exits from the labour market had upon each other. Without exception, it was taken for granted by both the women and the men that the wives should either retire before their husbands, or at the same time: women would not, or should not, continue in paid employment after their husbands had finally left it. Consistent with this finding, other studies have shown a pattern of women continuing in paid employment up to, but rarely after, husbands' retirement (Crawford, 1972; Peace, 1986).

However, in my study the empirical reality of the pattern of employment ending did not always match up to this normative ideal. Six wives did in fact retire before their husbands, two retired at around the same time, and five planned to retire when their husbands would, taking husbands' retirement as the marker. But in five of the 18 cases the husband had actually ended his employment first.

What is significant about this is the nature of explanation and justification given by husbands and wives to account for their 'deviant' sequencing of retirement and its discrepancy with the normative position. In the five cases where husbands made their exit first, unsolicited explanations of *why wives had not left employment* were given in every instance, and the situation was presented as problematic, or at least in conflict with the norm. These explanations included financial necessity; the woman's employment continuing only as a stop-gap until the husband either gained employment again, or retired; the woman's employment taking place at home and therefore 'not counting as a real job'. However, in the six cases where wives had made the first exit *no explanation of the husbands' continued employment* was deemed necessary, because it was unproblematic. In the seven cases where couples had retired together, or planned to do so, the pattern was always that the woman had or would give up her job on her husband's retirement.

The implication of this is that 'retirement' as a family life stage meant 'couple retirement', but that this was crucially defined by the ending of men's main life's paid employment. Other patterns of paid work ending did not really count at this normative level. This was the time when the men had finally left paid work and were spending most of their time at home ideally in the company of their wives. There was a clear normative message that men should not be left at home on their own in retirement. This implies that the ideological existence of the home is dependent on the presence of the wife.

In some ways this androcentric form of 'couple retirement' is not intellectually surprising, for although most of the women had been in paid jobs for most of their married lives – and were living testimony to the post-war increase in married women's employment – their employment had always been seen by them and their husbands as secondary, voluntary and supplementary in comparison to the staple employment of their husbands. Looking back over their lives it was evident that the women had tailored their employment around the servicing requirements of their families, negotiating absence from paid work following the birth of children, or during family crises. Seventeen of the 18 had taken part-time employment once their children were of school age or daily care for them could be easily arranged. All of the men had been employed full-time for most of their lives, and nearly all of their employment careers were uninterrupted. In all the cases it had been taken for granted that the women, not the men, should consider the domestic, health and servicing requirements of their children, spouses and sometimes elderly relatives in deciding whether or not to take paid employment and what type of employment would be appropriate. If one forgets structural gender divisions, together with prevalent ideologies of motherhood and familism (Barrett and McIntosh, 1982), it would be easy to suppose that the women were free to make choices, and the men were unfree, or constrained. Of course, both of these potential accounts are partial in different ways, but this was the scenario generally presented to me in the interviews.

Consequently the predominant view of men's employment and retirement was that it is more important and fundamental, and that women's employment and retirement – being chosen and voluntary – should accommodate it because it did not really count as retirement in its own right, or certainly not 'couple retirement' as a family stage. This of course meshes with popular concern about retirement and its construction as a social problem; for example the concern is about *men* stagnating, becoming 'disengaged', depressed, having heart attacks and so on. Also, I might add, it meshes with sociological concern. There is an abundance of research on men's retirement, but much less on women's (Szinovacz, 1982; Phillipson and Walker, 1986; Phillipson, 1987).

Ageing and the home

The second major factor having a bearing on the reconstruction of the meaning and experience of the home is ageing. Of course this is closely tied up with retirement, not least because the ending of paid work is a reminder, or a social marker, of one's age and its significance in our society. Other markers, such as age-related ill-health, adulthood of children and their departure from the parental home, birth of grandchildren, death of parents, and so on, provide very clear reminders for people of their social position in the last quarter of a life course and, very often, as the oldest living generation in their family. These issues were extremely important in all the accounts I gained from the interviewees, and the following extract from my interview with Sarah and Bob gives an idea of the ways in which they mesh together in people's lives:

> *Sarah:* I think apart from the obvious physical changes which go on, but inside I think . . . um it's hard to just describe it but if I can just say it very simply like this: when you're younger you tend to take lots of things for granted. You're quite sort of self assured in some respects and sort of very frightened and insecure in others. I think as you go through life and you sort of learn all your lessons and each one sort of helps you to adjust, and having got to this point I wouldn't want to be younger anymore, and go through all the hurts and upsets and the little things that happen to you that you take so much to heart. Because now, at this stage, somehow you see a reason for all this happening. It's helped to make you a more complete person//
> *Bob:* I think the biggest change is when the children go//
> *Sarah:* And I'd like to think that I've got more peace of mind now than I had then, so that's certainly a big change. I'm more afraid in other respects than I was then because I think, er, suddenly . . . some things become more precious. I don't mean material things, but your relationships probably become more precious at this point in life//
> *Bob:* Yes.
> *Sarah:* than they did when you were younger, because when you were younger you're very outgoing and you knew lots of people, and therefore it's all sort of hail and farewell and this is how relationships go on. And as you get older, you become . . . you judge situations, you become more critical, more wary, more withdrawn very often//
> *Bob:* This is because of experience over the years.
> *Sarah:* That's right.
> *Bob:* But I think that once children leave home it's like courting again, it's going back to courting.
> *Sarah:* Well I think that's because you haven't got any distractions and other people to consider. In a sense the relationship becomes more special then. You think, 'Ooh, isn't it marvellous'. Perhaps I shouldn't say this

[laughing]. When things are good you think 'Oh please God let them go on' you know, 'Don't let them stop now. Let everything last forever'.
Bob: But obviously when the children are becoming adult there are tensions that are there. They're feeling their feet and they want to do this and you're being a bit restrictive with them still//
Sarah: Which causes tensions within the family.
Bob: Which causes tensions, and of course when this goes it's a happy release because you realise that you've done all that you can do to prepare them for the outside world and they've got to find their own level outside. And it's like a weight off your shoulders, like a lot of responsibility's gone, and so you feel free.
Jennifer: Do you think everyone sees the children leaving as freedom?
Sarah: No. I think you never really stop feeling responsible, you know.

Within certain constraints, such as compulsory retirement, access to financial resources, health and physical capacity, people may of course interpret and deal with such markers in various ways. However, those very constraints, together with the social construction of ageing in our society, do help to produce certain similarities, or recognisable divisions, of interpretation. For example, one of my interviewees expressed a view common to most of them as follows: 'This is our last home, we won't be moving now, and we want to make the most of it.' And another said, 'We've been working at getting the house how we want it.' The practical manifestation of this kind of view varied. Four of the couples, for example, had moved house in anticipation of this 'last home' stage. One of these couples had made what they now considered to be a bad move to an isolated seaside resort, in a desire to 'retire to the sea'. Another had designed and built their own bungalow, the design reflecting their anticipated needs in old age. The other two had both lived in tied accommodation for most of the duration of the husbands' employment lives. One couple had kept and rented out what they considered to be their 'real family home', always with the intention, now fulfilled, of moving back in retirement. The other couple had always planned to buy a 'home of our own' for retirement, and had now done so. Other couples in the study had used inheritances, and sometimes 'golden handshakes', to pay off outstanding mortgages and become the outright owners of their houses. Some council tenants had bought their council houses, and without exception the ones who had not done so expressed regret at being unable to afford to do so. In every case interviewees were clearly angling for security and permanence as part of the 'last home' ideal, and this was mainly to be achieved through outright ownership and minimal ongoing financial outlay where at all possible. Class and other divisions between people, families, and households, of course set boundaries within which negotiations and choices like these can take place. In general terms it is clear that the inequalities which condition such choices are likely in turn to be magnified as a consequence of those choices in 'retirement'.

As well as self-consciously locating and securing their homes, some interviewees began to put more time and energy into home improvements, decorating, and in some cases into installing equipment and facilities which would enhance the possibility of their being able to remain in their own homes indefinitely in spite of anticipated frailty and incapacity. As a whole, the women in the study were either more aware of, or more ready to acknowledge, a necessity for planning for decreased capacity, indicating perhaps a knowledge grounded in household experience of the likely difficulties of doing housework under such conditions. Sometimes ideas for home improvements and so on had not got very far. Usually it was the men who hatched these plans, generally before retirement, and factors like bad weather, unanticipated lack of time, lack of appropriate skill, lack of money for materials or to employ formal labour, ill-health or simply 'not being as fit as I used to be', often hindered their completion.

Taken together, the two factors of ageing and retirement, and the reconstitution of the membership of the home, contributed to an emerging ideal image of the home: it was to be about relaxation, leisure, or at least non-work, it was to be secure, safe, comfortable, and 'ours', and to provide an environment conducive to a gentle process of ageing. Not only was it to be *an* environment, but *the* pivotal environment for the ageing couple, and for their newly-special relationship – whether that be ostensibly good or bad. Many of the men were explicit about having looked forward to, and worked towards, this very goal. As one of them told me: 'I've had a lifetime's slog. Now I'm looking forward to a comfortable retirement at home with my wife.'

WHOSE HOME?

However this ideal is clearly not a gender-neutral one, and looking behind it can reveal a good deal about the relationship between gender relations, ageing, and the significance of the home in family life. When considering each aspect of the ideal, we need to ask the question 'for whom?' For example, the ideal says the home in retirement is to be about leisure, but whose leisure? There is an increasing body of research showing that, for younger women at least, the home is a workplace, so that being at home does not automatically imply having time off (Deem, 1986). Of course a large part of being a housewife or a 'home-maker' does involve, literally, creating the home – establishing a comfortable and relaxing environment for the family (see Hunt, this volume). I want to suggest that the women in my study were producers of the home, and that this was done on two levels: first, for husbands and secondly for public scrutiny. The distinction between the two is akin to that between reproduction and social reproduction.

Producing the home for husbands was done in a number of ways. Most obviously, the women maintained responsibility for producing the domestic environment through housework and cooking. Although some of the men had begun to take more of a role in these labours, without exception the women held the overall responsibility, and generally performed most of the labour (Mason, 1987b). But the women also held a less tangible responsibility: namely for ensuring the well-being and health of their husbands, and specifically for smoothing their transition to retirement. This meant that the wives put both physical and mental labour into caring for and caring about their husbands on a routine and daily basis. One example of this is the pattern, mentioned earlier, for women to retire voluntarily at the same time as their husbands. One of the wives gave a particularly vivid illustration of this form of caring and its relationship to the home and gender relations:

Sarah: One of my friends had an operation in hospital. I went up to see her and while I was there – one of my colleagues at the office, about Bob's age, had had a heart attack and was in the intensive care unit – so I said to Bob, 'Oh I'll just pop along and see James'. And when I got there I looked at him and I thought, 'Good heavens'. Bob had been quite ill you know at times, especially at night times, having come home after the stress of the day . . . and as I stood there and looked at James I thought 'Goodness me, he's in the intensive care unit' and Bob looked ten times worse than he did. And it was *such* a shock I hardly slept that night. The next morning I went in and I went to my chief officer and I said 'Look I'd like to take early retirement' and I explained why . . . and I said 'I stayed up all night, I couldn't sleep just thinking about it, and I do really want to go, because I know that if I go and am at home, then Bob will retire'. Because he would have gone on for another four years, and I could see that at the rate he was going . . . well I didn't think he would last the four years, it was as simple as that. And so I had to make up my mind which was more important. Was the work more important, or was the fact of his health more important and the fact that he could relax? And so it wasn't really too difficult a choice because he was more important to me in the end.

It is, of course, significant that this was seen to be a special stage of life, and that Sarah's husband's health was in jeopardy. Sarah anticipated he would have a problem adjusting to home life if she was at work, and she felt acutely the responsibility to see this ran smoothly. She did this on an everyday, routine basis, although the example given is a rather more spectacular expression of this. The choice between her job and his life was a gendered choice. This is not because given the same circumstances a man would not make the same choice, but because a man would not be given the same circumstances – that is, women retiring first, or being at home alone, is not problematic.

Other women had similar stories of fairly dramatic accumulations of this routine well-being work. For example, Shirley told me:

Shirley: I'd done my job for years and it hadn't been a worry and it was suddenly becoming one. So I knew I should go. I think everything tells you that it's right. And the same with him you see. Because you know he was *very* ill last year and um, the same things were happening with him. Things at work were really getting on top, and it had never bothered him before. But you know I could see all the signs, all the things I knew that I was having the year before. And when you say to yourself 'What's the most precious thing, the most precious thing to us is being here, being together. What good is it if that isn't there?' And that's the way I put it to him actually, because that's the way I feel. And I'm sure again the decision's right. You can adjust your spending accordingly. You can't adjust anything else because you haven't got the power to.

In general, the responsibility for what Shirley calls 'being here, and being together', in other words for producing the home in its fullest sense, was a gendered one, and does not need to involve such dramatic manifestations. For example, other women talked of structuring their husbands' time, of worrying or 'having a conscience' about leaving them at home alone during the day, of curtailing visits to and from friends and so on. Indeed, despite differences between interviewees in styles of affective discourse, what was present in all cases and was strikingly gendered, was the women's accounts of the minutiae and detail of their husbands' states of mind, health and happiness, throughout their lives, but particularly in this last stage. At the very least they had all noticed and monitored these factors, yet there was little or no evidence that this was done in reverse in quite such a routine way.

On the face of it, these women were simply 'caring about' their husbands. They were not, on the whole, physically 'tending' or caring for them. The distinction between caring for and caring about has been rightly underlined in feminist critiques of those explanations of women's caring labour which suggest it is a simple extension of caring about, or of women's caring psyche. This is because it is all too easy to write off the labour intensive 'caring for' as though it were an integral part of, and no more than, being fond of someone (Graham, 1983; Dalley, 1988).

The point I wish to make adds another dimension to the distinction. It is that worrying about, noticing, monitoring, feeling guilty, promoting and ensuring everyday well-being and so on, are aspects of a particular kind of labour which sits more neatly under the heading 'caring about', than 'caring for'. It is mental labour, although it also involves particular kinds of practice. It is important not to lose these mental aspects of labour in an analysis which only counts physical labour as real. On the other hand, this is not to say that anyone who simply feels concern or compassion for someone else is engaging in labour. But it is to suggest that the daily, routine, constant, exhausting and indeed labour intensive nature of these women's mental worry work qualifies it as labour. Just as physical caring or tending should not be dismissed unproblematically as an aspect of the female psyche, neither should that mental labour which serves carefully to promote and meticulously to sustain the well-being of others. Indeed, just as it is possible to engage in caring for without caring about, so it is possible to engage in the labour of caring about without necessarily being fond of.

However, it is of course even easier to overlook the labour intensive nature of well-being or caring about work because it often is literally invisible in its performance in a way that, for example, changing incontinence pads is not. The everyday discourse used to make sense of it is one of love not labour, which also obscures its genderedness because if it is only love, then surely men are capable of that too. Of course I would not wish to deny that men are capable of love, but for these couples the structure and biography of the 'loving' relationship in which they were enmeshed did not give the men responsibility for everyday well-being work as part of their loving duties. If one were to focus on the conditions for this to develop, factors like the illness or disability of the wife are likely to be necessary, if not sufficient constituents (see Ungerson, 1987, chs. 3 and 5).

As suggested earlier, there is a second level of home production. This is related to the first, but involves the production of the home for public scrutiny: a process more akin to aspects of social reproduction. Again, in its fullest sense this does not simply mean making the physical environment of the home look nice for visitors, although that is an element of the procedure. Rather, it means producing the home – including its members – for public approval. In other words, producing the home means upholding in some public sense the status of the family household and making an appropriate private face publicly available. This comes close to what Papanek (1979) has called 'family status production'. She argues that this is a crucial aspect of women's work, centring on maintaining family status in the community through whatever means are culturally appropriate.

I am suggesting that the women in my study were engaged continually and routinely in this kind of process, in a way consistent with Goffman's concept of 'impression management' (Goffman, 1971), and that the culturally appropriate measure was the husbands' successful adaptation to retirement and home. For instance, many of the men and women told me 'horror stories' about what could happen to men after retirement, citing cases of male friends, neighbours, colleagues and even friends of friends, or 'someone I heard about'. Generally these involved descriptions of men who had become 'cabbage-like', and 'not interested in anything', or who 'stay in bed half the morning and don't shave or wear a collar and tie', or who 'sulk about the house', and sometimes of men who had died shortly after retirement. These images are indeed popular and familiar, and travel quite long social distances as is evidenced by the 'someone I heard about' route. But they are also images which champion a fairly rigid routine and high standard of domestic life, and the keeping up of appearances for the outside world. The images are of men and not of women. The wives in my study were engaging in mental and physical labour to ensure that their husbands and homes would not be viewed as 'horror stories' in a similar way.

Recognising that the wives were responsible for creating an appropriate home environment and public image, and that this involved gendered labour and responsibilities, raises questions about ownership and control of the home. The women clearly felt a prior claim to the control of the home, but this was also being renegotiated. Indeed, although most of them had worked in paid employment for most of their lives, they had always spent more time at home than their husbands. Their household responsibilities had always meant that they were grounded, if not always physically then certainly ideologically, in the home. Many of them were ambivalent about retiring husbands' apparent encroachment into the home. Sometimes their concern was simply about husbands 'being there' at new times, or being in parts of the house previously the wife's domain. Men's help with the housework, where forthcoming, was often perceived by wives (and possibly intended by husbands) as an attempt to take over their domestic routines and organisation (Mason, 1987a, 1987b).

It is in this context that we must view the ideals of togetherness and privacy at home: there was certainly a tendency for the women to be more ambivalent than the men about its merits. Women's responsibility not to leave husbands at home alone can produce an 'enforced' togetherness, hindering individual control of time and space. (See Mason, 1988 for a fuller account.) This underlines quite clearly the point that privacy *of* a location is not equivalent to privacy *in* a location. Thus any claims made that patterns of 'home-centredness' in this age cohort reflect privatism in a straightforward way need to take account of gendered dynamics such as these.

CONCLUSION

In this chapter I have focused on some of the ways in which transitions occurring in later life provide the conditions for renegotiation of the meaning and experience of the home. In general terms, these transitions and the consequent renegotiations express fluctuations in the meanings of concepts of public and private, but using the home as a central focus is more analytically productive since it provides a flexible although grounded way of looking at change, and avoids static conceptualisation of 'public and private spheres'.

Some of the renegotiations I have outlined centre on the inclusion or exclusion by married couples of other people from membership of their homes. I have identified ambiguities and contradictions in the process of establishing new 'rules' of membership and exclusion. It is in trying to discover the meaning of the home that these become visible. Other renegotiations are more directly concerned with interactions between husbands and wives. Seen in this light, the home is a contested domain of meaning and experience between men and women, and not only a principal site but also a component of gender relations.

8 Lone Parents and the Home

Michael Hardey

INTRODUCTION

The 'home' has become synonymous with the 'family' of husband, wife and their dependent children. In this conventional family the traditional role of 'mother' is that of the 'expressive follower' who caters to the needs of the children and her husband, the 'instrumental leader' (Parsons and Bales, 1955). It is the wife who 'makes' a home which becomes the centre of family life. These home-making activities give her a large degree of autonomy in the home but they also confine her responsibilities to it (Oakley, 1974; Pahl, 1985; Pahl, 1988). The home also forms the centre of the one-parent family but all the tasks of home-making and providing for the family are taken on by one individual. It is this socially constructed idea of the home as the centre of the family that is referred to as 'home' in this chapter as distinct from the physical space of the family's accommodation.

This chapter explores the nature of the home for women who are lone parents. The legal problems that confront lone mothers in relation to housing will be considered and linked to the economic situation of one-parent families. The experiences of lone mothers from a study of lone parents will be used to highlight some of the ways they have overcome these problems to make their own home. Sharing a home with other families will be discussed and the process of materially and socially constructing the home examined. The significance of the autonomy of lone mothers over all aspects of the home will be assessed and their degree of home-centredness discussed.

The sample of lone parents used in this chapter should not be regarded as representative of all lone mothers; however, in line with national figures, about half the women were divorced or separated while the remainder had never been married (Haskey, 1986b). This chapter is based on material from a research programme about lone parents which consists of in-depth interviews with male and female lone parents living in England with dependent children in 1988[1]. All the lone parents had pre-school or school-aged children and had been living on their own for at least a year. Only three of the lone mothers quoted in this chapter were employed full-time and Social Security was the major source of household income for all the other families. They all had their own households and none lived with their parents or in temporary hostel or hotel accommodation.

RIGHTS TO A HOME

The legal rights of women in relation to the family home have developed in line with the changes in divorce law. After both the World Wars the grounds for divorce were gradually extended and in 1950 the provision of legal aid made divorce far more accessible, especially to women. The Divorce Reform Act of 1969 finally made the 'irretrievable breakdown' of marriage the sole grounds for divorce. The guilt of one of the partners was no longer the central issue and within three years the number of divorces per year had doubled (Haskey, 1986a). In line with these changes the number of one-parent families grew. The 're-discovery of poverty' in the 1960s highlighted the extent of poverty amongst such families and helped lead to the setting up of the Finer Committee on One-Parent Families. Its report emphasised the housing problems faced by lone parents and stressed the importance of the continuity of housing for divorced and separated women (DHSS, 1974).

The Matrimonial Causes Act 1973 and the Matrimonial Homes Act 1983 recognised the housing needs of child-carers in a divorce above the strictures of property law which tended to favour the man. However there is still no legislation which gives unmarried women who do not have a formal financial stake in their home the kind of protection available to married women (Watson with Austerberry, 1986). The Domestic Violence and Matrimonial Proceedings Act 1976 provides short-term protection for women from violent partners who may be excluded for up to three months from the family home. The Act was originally designed for married couples with the aim of providing a 'breathing space' but was extended to cohabitees in Committee (Logan, 1987, p. 36). However the long-term position of cohabiting women is less certain and the effectiveness of the Act in practice questionable. In some instances courts have applied 'married-like' interpretations to cases and given priority to the needs of the child-carer while in others property and contract law has come to the fore (Logan, 1987). Local Authority tenants only gained security of tenure with the 1980 Housing Act. However this can create problems when the man and woman are joint tenants and the relationship breaks down (Watson with Austerberry, 1986). In cases where women were confronted with violent partners councils can be reluctant to re-house them.

Women who have never had a formal stake in property, and may not have ever lived with the father of their child have to rely on their own resources or the variable policies of local authorities towards them. One of the first studies of one-parent families revealed that young mothers in mother and baby homes were frequently unable to find accommodation and so had no alternative but to offer their children for adoption (Wynn, 1964). It was not until the Housing (Homeless Persons) Act 1977 that local authorities had to make a provision for such women. However they were likely to be classified as 'problem families' and offered the poorest housing on 'undesirable' estates (Harrison, 1983; Cashmore, 1985; Pascall, 1986). Lone parents may also be allocated accommodation with less space than a conventional family would be expected to occupy (DHSS, 1974).

Lone parents now have some degree of legal rights to a home. In this, widows are in the best position because the family home is not the subject of a dispute and insurance policies often pay the outstanding mortgages. However the majority of lone parents cannot afford to gain access to, or remain in, owner-occupied homes because of their low income, and are therefore disproportionately reliant on local authority housing or the private rented sector.

FINDING A HOME

The majority of lone parents have shared a home with the father of their children (Haskey, 1986b). When they become lone parents they have to re-constitute their home to meet their new status. Many face the problem of finding a new home due to the strictures of divorce proceedings and workings of property law. Those who lived with their partners in owner-occupied homes are the most likely to move, whether they desired the sale of their home or had it forced on them. The majority of these one-parent families move from the owner-occupied sector to the rented sector. This reflects a general movement into a lower income bracket that most lone parents experience. Those who initially manage to stay in owner-occupied homes often find that in the long term their income is not enough to support the mortgages and so are forced to move out of owner-occupied properties (Watson, 1987). In 1986 only 28 per cent of one-parent families lived in owner-occupied properties compared to over 77 per cent of two-parent families (Department of Employment, 1986). Lone parents who occupied local authority housing with their partners enjoy the greatest degree of security and frequently remain in the same property due to their recognised housing needs as child-carers. Public sector housing provided a home to over 56 per cent of lone parents in 1986 and as Eekelaar and Maclean note without its relative security the plight of many one-parent families would be far worse than it is (Eekelaar and Maclean, 1986, p. 78; Department of Employment, 1986).

The position of lone mothers in the housing market is shaped by their economic situation. Families headed by lone mothers make up by far the largest proportion of families in or on the edge of poverty. They also form the largest proportion of families with children dependent upon Social Security (DHSS, 1974; Layard, Piachaud and Stewart, 1978; Townsend, 1979; Popay, Rimmer and Rossiter, 1983; DHSS, 1986; Millar, 1987). Such inequalities compared to the conventional family lead to housing disadvantage with a disproportionate number of lone mothers living in temporary accommodation, overcrowded and inadequate housing (DHSS, 1974; Pascall, 1986; Watson, 1987).

Retaining or finding a home for the family is one of the first problems that confronts many lone mothers. Divorce proceedings and the reality of maintaining a home on a low income demand considerable adjustments. Joan's initial experiences of taking on the role of both home-maker and home provider are typical:

> I lived in a big house when I was married. It had two bathrooms and a large garden. When we first split up I thought I could keep the house on as I had the kids but we had to sell it because it had a mortgage and so on. Remember I was still upset about the end of my marriage and there I was having to find a home for me and the kids. We rented this place in the village but even with my share of the money from the house it was obvious I couldn't afford to keep it on for long. I suppose we were lucky because we got this place from the council after a year. I was upset at having to leave the village and come to the estate where I didn't know anybody. I know it sounds as though I'm being a, you know snobby, but it was also a shock to find myself living in a council estate. I'm used to it now but it is rather rough and not everybody looks after their houses and families as well as they might. That was the worst thing really, realising that it was

only you who had to find a home and if you didn't, well your family had nowhere to go.

The transition into lone parenthood for Joan and many like her is marked by the taking on of the traditional 'male role' of provider/ organiser while continuing the 'female role' of home-maker and experiencing a process of downward social mobility. Moving away from the old family home not only takes lone parents away from established networks but can be an additional disruption for school-aged children. However it is not necessarily completely disadvantageous and may be precipitated by the unwanted attention of a former partner from which the lone mother wants to escape.

Jane who had been a lone parent for four years lived in the same council house she had when she was married. When her husband left she had to arrange to transfer it to her name and claim Social Security benefits for the first time.

> I was the typical wife who thought it was my job to look after the house for my husband and children. All that changed when John [her husband] left. I didn't like having to go to the social [local Social Security office] and organise the housing people so we could stay on here. I mean all I had done before was to pay the odd bill because John would do all the other things. I went to the advice centre and they were very good to me. They told me I had to change the house over to my name and that they [the council] couldn't turn me out. So there I was going to all these offices with a young child and fixing up our own lives and making sure we could keep our home. I now feel that it somehow made the house mine instead of something left over from my time with John.

Joan and Jane had both been married for some years and began being mothers within the conventional family. As was noted earlier it is the women who have never experienced such domestic settings and had no recognised claim on a property that have the most marginal position in the housing market. Those who live with their own parents or relatives when they become parents have been labelled the 'hidden' lone parents as they do not make demands on local authorities and tend not to appear in official statistics (Popay, Rimmer, and Rossiter, 1983). Others, like Janet who became pregnant near the end of her college course, were virtually homeless. Her strict Catholic family had refused to have any more to do with her, as did the father of her child.

> It was awful when I first had Daren. The college were very nice about it but I couldn't stay there after I finished my course and we had nowhere to go. I went to the housing department and they thought I should go back to Ireland [and her family]. It was after that that I got angry and thought

'What right have they to tell me to go back there?' The welfare people at
the college told me that the council had to find me somewhere to live. So
me and Daren used to go to the council offices [housing department] nearly
every day and say we were homeless. In the end I think they got fed up
with us and gave us this flat to get us out of the way. It's one of the things
that I have learned about being a single mum; that is, you have to stick up
for yourself as no one else is going to.

For many lone mothers like Janet the local authority is their only
opportunity to find secure housing. However some councils have
closed their waiting lists and others may encourage people not to
apply to join them. In the face of such difficulties Janet was fortunate
to be offered a flat after a few months. Since the decline in local
authority building and the sale of council houses an increasing
number of one-parent families in Janet's situation have been housed
in bed and breakfast hotels or other temporary accommodation
(DHSS, 1974; Pascall, 1986; Watson, 1987).

ALTERNATIVE HOMES: SHARED ACCOMMODATION

Lone parents inevitably live in accommodation that was intended for
the use of families, couples or single people. The location and form of
this accommodation may not lend itself to the needs of a one-parent
family. This situation is exacerbated by the lack of power most lone
parents have in the housing market which means that their choice of
housing is more restricted than that of most conventional families.
Twenty-two per cent of lone mothers share their accommodation
with other adults compared to only five per cent of conventional
families (OPCS, 1984). Despite their limited housing opportunities
some lone parents have been able to make satisfactory homes by
sharing their accommodation with another family. Mandy, who was
in her early 30s and had a son of eight, provides an example of a
shared home arrangement. She lived in central London and rented
part of a Victorian villa together with another family.

There's a married couple with a daughter and just David and I in the
house, so everyone has got like a room each. It works quite well really and
we all sort of get on. We've all got our own little lives that we lead so we
don't really live communally, but we do sort of spend time together. I
always used to live with David by myself in Bath and I was forever having
people to stay at weekends so I wasn't constantly on my own. It does make
a difference living with other people and having a child around with other
adults. In some ways I wish I'd done it before, but I was sort of worried

about finding the right people to live with. You know, it's really worked very well all round really.

Mandy's home clearly overcomes some of the problems of isolation felt by many lone parents living in homes designed for the conventional family. However, Mandy was locked into the precarious private rented sector because the local authority had closed its waiting lists for council properties and her low income gave her little alternative to sharing accommodation. Lone parents who have a sufficient income may be able to enter owner-occupation by holding a joint mortgage with another lone parent. Mary and Sandra are a good example of such a household of lone parents. They had known each other for many years and they both worked as teachers in the local area. They had shared a Victorian terraced house alone with their three children for two years.

> We both thought it was the right thing to do. I lived in a flat and wanted a garden for Jenny [her daughter] and I knew that Sandra was unhappy, she was because the landlord wouldn't do any repairs. So we decided to try and get a house between us. We both have jobs but teachers are not well paid and I think building societies thought it a bit odd for two women to set up home together. I used to say that one of us should have a sex change! Anyway we found this house and got the money for it. It's been fine. We're both better off and our kids get on most of the time. We even share that old car out there which makes a lot of difference.

It is often difficult even for women with a sufficient income to enter owner-occupation by way of building societies and so the problems encountered by Mary and Sandra should not be unexpected (Austerberry and Watson, 1985). However within limits they had been able to choose their own accommodation and lifestyle.

MAKING A HOME

Making a home involves the expenditure of money which for the majority of lone mothers is in short supply. The Family Finances Survey suggests that 65 per cent of the total expenditure of lone mothers is committed to the essentials of housing costs, food and fuel so that the acquisition of household goods presents a considerable problem (Family Finances Survey cited by Millar, 1987, p. 172). Many unmarried mothers, like Dawn, began their home-making with money from the DHSS. She moved into a council maisonette with a cot, an old bed, one chair and an old television 18 months ago.

My health visitor told me to go to the social and ask them for money for things like a cooker. A man [from the DHSS] came to see me and wrote down all about what I needed. He told me that I should look around for secondhand things. Well I got this giro to spend on things for the house, so me and my sister went into town to get started. We went to these stores with cookers and things but even the cheapest cost more than all the money I had to spend on the whole house! I was very fed up because I only had a little camping thing to cook on. My health visitor told me about this warehouse place where they have secondhand things and put me onto these Christian Action people. I went to see them and they had this old hut full of stuff people didn't want but was too big to put in a jumble sale. They were really helpful and I got the cooker, a fridge, the washing machine, a couple of carpets and this furniture from them for nothing. I used the money from the social to pay off some bills and got a new bed for Mary [her daughter], some clothes for her and got some new curtains and wallpaper to make the flat more comfortable.

Through the help of a charity Dawn was able to use the money from the DHSS on what she considered to be essential items that would make her otherwise bare maisonette into a home. Since the changes to Social Security regulations in April 1988 lone parents in Dawn's situation would only be eligible for a grant which they would have to repay out of their Social Security income.

Women who have been lone parents for many years often become expert at 'making do'. Unwilling or unable to enter into credit arrangements new household goods have to be found through the secondhand market or by earning extra money. Charities such as Oxfam and the Salvation Army can provide a vital source of clothing which may be supplemented by clothing passed on by family or friendship networks. The initial purchase or replacement of the more costly items of household equipment presents many lone parents with a major problem. Joan had been a lone parent for 11 years and had three children the youngest of whom was 12. She lived in a 1950s council estate on the outskirts of a small town and occasionally worked part-time as clerk for a local building firm.

The biggest financial problem recently has been the washing machine. My old one broke down and couldn't be repaired. With my lot I couldn't do without a machine. I didn't want to get anything on credit so I got this job at the shop down the road just to pay for a new one. I knew the people that owned it and I could be home when my youngest came back from school. They said they'd give me cash in hand so I didn't have to declare it or nothing. They wanted me to stay on but I was worried in case the Social Security people found out about it so I left when I'd saved enough for the new machine. I'd do that again if I need something that I couldn't afford. I work and I get Social Security and housing benefit but that's not really enough to buy big things for the house. If I just put up with that, when things become too old to fix up like the washing machine we'd just have to do without. I don't see why my family should have to put up with that when I can do something about it.

Joan's pragmatic approach to maintaining her home pushed her into the black economy. She regarded her 'hidden' extra job as legitimate because it provided essential items for the home that she could not otherwise afford. However while she was earning the extra money she was constantly worried about someone informing the Social Security office about it and was happy to give it up.

Compared to conventional family households one-parent family homes lag behind in the ownership of durable goods such as washing machines and telephones which suggests that many lone mothers have to manage without household goods considered essential by most families (Department of Employment, 1986). Despite such problems lone parents are keen to provide a home that offers the same degree of comfort and security as any conventional family's home. Many like Christine are also keen to escape the public image that the one-parent family is inferior to the conventional family as a situation in which to bring up a child.

A lot of people think that single parents are all scroungers who can't bring up their children very well. I can tell you that this is not true. My home is as good as anybody's. The children's friends come in and wouldn't know I was on my own. It's tidy and we have the same things that they have at home. We might not have a video or computer games because I can't afford them but we have a good home which I think is the most important thing.

Making or repairing clothes, providing meals on a limited budget and other skills associated with living on a low income are important to all low-income families. However lone mothers have in addition to cope with the traditionally 'male' household tasks of home maintenance and repair. Many women had to learn how to do minor repairs and those who lacked readily available male help but wanted to decorate their home had another set of skills to learn. Sarah talked about how she had learned to cope alone with home-making tasks she once regarded as beyond her abilities. She moved into her council home after her owner-occupied home was sold because it proved too expensive for her to run alone.

When I first saw this place I nearly cried. I don't know who had it before but it was in a dreadful state. There was this blue paint everywhere that made it look very dark and depressing. I'd never done any decorating before but I couldn't afford to pay somebody to do it or know anyone I could ask to help. So I got a load of paint and so on and did it all over. I've learned a lot since I've been on my own. I can fix up plugs and so on. If I can't get on with something I'll ask a friend or get the shop to tell me how to do it.

An alternative strategy adopted by some lone mothers was to utilise their local social networks to provide the household skills that they lacked. This can have the advantage of allowing lone mothers to exploit some of their skills without the risk of losing part of their Social Security. Helen wanted to improve the kitchen in her house and although she worked part-time she could not afford to pay for new kitchen units.

The kitchen was very old and some of the shelves were falling off the wall. I can't afford one of these kitchens you see in the magazines but Jane whose son goes to the same school as Derek [her son] asked me if I could look after him after school for a while. It wouldn't have been worth me getting paid to look after him because I would just lose my benefit money but her husband's a builder so I asked if he could put my kitchen to rights for me instead.

Not all lone parents are able to cope as well as Sarah, Dawn, Helen and Joan. Lisa lived half way up a high-rise block of flats in an estate of 1960s system-built blocks. In recognition of the poor condition of the building the local authority was about to start a refurbishment programme and a neighbouring block had been sold to a private contractor. Life for Lisa and her young son and daughter was a struggle made harder by the extra costs of living in such accommodation (Knight, 1981). Their small flat was sparsely furnished and the only carpet threadbare.

I had no choice but to take this flat. I don't like being stuck up here, I don't go out much 'cos it's difficult to get the pushchair down the stairs and I wouldn't use the lift even if it was working. The flat is horribly damp in the winter 'cos the heating doesn't work very well and I can't afford to have it on much. The windows let in the rain and the flat is damp. I hate the winter most of all. I'm just stuck here with two children. I put up some wallpaper when I first came here in the children's room and in here to make it look nice but after the winter it got spots on it and came off in places [due to the damp]. It's very depressing. I'd like to get the flat more like I'd like it but I haven't the money and anyway nice things get spoilt. I really want a garden and a place that I can make a real home in.

The physical condition and design of Lisa's home undermined her attempts at home-making to the extent that she did not regard it as a 'real home'.

As noted earlier it is young unmarried mothers like Sarah who are likely to be given accommodation in the most dilapidated estates. Since the 1970s there has been a trend for the poorer sections of the population such as lone parents living in the large urban centres to become concentrated in specific areas of the cities. In Lambeth in inner London, for example over 32 per cent of all families with children were one-parent families in 1981 (Townsend *et al.*, 1987). This concentration of deprived groups in specific areas of the cities leads to a downward spiral of disadvantage and despair (Harrison, 1983). Amenities deteriorate and already hard-pressed local authorities find it impossible to cope adequately with the demands put upon them. Cashmore's study of lone parents described families living in the same conditions as Lisa (Cashmore, 1985). Like Lisa they wanted to leave the estate which they did not consider provided the basis on which to build a home for their family. The contrast between such areas where Lisa lived and the kind of home she aspired to was great. Some more fortunate lone mothers, like Norma, had been able to leave such urban high-rise flats.

> I've lived actually in Crawley for eight years. I got a mutual transfer [a system which enables council tenants to exchange accommodation with each other] from my flat in London to this house in Crawley. It was specifically for the benefit of my two young children, because I lived in a high-rise flat in London which was awful and my parents live in Crawley. When I was 20, I'd had enough of Crawley. I mean, it's a very dead-end town when you're 20 so I moved to London, and that's where I met my husband. I stayed in London until eight years ago. So this was the area I wanted to move to. I never had a garden in London, so it's obviously beneficial to everybody, I feel. I'm a full Londoner as you can hear from my accent. I love London, but not to live in. To work in, not to live in with children in a high-rise flat. I can make a better home here for them.

The shift in housing priorities noted by Norma reflect her desire to make a home for her children. She believed that she needed both more space than a flat in London could offer and a garden. Crucially lone mothers expect safe housing which does not have a high risk of direct or indirect violence or abuse from other people. High-rise and deck-access housing were seen as undesirable and potentially dangerous by lone mothers who lived in them. As a result they tended to spend a lot of time confined to their flats with their children. This could give rise to stress within the family that undermined attempts by the parent to make a home. Secure behind bolts and locks on the door, with bars at the windows to prevent children falling from them and blocked doorways to an unsafe balcony, flats like Lisa's took on the appearance of a fortress erected against a hostile environment rather than a home.

AUTONOMY IN THE HOME

In the conventional family the home is generally regarded as the domain of the wife and mother. It is here where she exercises day-to-day control and undertakes the tasks of child-care and home-making. However, the woman's power in the home is conditional upon the agreement and co-operation of her husband or partner (Finch and Groves, 1983; Brannen and Wilson, 1987). His presence in the home at weekends or more critically during times of unemployment can both be highly disruptive of the domestic routine and circumvent the wife's control over the home. Unlike women in the conventional family lone parents no longer have to be subservient to the domestic demands of a traditional male breadwinner (Parsons and Bales, 1955; Oakley, 1974; Oakley, 1979). Some lone mothers have left partners who ignored the needs of the family or were violent. Being a lone parent despite whatever new problems it might bring is seen as an improvement on such situations by many lone mothers (Pahl, 1985). Most women like Anne believed that they had a greater degree of freedom as lone parents with their own homes.

My marriage was a success at the beginning, I suppose. I wanted my marriage to be what I thought my mother's was. Looking after this man and being his possession, slave to his every whim. I can't imagine doing that now. Ten years ago I wasn't the same independent person I am now. I was the classic little woman staying at home bringing up the children, except that I did have the business [a small hairdressers]. I dashed home from the business to be home, iron the shirts, do the housework, cook the meal and that sort of thing. I thought that it was my responsibility whereas now in this house if we want food we get it ourselves, if we want something ironed or washing done there is a machine and we do it ourselves.

The control over all aspects of the home experienced by lone mothers allowed them to negotiate their own child rearing practices and set their own standards of domestic work. Helen who had been a lone parent for three years after leaving her husband talked about how she was now in control of her own home.

Looking back I think I must have been mad all those years making a home for my ex. Even when Joe [her son] came along the house would be all nice and tidy and a meal would be on the table when he [the husband] came home. We had all this furniture that I never really liked but David [her ex-husband] wanted it. So I just thought 'Oh that's alright then'. Now this is my home and I decide what goes in it and how tidy it is. I think it's great to have some toys around the floor and things. I could never have had all these plants in the house when I was married but I like them and it is now up to me to decide how I want to decorate the house. I always used to have to fit in with how David wanted things to look but now it's all up me. The whole house is mine, not just the kitchen!

Both Anne and Helen had accepted the traditional role taken by the husband as the 'natural' gender based division of labour in the home (Parsons and Bales, 1955). As noted earlier, taking responsibility for housing the family, which had for most women been the husband's prerogative, is one of the initial changes that many lone mothers had to confront. This does not necessarily imply that all lone parents are highly critical of the traditional gender divisions within a conventional family. Rather they recognise that it did not work for them or that they were unfortunate in their choice of partner.

Lone mothers have retained their nurturing roles of 'mothers' to which the responsibilities of the 'head of the household' have been added. This combination of roles can reinforce a feeling of isolation and estrangement from other adults. Janet for example was enjoying life as a lone parent but sometimes felt isolated in her home especially at times of tension.

It would have been nice to have someone to share the nice times as well as the bad times, you know. Often I've done things with him [her son] and it's just been me and him and I think well, nobody else knows about this apart from me. Other times when, like at the moment he's had problems sleeping for reasons which we haven't quite worked out, I find it tiring when I've had to go and tuck him in for the tenth time in the evening. It's at times like that, or when he was smaller and he'd cry and I couldn't get to sleep because he was crying or something and I'd think it would be so nice if someone else did this. I remember one day when there was a mountain of washing and loads of ironing, and I just found myself bursting into tears. I thought well, nobody's made me a cup of tea for about two weeks, you know. I'm sure if I was married I'd at least have one cup of tea at one stage. But on the whole, the sort of person I am, I think it does suit me to be a single parent because you are free to live the way you want to live and do what you want with your money. Everything's up to you. You don't have to argue about the way you treat your child or about your domestic arrangements. So from my point of view it suits me very well, it's a wonderful situation most of the time for me.

The majority of the lone mothers who had been married did not feel that the absence of a partner detracted from the quality of home life they experienced with their children. Partnership with a suitable man was inevitably regarded as necessitating returning to the gender-based divisions of responsibilities found in the conventional family. In part they were concerned about repeating a past 'mistake' by marrying but they were also keen to retain control over their own family and home. While most lone mothers had a low income, their ability to manage the household resources made a significant contribution to their sense of coping successfully (Evason, 1980; Pahl, 1985; Graham, 1987; Pahl, 1988). Jane expressed her desire to retain the independence and autonomy in the home that she had established.

> I have a boyfriend but it's not a live-in relationship. I see him some weekends, not every weekend. It's a faithful relationship on my part. I hope it is on his, but I don't want to marry him or let him move in. I don't want the commitment of marriage. I feel I can cope quite adequately as I am and I certainly don't want a man to have to look after. I'm sure if I was married I'd feel it was my sort of duty to get the meals and do the housework. When Frank [her boyfriend] is here at weekends it feels strange having somebody else in the house. If he moved in he would want to change things and I like it how it is. I'm not anti-marriage, but my life suits me as it is, thank you very much.

A number of lone parents believed that it was important to create their own space and time free from their children within the home. This 'adult space' was important to their sense of identity as an individual as distinct from that of a mother. Where space permitted this could take the form of a 'work room' where the parent pursued a hobby or did homework for an educational course. In other instances the main living room would be kept fairly free of children's toys and other impedimenta so that it could be quickly established as adult space once the children had gone to bed. The creation of adult space therefore requires the management of both physical space within the home and time within the domestic routine. Janet's use of space and time in her home illustrates this creation of adult space. She had a son and a full-time job with the local council but she was able to meet her son after the school's club had closed.

> My day finishes at five o'clock and it takes me about half an hour to cycle to collect Mark. His play centre used to open a bit later but now because it finishes at quarter to six I have to definitely make sure I'm there to collect him. There's a park which we go to on the way home from school if it's nice. We come home and I actually have to lie on my bed for about 20 minutes when I get home. I don't go to sleep, I just have this sort of zonking out time, during which he watches TV before we have supper. I think it's important that we have our own space. I try to keep his things out

of one room so that when he has gone to sleep I can have some room and time of my own. I might just watch TV or do some sewing. I just need to relax in a place that I have made comfortable for a while to recharge my batteries.

As Janet implies, 'comfort' in the home is equated by most lone parents with a sense that the domestic tasks are manageable. It is especially true for employed lone parents that the routine domestic tasks have to be fitted around the demands of child-care and work. For example Catherine, who was asked to describe her typical day, had a demanding domestic routine. She had two older children who were to some extent able to look after themselves but she also had two part-time jobs. Her family lived in a modern terraced council house near the centre of a small town.

I get up in the morning around half past seven. I do a small part-time cleaning job which I should do in the evenings but I can never find the time in the evening so I go and do it first thing in the mornings. It's in an office and they don't start work until nine so I get up at half past seven and I am away by half past eight. The children have got up by then and started having breakfast. When they have gone I do a bit of housework, have a snack for lunch and go into work. I'm back by about half past five and we all have a proper meal. I do a bit more housework, or do something with the children before they go to bed. Then I finish tidying up the house, perhaps watch TV. There is always something that needs doing!

Catherine's domestic routine was possible only because her children were old enough to co-operate and her home had modern amenities such as central heating and a washing machine.

Full-time parents like Lisa apparently have plenty of time to devote to domestic tasks. It will be remembered that her flat was in a poor condition and that Lisa had few domestic gadgets.

I try and keep the flat nice, you know clean and tidy but it is not easy. The children are always under my feet and their toys are everywhere. They haven't got anywhere else to go and play. The little one always needs something like a nappy changing so I don't get much time to do other things. It's difficult to keep clothes nice because they get damp and spoil. When they have both gone to bed and are asleep I'm just worn out. I have a bit of a clean up and then watch the telly for a bit. I hate it sometimes because I feel trapped up here in a place I can't really have like I want it.

Lisa coped in difficult circumstances but felt that she had become locked into what she saw as the isolated prison of domestic life. Living in dilapidated accommodation on an 'undesirable' estate increases the problems of isolation and reinforces the sense of hopelessness felt by many lone parents. As noted earlier the problems of high-rise and deck-access estates tend to make home-making more difficult and costly.

In contrast to Lisa, Angela lived in a pleasant house in a village. She had been able to keep the family home after her divorce with some help from her parents. She worked as a 'dinner lady' in the local school when it was term-time.

> Most of the time I enjoy being on my own with Sue [her daughter aged seven] but sometimes I get really down. Perhaps I've been at home all day and not seen another adult. I know I'm lucky to have such a nice home but it gets you down sometimes. I feel that here I am, in this home I have made for us that turned into a prison I can't get out of. But I don't feel like that often and if I do I ring up a friend and have a good moan!

Angela's feeling of being locked into the home is not confined to lone parents but is experienced too by many women in conventional families (Gavron, 1968; Hobson, 1978; Wearing, 1984). Like women in conventional families lone parents considered that keeping the home clean and tidy was one of the basic tasks that a mother undertook. Although some like Catherine expected her children to co-operate, the major part of the domestic chores were seen as naturally being part of the parenting role.

A study of the home and leisure activities in Nottingham found that lone parents 'faced the greatest difficulties in attempting to match diverse family demands to the poorer resources of space at their disposal' (Glyptis and McInnes, 1987, p. 152). They were also the most home-centred of all households with little adult leisure opportunities outside the domestic sphere. Those like Mandy, Mary and Sandra who share their accommodation with others have an important advantage in that child-care may be easier to arrange allowing them to lead a more active social life outside the home. For example, Mandy who shared the house with another couple, went out two or three times a week.

> There's about three adults in the house, there's usually someone at home. I very rarely go out before David has gone to bed. I always put him to bed and then I can go out. There have been sort of odd phases where there hasn't been anyone around that could baby-sit and I felt a bit sort of, a bit trapped. I can't imagine now living by myself. I do keep meeting people who are a lot younger than me and they're sort of surprised to see a single mother out sort of having a whoopee time!

It is important to note that Mandy's child-care arrangements were based on reciprocity and therefore did not present her with an extra financial cost. Lone parents frequently find it impossible to join child-care circles of parents which operate on an exchange basis because they lack a partner to care for their own children (Hill, 1987). Janet's home-centred and child-centred leisure activities are more typical of lone parents (Glyptis and McInnes, 1987). She was an active Gingerbread member and helped to organise trips and other events for lone parents.

> I do a lot for Gingerbread. It takes up most of my spare time but I enjoy doing it. We have meetings in each other's houses and can take our children with us. I arrange for some students at the college to baby-sit for people that want them. So we all get to the pub once a week and have a good time. Most of my friends I've met through Gingerbread, they're friends for life.

Lone-parent organisation like Gingerbread offer an important source of leisure activities for many lone mothers. Organised by lone parents to meet their needs, they offer the opportunity for lone parents to construct a social life to suit their situation.

Other lone mothers seek to separate their leisure time from their home and family. This presents a problem for women like Joan who discover that there are few places where a single woman in her 30s can go alone.

> I belong to the DSS Club which is the Divorced and Separated Club. I can honestly say I've been going there for about two years and I go there once every three or four months, not on a regular basis. I didn't go there to meet my ideal man but to go out somewhere where I could feel comfortable with similar people. I did meet a guy there once and built up quite a nice relationship with him, but he was married and I never knew. He lied. And I thought 'Huh, who needs them sort of places, where they go to pick up women and lie to them!' Nine times out of ten the guys are married that go there. I mean I'm genuinely divorced and they say they are. They tell you so many lies. Initially it's quite fun, but I don't really give them a lot of time, them sort of places. I don't belong to any single-parent clubs or whatever that involve the children. I just go around as a little family or else as a single woman.

The problem of getting baby-sitters and the difficulty of finding leisure activities outside the home which a single woman can enjoy encourage lone parents to remain in the home. The location of the home can make mothers like Lisa unwilling to go out even if they could afford outside activities. The home-centredness of lone parents is therefore often due to lack of alternative opportunities rather than choice. Making a home with room for both parent and children is important to the well-being of the family. However, even a comfortable home such as Angela describes may at times seem like a prison.

CONCLUSION

Many one-parent families have to make a home in accommodation that they believe is not suited to their needs. In some cases the physical form of the housing and its immediate environment may trap the family in the home which becomes a fortress against the outside world. Strategies such as sharing owner-occupied housing may increase housing choice for those lone mothers with sufficient earning or borrowing power. However the majority are dependent upon local authorities for housing in which they must then create a home for their family. Lone mothers are often reliant on charities, family networks or their ability to earn an additional income for the consumer goods that are needed by home-makers. The changes to Social Security in April 1988 make it more likely that lone parents will have to manage without some of the basic household goods or be forced to consider the black economy in order to purchase them. The new, younger lone mothers will be one of the groups most affected by the changes to Social Security in April 1988. They are the most marginal in the housing market and lack the supportive networks and 'make do' knowledge of the more established lone parents.

Lone mothers are the most home-centred and child-centred of all households with few adult leisure opportunities outside the home. This home-centredness may contribute to the sense of being imprisoned in the private sphere of the home. Thus the creation of 'adult space' within the home is important to those lone mothers who have little choice but to lead home-centred lives. This involves the organisation of both the domestic routine and the physical space in the home which suggests that lone parents require as much space within the home as the conventional family. A restricted number of bedrooms and combined living, dining and kitchen areas designed for childless couples or single people make it impossible for lone mothers to create such space.

The control that lone mothers have over their home-making activities and domestic arrangements is seen by them as an advantage they have over women in conventional families. However the relative lack of household resources in one-parent homes compared to that of conventional families means that home-making skills of a 'make do and mend' kind are important, as is the ability to develop strategies to overcome the restrictions imposed by limited household budgets. Despite these difficulties making a home for their family was regarded by the lone parents as an important achievement. The combination of inequality in the housing market and low income create housing and home-making problems for lone mothers. Their ability to make a home in the face of such difficulties is seen by them as symbolising their success in providing for their family and demonstrating their own independence.

Notes

The data on which this chapter is based were collected as part of research for the Alvey DHSS Demonstrator project, funded by the SERC and the DTI. I am grateful to my colleague Nigel Gilbert for his comments and criticisms. I must also thank all the lone parents who allowed me to talk to them, and the Gingerbread organisation.

1. A sample of 50 lone parents was constructed through the help of lone parent organisations, schools, training agencies and snowball techniques. Lone parents were interviewed using an open-ended technique and these conversations were taped and transcribed into a microcomputer. Additional material was gathered from lone parent meetings, social events and other activities.

9 Insiders and Outsiders: Boundaries around the Home
Graham Allan

The home is seen as an essentially private sphere. Yet, as other chapters in this volume have argued, both the concept of 'home' and the distinction between public and private are more problematic than is often recognised. Certainly the boundaries that are constructed around the home which give it its sense of privacy have not been examined very fully. A starting point for a fuller analysis lies in the recognition that the home comprises both a physical setting and a matrix of social relationships. In everyday life the correspondence between this social matrix and the physical setting, the ways in which they each define and give meaning to the other, is rarely a matter for concern. Yet given that the idea of the home as a private sphere, as a place which is 'ours', where we can exercise control and keep 'outsiders' at bay, is so significant within British culture, the distinctions entailed within this social construction warrant some discussion.

The purpose of this chapter then is to examine the social boundaries that are drawn around the home and the distinctions which are maintained between it and the outside, public world. Who is allowed into the home? Under what circumstances? And for what purpose? Who is excluded? These are not straightforward issues as the control exercised over the physical space varies a good deal. Even the apparently simple question of whose home it is is more complex than it first appears, as people's residential arrangements are quite often less tidy than standard categorisations would have them (Wallman, 1986). Moreover, even if the issue of whose home it is is clear-cut, some of those living in it will have more control over its use than others, for example, owners more than lodgers; adults more than children; sometimes husbands more than wives, sometimes *vice versa*. So too, which outsiders are allowed into the home varies between households, as do the elements of home life which they are permitted to participate in or observe.

In addition to these topics the chapter will also give some consideration to the manner in which different 'outsiders' are treated within the home. Although relatively little research has focused directly on these matters so that only broad generalisations are possible, the style and content of people's reception in the home are important not just for what they reveal about each particular relationship, but also for what they collectively signify about the ordering of the home (Seeley, Sim and Loosley, 1956). So, for example, such issues as the rooms that people are allowed in, the types of food and drink they are offered, the formality or otherwise of the way they are entertained, and so on, are all indicative of the social distinctions and divisions that members of different households make which inform the boundaries between the private sphere of the home and the public world outside.

Using the concept of 'boundaries' to analyse the differential access that people have to the home raises certain difficulties. While the home does comprise a private bounded space, with household members having quite a high degree of control over who is invited or allowed into it, the concept of 'boundary', with its rather rigid geographical or mathematical connotations, does not provide an entirely satisfactory model for social relationships. Certainly the social boundaries constructed around the use of the home and the sort of access that different people have to it are rather more blurred and diffuse than the concept normally suggests. For example some people invited into the home may at times be privy to more personal matters than their hosts would wish. Others usually excluded may be given entry on special occasions – funerals, emergencies, and such like. Perhaps most importantly, social relationships change over time so that the degree to which people have access to different aspects of home life is likely to vary quite significantly as their relationships develop or wane.

So too the distinction between 'insiders' and 'outsiders' is less than perfect. As well as there being different degrees of 'outsider', 'insiders' are not always as cohesive or as revealing to one another as the category implies. They have their separate identities outside the home which may in no small part be valued because they provide a personal 'escape' from the domestic world. An obvious example is the way many adolescents try to stop their parents ever fully keeping track of their activities. But so too, adults often appreciate being able to keep parts of their lives separate from their family and domestic roles. One of the benefits of employment, for instance, or membership of a social organisation, is that they offer some opportunity for displaying a different identity or persona to those generated at home.

While these considerations make the ideas of 'boundary' and of 'insiders' and 'outsiders' somewhat problematic, they are still helpful concepts for analysing the social distinctions which are embodied in the social use of the home. However it is necessary to remember that these dinstinctions are not totally rigid or set. Rather the boundaries being referred to are somewhat permeable, fuzzy and liable to alter. Indeed the relative rigidity of the categories in practice in different homes is itself a measure of some consequence in understanding the meaning that the home has for those involved.

WHOSE HOME IS IT?

As has already been pointed out in this volume, there is a large degree of overlap between our everyday conceptions of 'home' and of 'family', to the point that the two terms are often treated as synonymous (Oakley, 1976). This tendency to conflate the two terms reflects the shifts that have occurred in the nature of domestic experience, and in particular the potential for greater privacy that there now is, in comparison to the past (Laslett, 1969). The higher quality of housing obtainable by the majority of the population, the greater facilities and improved ambience of the home, the increasing emphasis on the ideology of conjugal marriage and 'family-centredness' all foster the identification of 'home' with 'family'. In this context, the home can be thought of as the family's 'natural habitat'. Members of this (narrowly defined) family do not have to *make* themselves at home, they *are* at home. Similarly, how domestic life is organised and what goes on in the home are a consequence of the negotiations that occur within the family, though of course not all members have equal say and the negotiations may not be as peaceful as the idyll would imply. Relations between parents and adolescent children, for example, often become quite strained over the setting of household rules and practices.

Yet while conceptually 'the home' is closely associated with 'the family', quite often those who share a home do not fit the convention-al conjugal family model. While there may now be rather less diversity in household composition than there was, say, at the turn of the century when lodgers and servants complicated matters, still many people's household arrangements differ from the assumed 'normal' pattern. Thus not only do many people live alone, but many also share houses or flats with unrelated others. Even when the acknowledged 'core' of the household does consist of the stereotypical couple with or without dependent children, others, such as elderly parents, adult children, siblings, lodgers, *au pairs* and so on, may live with them (Bernardes, 1986). Not all these people are likely to experience the home in the same way as those who are recognised as having fuller rights over it. Indeed many may not feel a sufficient sense of belonging or unity to regard it as 'home'. They happen to live there but it does not have the identity of home.

This is particularly likely to be so for non-kin residing in a family home on a relatively short-term basis. For example, lodgers, *au pairs* and live-in nannies are likely to be conscious of their status as outsiders, even though, in contemporary fashion, they may to some extent be encouraged to treat the house as their own. They are usually aware of having to fit around arrangements others determine rather than having much right to impose their own ways. Indeed, it would seem that tensions quickly develop if *au pairs*, lodgers and the like ever do take the invitation to treat the house like their home too literally. Often these relationships can be quite fraught because of the difficulty of maintaining the required though largely implicit boundaries. It is not wholly in jest that this may be regarded as the 'servant problem' in contemporary guise! (See Craik's chapter in this volume.)

The position is far more complex with 'extra' kin residing in the home. As 'family' the home is in some respects your home, yet control of it lies in the hands of others. One has to fit into patterns other people set rather than controlling them oneself. For instance, the disadvantages of starting married life living with parents(-in-law) has long been recognised. Aside from possible overcrowding, couples generally want to have space to themselves and be able to plan and organise their own home in their own ways (Holme, 1985a; Wallace, 1987; Mansfield and Collard, 1988). Having to share a home with parents, however amenable, and follow their routines is regarded as distinctly second best. In a rather similar vein, young adults who have experienced living away from (their parents') home often feel constrained if they return to live there. Students, for example, may still refer to the parental home as 'home', but often lack the previous sense of belonging and find returning to live there somewhat 'claustrophobic'. Following other people's rules and timetables can be resented once a form of independence has been experienced. In turn, as Mason (this volume) discusses, parents may also feel a degree of intrusion when children's renewed presence in the home disrupts the routines which they have established since their children left.

Recent demographic changes have made these issues increasingly pertinent for some of the population. For example infirm elderly people may be encouraged to give up their own home and move in with one of their children. Whatever the other benefits of this, many of the elderly people involved appear to feel a sense of loss, or even lingering resentment, at having to give up their home. Even if they have specific rooms set aside for their exclusive use, they are unlikely ever to come to regard the new arrangement as equivalent to being in their own home. The sad irony is that the younger generation also sometimes feel that their home has been invaded and that they are no longer able to mould it as they wish.

Somewhat similarly, increases in the numbers of step-children raise questions about whose home a home is. In particular, where children visit the parent they do not normally live with, especially if he or she has remarried, to what extent is this home regarded as theirs? Again here, supposedly re-assuring statements to the effect that the children should treat this home as their own signify the fact that it actually is not. Moreover should the children take such invitations at face value, it is quite likely that tension will develop, especially in the early phases of the re-marriage before separate 'rules' have been learnt, either between them and the step-parent or between the two adults.

Examples like these illustrate how drawing the boundaries between 'insiders' and 'outsiders' in the home can be more complex than it first appears. Even where specifying who lives in a house is straightforward, not all those there may think of it equally as 'home'. As Higgins's discussion in this volume highlights so well, 'home' involves far more than just sleeping or eating in a place. Amongst other emphases, its referents include a sense of belonging and commitment; the exercise of control over space and over the 'rules' governing home life; the notion of having created a domestic arena that in a myriad personal, yet ephemeral, ways reflects your choices, experiences, and relationships. Clearly the inadequacy of some people's housing conditions (not least families in bed and breakfast accommodation) is likely to limit the sense of 'home' they have (Watson with Austerberry, 1986). But equally, even with adequate housing, many of those who, for whatever reason, live in other people's homes are likely to see themselves as something of 'outsiders' and be ambivalent about the extent to which they are genuinely 'at home'.

KIN

As has been pointed out already, the home is seen as being the place for the family. Home and family go together and draw their meanings from each other. Yet the term 'family' is rather a vague one, referring to a different membership in different contexts. Normally when considered in terms of the home, the family is taken to be the family narrowly defined, that is those family members who usually live within the home. But what about family in a wider sense? What sort of boundaries are drawn around the access that 'non-residential' kin have to the home? Clearly the answer depends on how 'close' the kin in question are, that is, the extent to which in conventional terms they are regarded as 'family'. Here 'closeness' involves both genealogical and emotional elements, though the consequence is generally the same: primary kin are usually allowed a fuller vision of the home than secondary kin.

The most significant point to make about kinship and the home is also, on reflection, the most obvious. To a far greater degree than with non-kin ties, the home is the normal, expected place of kinship interaction. Certainly interaction with primary kin is not necessarily limited to the home, but equally there is no question that the home is defined as a suitable, indeed the prime, arena for meeting with these kin. To a degree this privileged access to the home symbolises the solidarity of kinship. Yet of course there is much variation in the actual patterns of home visiting which develop between kin. For example some parent/adult-child relationships involve frequent, yet largely unplanned, visits, much like the pattern described in the 'traditional' working-class community studies. Others are less spontaneous, though equally routine – the regular visit for Sunday tea, for example. In other relationships, visits may normally be fixed more formally beforehand; whilst in still others geographical factors may result in weekend or longer visits being necessary. Whatever the pattern that develops though, the centrality of the home for these close kin relationships is evident.

Yet while primary kin are usually privileged in their access to each other's homes, they nonetheless remain 'outsiders', at least to the extent of not being fully 'insiders'. Thus for example they tend not to feel the sort of restrictions others may feel about entering different parts of the house. Few rooms – adults' bedrooms being the main exception – are not to some degree 'open' to them. On the other hand there are quite strong conventions about their not being 'nosey' or prying too greatly. They have access to rooms others would hesitate to enter uninvited so long as there is reason for their being there. Similarly, except perhaps where there is frequent, spontaneous calling in on each other, some effort is generally made to prepare the home for visits by these kin. For instance special efforts may be made to tidy the house when parents or parents-in-law are coming, even if this just means a quick 'whizz round' putting things in their place. Equally it is not uncommon for the food that is provided to be in some sense special. As an illustration, stories of mothers routinely preparing a special Sunday dinner or tea in which a far greater range and variety of food is presented than is either normal or necessary are not uncommon.

The 'outsider' status of primary kin within the home is also indicated by the tensions which can arise from visits. Unlike conflict amongst those whose home it is, the existence, or even just the fear, of such tension, especially between the generations, signifies that the routine of the home is being disturbed. Thus, for example, when parents come to visit, whether it be for an evening or a longer period, the younger generation may at times feel their domestic styles are being judged. Whether meant as such or not, suggestions, criticisms, advice about the 'right way' to organise the home, and so on, can easily be experienced as judgemental and interfering. Children may also at times criticise parental standards, but this probably has less force as the history of social control within the relationship lies in the other direction. While the criticism is 'insider' in that it normally does not get expressed outside the primary kin group (in contrast to criticisms made by 'outsiders' which are normally directed outwards to others), the tension which can be generated indicates that these kin are defined in these respects as 'outsiders'. Similarly, the very fact that these kin, whatever the actual relationship, can 'outstay their welcome' in the sense of disturbing the routine organisation of the home for too long also indicates their 'outsider' status relative to those whose home it is (Mason, this volume). Overall, the point here is that while primary kin do have privileged access to the home in comparison to many others, this access is not as open as it is for the 'insiders' who actually live there.

NON-KIN

As argued above, the home is the routine site of family life. The family here is usually taken to be narrowly defined, that is typically a couple or adults and children. However to some degree other close kin are recognised as also having some limited, if ill-defined, rights to be involved in aspects of home life. The same is not true of non-kin as an overall category. In general the boundaries between family and non-family are here quite firmly constructed (Morgan, 1975). The home is the family's territory and space; non-family/outsiders enter only when invited and then often for reasonably well-defined purposes. Obviously there is much variation in this. Some families/households have a more 'open door' than others. In turn some individuals are closer friends than others and may be deliberately excluded from relatively little that goes on in the home. This though does not alter the main point. Because the home is seen as private, bounded, family space, the family – though not all with an equal voice – control and limit non-family members' access and participation.

NEIGHBOURS

Relationships between neighbours are particularly interesting in this context. Because of their proximity, the capacity of neighbours to interfere and disrupt each other's privacy is quite large. Yet while many people have at some time or other experienced some form of tension with particular neighbours, neighbour relations are surprisingly conflict-free overall. In no small part, this is because there is a widely-held consensus concerning the appropriate way for neighbours to behave towards one another. Encouraged by the obvious dangers of reciprocated annoyance, there is a general norm that neighbours should be friendly yet respect the privacy of each other's household by 'keeping their distance' (Bulmer, 1986). What is called for, in other words, is a general cordiality, without this becoming prying or interference. The spirit of contemporary neighbouring is best captured by a notion like 'friendly distance'.

In general there is no expectation that the neighbour relationship of itself normally involves people mixing with each other in their homes. Indeed the neighbour tie is one which is usually activated around the periphery of the home – chatting over the fence or greeting each other in the street. Obviously this applies to some neighbours more than others. Children, for example, may be allowed in the home more readily than adults. Some neighbours will become friends so that different principles govern the relationship. Those neighbours who help each other out by, say, keeping an eye on the house or taking in parcels are also likely to entertain each other in the home on occasion. This however is not the way most neighbour ties are organised. Within British culture there is a strong – and sociologically sound – belief that caution should be exercised over allowing neighbours into the home for fear that once there these relationships may become far harder to limit and control. Consequently with the majority of neighbours the boundaries around the home are quite tightly drawn so that domestic privacy can be protected.

This concern for drawing a wall of privacy between home and neighbours is not new (Crow and Allan, 1989). Davidoff and Hall (1987) have shown how the middle-class home emerged as a private, family-centred space during the first half of the nineteenth century with hedges, walls and gates serving to mark the boundaries between public and private spheres. Before the end of the Victorian era the privacy of the home had become a central aspect of much working-class life too. In particular, maintaining a strict division between the private domestic sphere of the home and the world of work and neighbourhood outside it was a principal means by which 'respectable' working-class families sought to protect their status (Daunton, 1983). As numerous accounts make evident, this concern for domestic privacy continued to prevail in much working-class life until well after the Second World War, not least in those 'traditional' working-class localities where gossip flowed so readily (Hoggart, 1957; Young and Willmott, 1957; Klein, 1965).

The link between domestic privacy and respectability is still quite strong in the late twentieth century, and not just among the working class. Certainly there is a general acceptance that domestic problems, conflict and tension should be kept within the family. As the saying goes, 'dirty linen' should not be washed in public. Yet equally it is clear that the reasons for this are not now the same as they were in those traditional working-class communities studied a generation or more ago. There the concern was with limiting the gossip which spread so quickly through neighbourhood networks. Now the social conditions which generated such networks rarely exist (Abrams, 1980). Rather than tight-knit networks of acquaintanceship and knowledge within particular localities, contemporary neighbourhoods are far more amorphous. People rarely know many others living nearby to any great degree, and furthermore most have no strong interest in getting to know them any better.

This is not so much a question of unfriendliness, nor even of rapid geographical mobility. The issue is rather that many people are not in any real sense dependent on those near to whom they happen to live. As geography has become less constraining with the development of more efficient transport systems, so many people come to rely less and less on those who live in the locality. They are unlikely to be involved with them in any context other than that of neighbouring, and this is rather a weak basis for solidarity. For example neighbours usually do not work together; they are not related through kinship; they often did not grow up in the same area; they have separate sociable networks and different leisure interests. What they share is a common locality, but for many this does not mean that they have any need to be embedded in a set of local relationships. The neighbourhood is just a place to live. This, of course, is too bald a statement. While many of us are not dependent on the locality in which we live, we still have some desire to be integrated and involved in local organisations and relationships, but on our own terms. The norm of maintaining cordial but distant relationships with neighbours facilitates this. Particular, selected relationships may be developed more fully, but domestic and personal privacy is secured from the majority.

Of course the emphasis on domestic privacy between neighbours can result in dissatisfaction and tension. For example those whose movements are more confined to a local area and who are consequently more dependent on local relationships may wish for greater involvement. Thus some full-time mothers of young children and some of the less mobile elderly may feel rather isolated and wish for greater contact with their neighbours, whilst still valuing their control over domestic privacy. Conversely some people may feel they have too much contact with neighbours and too little privacy. For example commonly expressed antipathy about living in high-rise flats or in tenement buildings is partly explained by the reduced boundaries of private space associated with these forms of housing. Apart from often having neighbours on all sides – including above and/or below – the area immediately surrounding the home is 'semi-public' and so outside the household's exclusive control. As a consequence, there is an increased potential for neighbours to impinge on one another's domestic environment, not least when the cleaning and security of stairwells, landings and other common territory is felt to be inadequate. As Roberts's study (this volume) indicates, under these circumstances the respectability of neighbours looms large in people's concerns.

FRIENDS

Whereas neighbours, as a general category, tend to be excluded from the home, friends are usually invited into it. Indeed socialising in the home can, to a degree, be taken as indicative of friendship. Yet in a sense friends have less 'right of entry' into the home than primary kin. They are there as individuals by invitation, and not because they are part of the wider family group. Thus in terms of the boundaries constructed between insiders and outsiders, the involvement and treatment of friends in the home is particularly interesting. The extent to which different friends are invited into the home, the way they are entertained when they are there, the aspects of home life they are, at different times, allowed to see, and so on, can reveal much about the way in which people construct their domestic life and the image of the home they hold.

Elsewhere it has been argued that important class differences exist in the use of the home (Allan, 1979). While the middle class regularly use their home to entertain friends, much of the research literature suggests that this is quite rare in working-class patterns of sociability. For this group, the home is more likely to remain the preserve of family, with mates being seen in other settings and contexts. Two main criticisms can be made of this argument. First, the literature that reaches these conclusions is now rather old, much of it dating back to the 1950s. New ideologies of marriage and new housing conditions are likely to have had some impact on the patterns reported. Secondly, as this implies, other factors than class affect the boundaries that are constructed around the home. Williams (1983), for example, in his study of London families, argues that while entertaining non-kin in the home is still unusual in the 'traditional' working-class boroughs, it is quite common amongst the working class who have migrated outwards to other parts of the city. Aside from anything else, increasing levels of owner-occupation among the working class are likely to foster new conceptions of the home and alter patterns of home usage.

Other social changes though are also likely to have modified the exclusiveness of working-class homes. As an example consider the position of mothers caring full-time for young children. According to the literature on 'traditional' working-class localities, these mothers were likely to spend much of their time with their mothers and/or sisters. Isolation was not a problem, and likewise most had no great need to develop neighbourhood ties. These existed in abundance. The situation is quite different for many today. Geographical mobility, married women's increased participation in employment and smaller families have meant that many of those caring for young children do not have close kin available during the day (Devine, this volume). As many studies have shown, loneliness can consequently be a major problem (Gavron, 1968; Oakley, 1974; Hobson, 1978). Structurally there are relatively few opportunities to meet others in a similar position or places to interact with them if they are met (Allan, 1985). The obvious 'solution' is to socialise in one another's home, however unlikely this might have been a generation or two ago.

Whatever the class of the mothers involved, the form that such socialising takes tends to be quite informal. Importantly the interaction is usually seen as part of the mothers' work routines in a way that other entertaining in the home tends not to be. Indeed in a sense the interaction is not seen as 'entertaining' *per se*, for usually little effort has been made to prepare for it, especially where the people involved know each other quite well. Normally the house is not tidied up to any great extent beforehand, nor is any special food prepared. Thus these occasions have quite a different character from more formal 'coffee-mornings' when a number of people may be specifically invited round and a good deal of effort made to present a particular image of the home. Instead they involve the home 'in use', as it were, with the mothers talking over tea or coffee as they share, and thereby gain some relief from, the demands of children.

Usually this type of home socialising occurs during the 'slack' periods of the women's routines, typically at times during weekday mornings or afternoons when meals are not being prepared or cleared and when older children are still at school. Certainly there is some pressure for such visits to draw to an end once husbands return home. Yet this is not just because the day now takes on a different tempo as the home is once more tidied, an evening meal produced and children prepared for bed. It is also because the women are no longer in control of the home as a physical and social setting. While the home is generally seen as the wife's domain, when husbands are present they often exercise a strategic control over its use in much the same way as they do over household finances. Thus, as researchers like Finch

(1983), McKee and Bell (1986) and Mason (this volume) indicate, wives can experience the presence of their husbands in the home during the day as quite constraining.

The character of these relationships can, of course, vary a good deal. Most pertinently, differences occur in the boundaries governing their involvement as outsiders in home life. To begin with, there is the extent to which relatively 'privileged' information about domestic relations is disclosed. In many of these friendships a good deal of such knowledge may be gained as problems to do with running the home and 'managing' family relationships – both of which are, of course, integral to their common work as housewives – are talked over. In addition though, there is the question of how restricted these friendships are in context. Some may only ever involve the individual women meeting during their housework schedules. Others will be broader and also involve sociability during evenings or at weekends as couples or families. What this indicates is that the access which friends have to home life depends in some measure on the nature of the relationship that exists between those whose home it is. Thus where, in Bott's (1957) long-established term, marriages are 'segregated', not only is it unlikely that the couple will socialise jointly with friends, but moreover the use of the home for entertaining non-kin will probably be limited, possibly to times when the husband is at work or otherwise absent.

Even by considering simple illustrations like this, it is evident that the extent to which friends and other 'outsiders' are given access to domestic life in the home can vary quite substantially. As indicated above this will be patterned to some extent by 'household' factors, such as the organisation of the marital tie or the extent to which the household as a unit welcomes or discourages visits from 'outsiders'. This in turn is likely to be influenced by the degree to which the home is felt to meet normative conventions about 'normal' family life. For example, there is often reluctance to invite people in if the home's material standards are thought to be below par; or if there is domestic conflict and/or violence; or, indeed, if a dependent elderly person being cared for in the home causes embarrassment through, say, dementia or incontinence (Mogey, 1956; Dobash and Dobash, 1980; Briggs and Oliver, 1985).

However it is not only these types of 'household' factor which influence how much, and which, aspects of home life are revealed to friends, any more than it is simply a question of personality or individual trust. The style or manner with which people are treated when they are in the home is also important. Obviously this will not be uniform. Some people will normally be treated one way, others another. Indeed closer friends may at different times be treated quite differently depending on the reason and context of the visit. A central distinction to make here concerns the degree or level of formality which pertains to the visit. For the sake of simplicity, consider the differences there are between entertaining friends and having them 'pop in'.

Friends who 'pop in' to each other's homes rather than always being explicitly invited are likely to be good friends who live nearby. Whether these visits are haphazard or regular, the fact that the friends have developed the sort of relationship that allows them to enter each other's private arena without forewarning indicates the level of trust that exists between them. In this sort of relationship each sees the home – or at least its downstairs, living areas – as it normally is, without its being put into any special sort of order beforehand. Equally they are likely to see aspects of domestic routines and relationships generally hidden from less close friends.

Yet the 'outsider' status of these friends clearly remains apparent in a number of respects. Thus, while they do have a freer access to the home than most, there are still areas of domestic life and the home which are less visible than others. So too friends usually only call round at times which will not interfere with the household's normal routines. Early mornings, meal times, late evenings are generally seen as inappropriate times to visit. More interestingly those visited are likely to make some effort to tidy their house up a little in front of their friends. The point here is not really to pretend that the home is normally less disorganised than it currently appears, for these friends will know the normal state. The tidying up, however token or otherwise it is, is more a reflection of the visitors' outsider status and a way of demonstrating hospitality. Similarly offering food and drink – tea, coffee, alcohol, biscuits, cake, or whatever – also indicates 'outsider' status. Even if the guest is familiar enough to offer to make it – 'Shall I put the kettle on?' – the fact of asking serves to underscore the distinction.

Entertaining friends in the home generally has a rather different character to their just 'popping in'. It usually involves a greater preparation and a degree of formality, even though the intention may be to generate an ambience of informality. It also entails a different presentation of the home as organised space, which itself is influenced by the social position of the households involved. To see this, first consider the traditional style of entertaining associated with the 'respectable' working class of a generation or two ago. As various community and family studies show, non-kin were only quite rarely invited into the home. Relationships were by and large maintained in other settings – work, social clubs, the street. (See Allan, 1979 for a summary.) Where friends were entertained in the home, they generally seem to have been treated in a quite formal way. They were likely to be taken into the front room or parlour, which was typically kept 'for best' rather than used for everyday living, sat down and given tea and specially prepared cakes served on the best china.

This highly stylised form of entertaing non-kin, dominant amongst the 'decent' working class in the middle decades of this century and in some respects reflecting earlier middle-class patterns, indicates well the careful boundaries constructed around the home. Although welcomed in as a special friend, the 'outsider' status is pervasive. They may be told to make themselves at home, but everything about their treatment shows that they are not. Aside again from the significance of the food and drink specially prepared and served for them, the use of the parlour for entertaining is particularly telling. Here was a room which was kept tidied and uncluttered, not suffering the wear and tear of other parts of the home, reserved for special events such as Christmas and other family rituals. The placing of visitors and guests in this room certainly demonstrated their status and the regard with which they were held, but also of course it served to keep the rest of the home somewhat hidden. In other words, this room can almost be seen as an interstitial or 'halfway' space, acting as a barrier to the 'real' home yet simultaneously allowing a perfected view of it.

Contemporary middle-class patterns of entertaining are in marked contrast to this traditional working-class form, even though the home is still displayed in a manner which disguises its routine practices somewhat. Although those being entertained may often have seen the home in a less organised state, an effort is still made to present the home in a pristine and tidied fashion that reflects respect for the guests as well as demonstrating the host's capacity to put on an appropriate display. Consider here the classic middle-class form of entertaining – the dinner party. Notwithstanding the variation there can be in details, the central element of dinner parties is the traditional practice of expressing communion through the sharing of food. Importantly, of course, the meal given is no ordinary, run-of-the-mill meal. Much time and effort goes into its planning, preparation and presentation. On such occasions the meal not only serves as the focus for the interaction but also reflects on the capability, skill and virtuosity of the host. In this respect conspicuous display is a significant element within this style of entertaining.

It is not just the food which is on display. What matters is the creation of an appropriate ambience: relaxed and informal, yet stylish and different. To this end the home is also ordered so as to create, or at least encourage, a particular mood. The room(s) to be used are especially arranged and tidied; appropriate lighting, frequently featuring candle light, is organised; the table is formally laid out with best glasses, table-ware and napkins; particular music may be selected for later in the evening; and so on. all this effort is to make the event a little special for those involved. Yet it also serves as a display of the way in which the home as private space has been constructed. It is a statement to outsiders, however familiar they may be, about the style, values and taste of the individual(s) whose home it is. (For a discussion of the way in which the home is seen to express personality, see Craik's chapter in this volume). Thus the dinner party is a mode of entertaining which uses the home as an arena, yet which in the process clearly manipulates those aspects of it available for scrutiny.

CONCLUSION

The focus of this chapter has been on the permeability of the social boundaries which people construct around their homes. The concern has been with the extent to which different 'outsiders' are permitted entry to the privacy of the home. The chapter has, of course, concentrated on rather broad categories and so ignored the more subtle distinctions and discriminations made by households in their day-to-day affairs. Equally it has had little to say about the differences and variations which occur between households, whether these be a consequence of major structural factors like gender, life course position or ethnicity, or the result of more personal and idiosyncratic aspects of sociability styles. One difficulty here is that there is so little contemporary research into the ways in which different people regard and treat their home. (As Morgan (1975) suggests, Seeley *et al.*'s (1956) study of *Crestwood Heights* remains one of the few which include a developed analysis of the social meaning and significance of the home.) Despite its acknowledged problems, fresh research in the tradition of ethnographic community studies would in this respect be welcome.

If the data were available, it would undoubtedly show both that the boundaries constructed around the home by any household change over time as their circumstances alter, and that there are more general temporal shifts in the way that the home is defined and used. A predominant view is that people's lives have become more home-centred and privatised, though exactly what this entails is often unclear (Saunders and Williams, 1988; Crow and Allan, 1989; Devine, this volume). One aspect of it is that the home has become more significant in people's world view. They take a greater pride in their home; commit more resources to it; gain more of their sense of identity from it; spend more leisure time in it; and so forth. The corollary of this is often taken to be increased privatisation: because people spend more time in their home they are less involved with non-domestic social relationships to the detriment of work, neighbourhood and other forms of collective organisation.

However these two elements do not necessarily go together, at least not in the way usually envisaged. While the home and all it represents may now be more central in people's lives generally, (though this itself appears to be a very male vision), it does not follow that non-domestic relationships have become of little consequence. Instead these relationships may themselves have become 'privatised'. That is, rather than taking a public, collective form, as the home has developed so the more important of these relationships may more frequently be framed within this private domain. Although the absence of recent studies makes it hard to demonstrate, what is being suggested here is that the boundaries constructed around the home are likely to have shifted and become somewhat more open as the standards of people's homes improve and it becomes more significant in their lives.

Thus changes in the comfort of the home; the increased amenities and facilities found there; the efforts which go into personalising and moulding homes; architectural shifts in the use of space, especially the creation of 'through lounges' and the modification of kitchens into more social areas; all these types of change are arguably more likely to encourage the display of the home and open up the boundaries around it as to lead to its being privatised in the restricted sense usually meant. Similarly lower-density housing and improvements in noise insulation may make it less necessary to keep neighbours clearly at bay as privacy can be assumed rather than needing to be guarded continually. It would certainly be curious if, with so much effort, money and time currently being spent on creating the right 'style' or 'feel' in the home, there was not a concomitant shift in the willingness of people to display the effects to those they know. Recent developments in home-centredness, in other words, may well have resulted in the boundaries around the home being less tightly forged.

10 Homes and Institutions
Joan Higgins

All the earlier essays in this book have been concerned with the social relationships of people who live in domestic settings which they regard as 'home', but there is, of course, a small but growing proportion of the population who live, on a long-term basis, in settings which are not their own homes nor those of friends or relatives. They live in prisons, hostels, boarding houses, hotels, boarding schools, long-stay hospital wards, children's homes, residential care homes and nursing homes. They do so sometimes out of choice but often out of necessity. In many cases they are dependent in some way, either because of physical or mental infirmity, or they have special needs which cannot be met in a domestic environment. In the case of criminal offenders, they may be regarded as a threat to society and deliberately removed from their own homes. Many of the institutions in which this diverse group spend their lives are either owned by the state or are governed by state policies which are designed to ensure certain standards of care and facilities. In a number of cases the state intervenes to create a substitute home and a 'home-like' or 'homely' environment. This kind of intervention affords us a unique opportunity to examine how public agencies (as they see it – representing public opinion) set out to create a 'home' *ab initio*. It brings into sharp focus the kind of criteria we employ when defining a 'home' and the kind of structures, relationships and facilities we seek to replicate when providing a home for those who do not have one.

The main focus of this chapter will be upon the ways in which social policy reflects attitudes to the home and to home life and at the attempts to re-create domestic environments in institutional settings. The development of residential care and the evolution of institutional regimes, in which people spend all or part of their lives, involves both explicit and implicit statements about the nature of domestic environments and routines. There is hardly a better testing ground for examining the essential nature of 'home' and the power of the modern domestic ideal.

It is important to begin by distinguishing between the types of residential setting described above. Some of them, such as prisons or some long-stay hospital wards, have what Miller and Gwynne (1972) describe as a 'warehousing' function. They are essentially for 'storing' people, either for the purpose of punishment or because no alternative accommodation is available. In these cases, although there may be some attempt to provide minimal domestic comforts (televisions, pictures, personal possessions) there is no intention to provide a substitute home or a home-like environment. Equally, there are institutions (such as boarding schools) which provide special facilities and where people live for part of a year. Once again, they are not designed to substitute for their own homes (to which they are expected to return) and there are only symbolic gestures towards domesticity. The real concern of this chapter is with settings such as residential care homes and nursing homes where residents live on a permanent and long-term basis, usually for the rest of their lives. Their own homes are often sold or otherwise disposed of and the institution to which they move or are moved is now their only home. Although a small number of people with a mental or physical handicap also live in such institutions this chapter focuses primarily on elderly people in homes. It looks at four main issues: the numbers of people in homes and who they are; the concept of 'home' in residential care; the realisation of the domestic ideal in institutions; and the physical and metaphysical meaning of 'home'.

PEOPLE LIVING IN 'HOMES'

The number of elderly people living in residential homes has risen significantly in the last decade. In 1986 there were a total of 233 600 people living in this type of care in the United Kingdom. 120 900 were in homes provided by local authorities, while 112 700 were in voluntary or private homes (more than double the numbers in this sector a decade earlier). In addition there were 13 300 physically handicapped people (under 65 years) in 'homes' as well as 9500 people with a mental illness and 27 800 with a mental handicap. The number of places in voluntary and private homes for these last two groups has increased substantially in recent years but the majority (and in the case of people with a mental handicap a large majority) of people are still housed by local authorities (Central Statistical Office, 1988, p. 128). The National Health Service provides over 40 000 long-stay beds for elderly people and the private and voluntary sector slightly fewer. In total there are just four per cent of over 65 year olds in the UK living in residential accommodation of some form and this is a substantially lower proportion than in many European countries and countries like Australia (Laing, 1987, pp. 161–81).

As the numbers of people in these groups in residential homes (with the exception of the physically handicapped) has risen sharply in the 1980s the number of children in care has gone down. In 1985 there were 72 800 in care, with around half of them 'boarded out' with foster parents. Only a fifth of them were in community homes compared with one third in 1977. A very small proportion were in voluntary homes or hostels (Central Statistical Office, 1988, p. 129).

A study carried out by Wade *et al.* in 1980 of four representative Social Services Departments and four Area Health Authorities provided detailed information about the characteristics of elderly people in 'homes'. Residents were predominantly older (over 75 years) women, the vast majority of whom were either single or widowed, divorced or separated. Women outnumbered men by a ratio of 1 : 2.6 in local authority homes, 1 : 2.2 in voluntary homes, 1 : 5.0 in private residential homes and 1 : 15.3 in private nursing homes (Wade *et al.*, 1983, p. 46). With the exception of the figure for private nursing homes (which is unusually high) these figures are consistent with other national samples. The ratio of 1 : 5 men to women obtained in a study of nursing homes by Challis and Bartlett (1988) is perhaps a more realistic figure and is substantiated by other studies (Andrews, 1984; Lowrey and Briggs, 1988). Wade *et al.* (1983) show that older women are much more likely than men to be living in 'homes', first of all because of their longer expectation of life, second because they are less likely to have a living spouse who could help care for them at home and, third, because they are likely to live longer than men after admission to residential care. Lowrey and Briggs (1988) add that some 'homes', especially smaller ones, take 'ladies only'. Conversely, there are only small numbers of married men living in residential homes and a very high proportion of them receiving care in 'the community'. Two factors seem to emerge from many of the studies: the first is that more men than women are being cared for by their spouses outside institutions and, second, that the men who do live in 'homes' are fitter and less dependent than women in 'homes'. It is, of course, well known that so-called 'community care' is, in most cases, care by female kin rather than by 'the community' at large. What these studies also appear to demonstrate, however, is that men requiring care benefit from a double 'advantage'. In the first place greater efforts are made, by statutory and voluntary agencies as well as informal carers, to support men in their own homes so as to avoid their admission to institutional care. Where care in a 'home'[1] is sought, on the other hand, men achieve admission to care in less severe states of dependency than do women. One small exception to these two firm conclusions is that Willcocks *et al.* (1987), in a study of private 'homes', suggested both that men may be more socially isolated in 'the community' and that more women than men in the private sector attributed their admission to care to the death of their spouse. However, the numbers involved were relatively small and do not significantly weaken the general observation that, on the whole, men receive more support in their own homes especially in tasks normally defined as women's work (cooking, cleaning, laundry, ironing) (see Wenger, ·1984, pp. 121–2) and that men are more likely than women, in similar states of dependency, to gain admission to a residential home.

The categorisation of residents according to social class throws up some interesting distinctions. Taking account of the difficulties of allocating elderly people to social classes, especially elderly women, Wade *et al.* (1983) show that residents of local authority homes are predominantly from the Registrar-General's social classes III, IV and V (but especially V) whereas residents of private sector homes are almost exclusively from classes I, II and III. However, increased Social Security subsidies to low-income residents in the private sector since 1980 may have altered the picture. Studies of children in residential care also suggest similar patterns of admission according to social class. As Davis argues, this is not because of any evidence that families in social classes IV and V are more likely to reject or neglect their children but because better off families are more able to purchase more attractive (and less stigmatising) alternatives (Davis, 1981, p. 17). Overall, studies of institutional care – as I shall argue later – demonstrate that gender inequalities and class inequalities in residential homes closely replicate those in domestic settings in the outside world.

THE CONCEPT OF HOME IN RESIDENTIAL CARE

There is now a considerable literature on residential institutions as substitute homes, deriving from two main sources. First, there has been a strong tradition in Britain of ethnographic studies of institutional life from Peter Townsend's *The Last Refuge* in 1962, to the studies by Willcocks, Peace and Kellaher in the 1980s. Second, from the beginning of the twentieth century there have-been consistent attempts to introduce legislation and regulations governing standards of care in institutions, especially nursing homes. In more recent years the focus, in regulation, has been upon creating not just minimum physical standards in long-stay institutions but also a 'homely' environment based upon principles of privacy, dignity and so on (see, for example, Centre for Policy on Ageing, 1984; NISW, 1988).

A good deal of the early sociological literature was critical of institutional regimes for failing to provide 'homely' atmospheres and, by implication, enumerated those qualities of home life which are highly valued. Townsend (1962), for example, talks about the 'loss of occupation' in residential homes, the isolation from family and friends and the 'tenuousness of new relationships'. He talks of loneliness, the loss of privacy, identity and individuality and the 'collapse of powers of self-determination'. Goffman (1961) criticised the routinisation and depersonalisation of institutional life, the 'batch living' where all residents did the same things (eat, sleep, take their leisure) at the same time, in the same place, with the same people day after day and also the enforced distinctions between staff and residents. More recent literature has focused upon questions of 'choice' in residential homes, on 'personal space', on 'induced dependency' and on control of one's own lifestyle (Clough, 1981; Booth, 1985; O'Connor and Walsh, 1986; Willcocks *et al.*, 1987; Challis and Bartlett, 1988; NISW, 1988).

Reflecting these concerns, the various measures which have been taken to re-create 'homely' environments have set out minimum standards and principles which residential care must meet if it is to provide acceptable substitute long-term provision. *Home Life*, for example, which is used as a handbook by local authorities inspecting residential care homes, sets out eight 'principles of care' which it expects every 'home' should observe. It begins by suggesting that 'homes' should ensure individual *fulfilment* by encouraging each resident to maximise her/his potential. It emphasises that residents should be treated with *dignity* and that they should be enabled to have some personal space both in a physical and an emotional sense. Residents have a basic right to self-determination and *autonomy* and should be given as many choices as is compatible with harmonious community life. Staff are asked to respect *individuality* and to encourage the self-confidence and independence of residents and are required to be responsive to personal tastes and different religious

and cultural requirements. The *self-esteem* of residents is also emphasised as are their *emotional needs*. Staff are encouraged to regard
responsible *risk-taking* as normal and to involve residents in as wide a
range of 'normal' activities (shopping, going to church, to the pub,
cinemas, theatres, etc.) as possible, so as to enhance their *quality of
experience* in the 'home'. There is an emphasis on personal clothing
and personal possessions and a particular concern that residents
should be addressed in the manner which they prefer – rather than by
their first name (if they regard that as over-familiar) or as 'Granny' or
'Grandad' (Centre for Policy on Ageing, 1984). The National Association of Health Authorities (NAHA, 1985) has issued a similar
guide to District Health Authorities who are responsible for nursing
homes.

What do this critical literature and these policy documents tell us
about the way in which the home is viewed in the public arena? There
is an assumption, above all, that the home is a private place, a place
where one has personal space and some control over who moves into
that space and on what basis. It is assumed that people living at home
have some form of occupation (housework, leisure, caring for others)
which gives them a sense of purpose and occupies their time
constructively. It assumes that the security of home life gives people
choice – a choice of friends, a choice of lifestyle, a choice of when to
eat, what to eat and when to sleep and a choice of how they will be
addressed and identified by those around them. Nicknames devised
by friends and family may be affectionate and endearing; being called
pet names by outsiders can be humiliating and degrading. It is
assumed that, at home, people can express their individuality, where
they are not a number or just one of a crowd, and can satisfy their
emotional needs. They can take risks or behave eccentrically without
the threat of sanctions or abuse. Perhaps most important of all, it is
argued, they can form social relationships on a voluntary basis rather
than as a consequence of being forced together around a communal
dining table, sitting room or a shared bedroom.

ACHIEVING THE DOMESTIC IDEAL IN AN
INSTITUTIONAL SETTING

Any attempt to create a 'home-like' environment in a residential
home faces two major obstacles. First of all, the history of institutional care in Britain has been characterised by an emphasis upon the

deterrent nature and stigmatising effects of that care. The image of
the institution, especially in the minds of many elderly people, is that
of the workhouse, and it is a negative and uncomfortable image.
Many people entering 'homes' (and their relatives) see admission to
care as a sign of failure and a sign of their inability to cope. As Davis
has argued, going into a 'home' may be a public declaration that one
lacks family or 'community' support and, even more, a 'general lack
of social standing'. She quotes Miller and Gwynne's observation that
residents in 'homes' face a 'double rejection': they see themselves as
people rejected by their families but also as 'a rejected category of
non-contributors to and non-participants in society, and indeed as
virtually non-members of society' (Miller and Gwynne, quoted in
Davis, 1981, p. 14). Even the best and most welcoming 'homes' are
regarded by many as a last resort – a place to die.

The second problem is that, however well prepared for admission
the resident may be (and few are prepared at all), going into a 'home'
inevitably involves what Willcocks *et al.* call 'environmental discon-
tinuity' (1987, p. 52). Individuals frequently lose all that is dear to
them, their home, their furniture, their freedom and, most upsetting
of all for many of them, their pets. Treasured animals are given away
or, at worst, put down. Many writers have used graphic terms for the
movement from one's own home into residential care, a move which
has a symbolic meaning of major significance. Goffman (1968, p. 23)
spoke of the process of 'disculturation' which occurred on admission
to care – not just an unavoidable dislocation of an individual's
environment but sometimes a deliberate stripping of identity. 'Disculturation', Goffman argued, consists of 'untraining' individuals so
that they become incapable of managing aspects of daily life if and
when they ever return to their own homes. Willcocks *et al.* (1987,
p. 31) talk of 'crossing the threshold' from the community to institutional care and Blythe (1979, p. 131) writes about 'the mark of
dissociation' which comes on entering the door of the institution.

Given this inauspicious background how well do 'homes' succeed
in achieving the 'domestic ideal' or even some approximation to it?
Four issues are of particular significance here: social relationships in
the 'home', the physical environment, the nature of the institutional
regime and the pattern of inequalities in residential care.

What is striking about life in residential homes is that, like
so-called 'community care', it is predominantly care by women, for
women. In this case, however, the carers are not female kin but
low-paid, low-skilled, usually part-time, employees. There has been

some debate about the extent to which paid caring in 'homes' could be used more extensively to liberate female kin from their concern for dependent family members (see, for example, Finch, 1984). However, we are concerned here more with the consequences of this type of provision rather than with its potential. Two seem particularly significant. The first is that the kind of personal and sexual relationships which we take for granted in our own homes are almost entirely absent in residential care. Despite the opportunities which 'homes' create for making friends with one's own age group many residents complain of the enforced familiarity which comes from sharing a bedroom or dining table with strangers, whom they may not like and whose company they have not sought. Willcocks *et al.*, in their study of 100 homes, for example found that 'close friendships between residents were rarely observed' and that one-third of the people they interviewed 'no longer had anyone to talk to about personal things' (1987, pp. 46–7). Wade *et al.* found that 48.5 per cent of their sample in local authority homes had not made friends with other people in their 'home', compared with as many as 63.6 per cent in private 'homes' (Wade *et al.*, 1983, p. 199).

Wilkin and Hughes found a similar picture. They compare the social relationships in the lounge of a residential home not with those in a domestic setting but with the kind of contacts people might have on public transport or in a waiting room. 'Relations between the actors', they argue, 'are characterised by formal politeness and an avoidance of personal contact which might invade the individual's right to privacy' (1987, p. 183). Many people talked of 'keeping themselves to themselves' and spoke of 'being friendly' rather than of having friends. Only a quarter of the sample said they had a friend in their particular 'home' but the interviews demonstrated that many of these feelings were not reciprocated. In practice, for many people, friendship meant tolerating the physical proximity of another resident rather than actively enjoying or seeking out their company. Even allowing for the less than idyllic relationships which some people have with family and friends in their own homes, the opportunities for satisfying social relationships which exist in residential homes seem markedly fewer.

Similarly, the chances of any relatively 'normal' relationships between the sexes, especially of a physical nature, are extremely remote. As far as staff/resident relationships are concerned there are significant gender differences. The vast majority of staff in residential homes are women. In Clough's survey, for example, 90 per cent were women (1981, p. 148) and in Willcocks *et al.*'s sample 93 per cent were women (1987, p. 62). In the 'ladies only' homes women were living almost exclusively in the company of other women and even in 'homes' where this is not an explicit policy it may nevertheless be a fact. For many people, then, this ruled out the possibility of even the most superficial relationship with the opposite sex and, as Clough observed in his study, 'the possibility of a mildly flirtatious relationship between male residents and female staff was ten times greater than between male staff and female residents' (Clough, 1981, p. 149). The prospects of anything more than mild flirtation between the residents themselves seems virtually ruled out, not only because of the gender ratio in 'homes' but also by the geography of residential homes and the attitudes of staff. Wilkin and Hughes argue that anything other than social relationships between male and female residents are extremely rare and that this may be 'a reflection of attitudes towards heterosexual relationships among the elderly, in general, but particularly people in institutional care' (Wilkin and Hughes, 1987, p. 185). The response of the staff, in their study, was ambivalent. They tended to joke about relationships between male and female residents but tolerated them as long as they remained entirely social.

The other main consequence of the gender imbalance in residential homes is that some residents feel that the jobs which were once their 'women's jobs' at home (cooking, washing, ironing, cleaning) are now being done by female staff, so that they are left with no real role in life. Certainly it is true that some residents feel grateful to be relieved of these tasks, especially when they are frail and ill, but others are resentful that their functions have been usurped by other women. In Willcocks *et al.*'s study, for example, they found that 'the feeling of uselessness and that everything was done for them was prevalent amongst residents' and that more women than men felt that they 'no longer do anything that is of real use to other people' (Willcocks *et al.*, 1987, p. 46). Some residents are not only resentful at the loss of occupation but are also profoundly bored. One resident interviewed by Wilkin and Hughes, for example, found the provision of what they call 'total care' a complete shock after a lifetime of activity. As she explained, she had looked after her own children and then her grandchildren and her daughter and son-in-law when they were ill: 'I did everything and you see coming here floored me . . . everybody doing things for me' (Wilkin and Hughes, 1987, p. 181). Where 'homes' do encourage women to take part in daily activities, such as baking or making drinks, levels of resident satisfaction seem to be much higher.

A second key factor in the development of domesticity in residential homes is the physical environment. Here the reality is very far from the ideal. Although there have been many attempts since 1948 to create a domestic rather than an institutional atmosphere in homes for elderly people, the physical arrangements of most 'homes' still do not conform to conventional models of home life. The lack of single bedrooms and sitting rooms in many 'homes' are the areas of obvious deficiency. Challis and Bartlett (1988), in their survey of private nursing homes, found that only 50 per cent of residents were in single rooms and 22 per cent of homes did not provide a sitting room. The study by Wade *et al.* (1983) drew rather different conclusions. Two-thirds of private nursing home residents were in single rooms but less than 60 per cent of them had the use of a sitting room. In contrast, residents of local authority homes were more likely to be sharing a bedroom but all had a sitting room. This is partly a reflection of the standards which local authorities set for their 'homes' but also reflects the fact that, in the private sector, there is little profit to be made in providing public space.

The significance of the physical environment is important for the kind of social relationships it encourages and permits. The loss of privacy in residential homes is keenly felt by many residents and there are strong feelings about being required to share a bedroom, perhaps for the first time in their lives (and perhaps for the rest of their lives). Furthermore, as Woodroffe and Townsend (1961) discovered, life tends to be centred around the resident's bed because of the lack of sitting or communal space. Thus, relatives and friends visit by the bedside as they might do in a hospital rather than in a sitting room or kitchen as they might do at home. This reinforces the sense that residents are outside the mainstream of life, that they are in some sense 'sick' or 'abnormal' and that they have different identities from those they had at home. As Graham Allan has argued elsewhere in this volume, even close friends and kin will generally regard adult bedrooms as 'out of bounds' when visiting each other at home. In contrast, in residential care, those areas – such as bathrooms, toilets and bedrooms – which are normally considered areas of intimacy or private space become some of the most public rooms where personal territory and dignity are frequently invaded.

A number of writers (Davies and Knapp, 1981; Willcocks, Peace and Kellaher, 1982; Booth, 1985) have written in some detail about the effects of the physical features of residential homes upon the individuals who live in them. All agree, as Willcocks *et al.* put it, that: 'In contrast with the domestic home, these buildings fail to convey any sense of personal ownership, of territoriality, or of individual influence over external appearance'. They create an impression that the residents are 'a homogeneous group of "old people" lacking personal identity or individuality' (Willcocks *et al.*, 1987, p. 79).

In recent decades local authority homes have been growing in size, usually making it more difficult for residents to have control over aspects of their environment. However where they do exercise some choice men and women appear to experience their environments differently. Men tend to move around more in the public areas and socialise with other residents whereas women establish their territory (usually a particular chair) and remain there. Similarly women have a greater chance of being in a single room than do men. As Willcocks *et al.* (1982, pp. 119–20) show, after spending some time in a 'home' men tend to graduate to a shared room and women to a single room. This is sometimes a reflection of residents' own preferences but also a reflection of assumptions made by staff about their needs (Willcocks *et al.*, 1982, p. 120).

The third – and perhaps most important – factor influencing the attainment of the domestic ideal in residential homes is the regime or organisational structure of each 'home'. Here the extent to which residents can exercise choice and achieve autonomy are the key factors. In recent years many proprietors and local authorities have become conscious of the need to enlarge the freedom of residents and small improvements have taken place to allow more participation in decision-taking. The better 'homes' in the surveys above, for example, allowed residents to buy their own clothes and to choose what to wear each day. Others provided choices of menus, mealtimes, bathtimes and bedtimes although staff could sometimes subvert good intentions. Wade *et al.*, for example, quoted one member of staff who commented: 'Yes, we have got a choice of menu, but we choose for them', and another who said: 'I think it is better to more or less think for them.' (Wade *et al.*, 1983, p. 186).

Most writers identify a variety of institutional regimes in residential settings but essentially they distinguish between those which are orientated towards the needs of the residents and those orientated towards the needs of the institution (and its routines and staff). Even where 'homes' are quite consciously resident-orientated the environment they create is still far removed from that of the average domestic setting.

The fourth factor which is significant in examining the attainment of the domestic ideal in institutions for elderly people is the issue of inequality. It is an irony that the features of residential homes which most reflect those in the home environment are the persistence of gender inequalities and of social inequalities. I have demonstrated above that elderly men are advantaged in two respects in relation to residential care; not only are they more likely to receive support at home (from both kin and statutory and voluntary agencies) to prevent their admission to a 'home', but when they do request admission they are able to gain access to a 'home' more easily than women with similar needs. Once in a 'home' they are more likely to enjoy a relationship with the opposite sex than are women but they are less likely to be offered a single room.

The small amount of evidence which exists on the subject also suggests that social inequalities outside institutions are replicated in residential homes. Wade *et al.*, for example, show that in their survey (which is consistent with the results of others) a very high proportion of residents in local authority homes (where facilities were relatively poor) were from social classes III, IV and V, whereas residents in private homes (where facilities were somewhat better) were typically from classes I, II and III. The figures they provide show that 83 per cent of the residents in local authority Part III homes were from classes III, IV and V compared with only 55.2 per cent in private homes (Wade *et al.*, 1983, p. 120).

Bedrooms in the local authority homes were likely to have rugs but not fitted carpets, and furniture was of a uniform design. Half the rooms had pictures and bedside lights and most had patterned wallpaper. In contrast, bedrooms in private homes had more domestic furniture and lighting and residents were often offered the choice of curtains and bedcovers. There were pictures on the walls and flowers in many rooms and bedrooms were described as being 'more homely and personalised' than those in the local authority sector (Wade *et al.*, 1983, p. 184).

Social inequalities in residential care reflect both differentials in ability to pay and differences in the exercise of informed choice. They may also reflect selectivity in admissions policies. Inequalities within 'homes' closely resemble inequalities outside them, but in virtually every other respect residential life runs in complete contradiction to the domestic ideal. 'Homes' for elderly people, with a few exceptions, have been largely unsuccessful in providing privacy, personal space, intimacy, friendship, autonomy, choice and dignity. Residential homes tend to provide most satisfaction where they replace some of the elements which their elderly residents feel they have lost at home, for example security, support and companionship. However, even when 'homes' are at their best, many residents find it difficult to regard them as their real homes. As Willcocks *et al.* put it: 'In reality, the ideal of providing a "homely" setting is a genteel facade behind which institutional patterns, not domestic ones, persist' (1987, p. 1). The final section of this chapter is concerned with one particular question: what is it about the home which cannot be replicated artificially in an institutional setting despite the best intentions?

THE METAPHYSICAL MEANING OF HOME

It is clear when studying institutions that although the physical features of the domestic environment are important in creating a 'homely' atmosphere they are insufficient, on their own, to provide a true sense of home. For many people removed from their own homes there is a feeling of having lost a sense of belonging and a sense of place. Home is associated with familiarity, both in a physical and an emotional sense. It involves a set of affective relationships, currently or previously, based upon kinship and friendship. It also re-inforces an individual's sense of identity, partly through memories and associations with the past. As earlier chapters in this book have shown, although the physical aspects of housing may both reflect and determine particular types of social relationship (especially between the sexes) it is the nature of the relationships themselves which often mark the difference between a house and a home. Homeliness may simply not exist even in the most carefully designed housing. On the other hand people can 'feel at home' in the most unpromising physical surroundings.

As Goffman has observed, entry into institutional care frequently entails what he calls the 'curtailment of self' (Goffman, 1968, p. 24). The individual casts off one set of roles (mother, daughter, husband, wife) and – often involuntarily – takes on another (resident, patient, inmate). In the case of elderly people it is often a case of a transition from 'doing for' to 'being done for', as well as a transition from independence to dependence.

In their own homes even the frail and housebound have some areas of life over which they exercise control, perhaps in relation to eating, dressing or sleeping or in whom they choose to admit through their front door. This is a very real contrast with life in a residential home. The fact that the Wagner Report should see the need to emphasise the importance to all residents in institutional care of having a personal key to their room highlights a central feature of domestic living which is taken for granted when people live at home but which is conspicuously absent when they live elsewhere (NISW, 1988, p. 41). The ability to exercise discretion about who is admitted to one's personal space, whether it is a house, or a bedroom, or simply a favourite chair in a residential home, is not just a question of exercising a right to privacy but it is also about power. The concept of home involves not only the creation and protection of personal space but it also involves profoundly important issues of territoriality and of security. This is illustrated very crudely in the notion that 'an Englishman's home is his castle'. Even at its least satisfactory, home is a place where people can feel comfortable and at ease, where the 'public face' can be allowed to slip and give way to a more relaxed and intimate sense of privacy. It is a setting in which people exercise a degree of choice and of control, where they can disengage from external relationships which appear damaging or threatening.

The real sense of home is essentially a metaphysical concept which transcends particular sets of physical arrangements designed to foster domesticity. For people to 'feel at home' there has to be a meaningfulness about those arrangements which reflects their sense of identity and sense of self. The desire of elderly people in residential care to hold on to a few treasured possessions symbolises their need to make a statement about themselves, their tastes, preferences and personalities as well as a wish to hold on to memories and fragments of the past.

The critical literature on institutional care, by implication, highlights some key features of home life which may be absent in residential settings. The Wagner Report (NISW, 1988), for example, emphasises the importance of allowing residents to take risks and of having a degree of autonomy (especially in a financial sense). Social policies for dependent people are frequently paternalistic and overprotective. They provide a level of protection which few people would have at home and which many people find stifling. The domestic environment, in contrast, permits a high degree of risktaking which allows people to make what may be 'unsuitable' or damaging choices. It permits them sufficient autonomy to succeed or fail in a whole range of experiences from the choice of food they eat to the kind of intimate personal relationships which they form.

In summary, this chapter has shown that by examining the attempts to recreate 'homely' environments and domesticity in institutional settings we can demonstrate how the essence of home is seen by policy-makers, planners and proprietors. The artificial reconstruction of homes in institutions, almost uniquely, necessitates explicit description of those elements which we regard as constituting the core of home life. It is perhaps inevitable that residential institutions, where they have considered the matter at all, have concentrated upon improvements in the physical and organisational environment (more single rooms, more privacy, more choice, more resident involvement, etc.) It is also inevitable that they have been unable to replicate the conditions of home which make it something other than simply a place to live since these, in the most literal sense, are metaphysical qualities which go beyond the physical arrangements of place and time which have become the concern of those who make and execute public policy.

Note

1. In the rest of this paper, where there is risk of confusion inverted commas will be placed around the word 'home' when it refers to institutional settings rather than the conventional domestic setting.

Bibliography

ABRAMS, M. (1970) 'Family and society', in Butterworth, R., and Weir, D. (eds) *The Sociology of Modern Britain*, London: Collins.

ABRAMS, P. (1980) 'Social change, social networks and neighbourhood care', *Social Work Service*, 22: 12–23.

ABRAMS, P. and McCULLOGH, A. (1976) *Communes, Sociology and Society*, Cambridge: University Press.

ADAMS, C. and LAURIKIETIS, R. (1976) *Education and Work: The Gender Trap*, Book 1, London: Virago.

ALDRIDGE, M. (1979) *The British New Towns: A Programme Without a Policy*, London: Routledge and Kegan Paul.

ALLAN, G. (1979) *A Sociology of Friendship and Kinship*, London: Allen and Unwin.

ALLAN, G. (1985) *Family Life: Domestic Roles and Social Organisation*, Oxford: Basil Blackwell.

ALLPORT, C. (1983) 'Women and suburban housing: post-war planning in Sydney, 1943–61', in Williams P. (ed.) *Social Process and the City*, Sydney: Allen and Unwin.

ANDERSON, M. (1985) 'The emergence of the modern life cycle', *Social History*, 10: 69–87.

ANDREWS, K. (1984) 'Private rest homes in the care of the elderly', *British Medical Journal*, 288: 1518–20.

AUSTERBERRY, H. and WATSON, S. (1985) 'A woman's place: a feminist approach to housing in Britain', in Ungerson C. (ed.) *Women and Social Policy*, London: Macmillan.

BACHELARD, G. (1969) *The Poetics of Space*, Boston: Beacon Press.

BACKETT, K. C. (1982) *Mothers and Fathers*, London: Macmillan.

BALCHIN, P. (1981) *Housing Policy and Housing Needs*, London: Macmillan.

BARKIN, C. (1981) 'Electricity is her servant', *Heresies*, 3: 62–3.

BARRETT, M. and McINTOSH, M. (1982) *The Anti-Social Family*, London: Verso.

BASSETT, K. and SHORT, J. (1980) *Housing and Residential Structure*, London: Routledge and Kegan Paul.

BAUER MAGLIN, N. (1981) 'Kitchen dramas', *Heresies*, 3: 42–6.

BEATON, L. (1985) *Shifting Horizons*, London: Canary Press.

BEETON, I. (1861) *Mrs Beeton's Book of Household Management*, London: Chancellor Press.

BERNARDES, J. (1986) 'Multidimensional developmental pathways: a proposal to facilitate the conceptualisation of "family diversity" ', *Sociological Review*, 34: 590–610.

BETTER HOMES AND GARDENS (1987) *Kitchens, Bathrooms and Laundries*, North Sydney: Advertiser Magazines Pty. Ltd.

BINNS, D. and MARS, G. (1984) 'Family, community and unemployment: a study in change', *Sociological Review*, 32: 662–95.

174

BLYTHE, R. (1979) *The View in Winter*, London: Allen Lane.
BODDY, M. (1980) *The Building Societies*, London: Macmillan.
BONNERJEA, L. and LAWTON, J. (1987), *Homelessness in Brent*, London: Policy Studies Institute.
BOOTH, T. (1985) *Home Truths*, Aldershot: Gower.
BOSE, C. (1979) 'Technology and changes in the division of labour in the American home', *Women's Studies International Quarterly*, 2: 295–340.
BOTT, E. (1957) *Family and Social Network*, London: Tavistock.
BOYS, J., BRADSHAW, F., DARKE, J., FOO, B., FRANCIS, S., McFARLANE, B., ROBERTS, M., and WILKES, S. (1984) 'House design and women's roles', in Matrix Book Group (eds) *Making Space: Women and the Man-Made Environment*, London: Pluto.
BRANNEN, J. and WILSON, G. (eds) (1987) *Give and Take in Families*, London: Allen and Unwin.
BRIGGS, A. and OLIVER, J. (eds) (1985) *Caring: Experiences of Looking After Disabled Relatives*, London: Routledge and Kegan Paul.
BROWN, M. and MADGE, N. (1982) *Despite the Welfare State*, London: Heinemann.
BULLOCK, N. (n.d.) 'First the kitchen – then the facade', *A. A. Files*, 6: 59–67.
BULMER, M. (1986) *Neighbours: The Work of Philip Abrams*, Cambridge: University Press.
BUNNING, W. (1945) *Homes in the Sun: The Past, Present and Future of Australian Housing*, Sydney: W. J. Nesbit.
BURGOYNE, J. and CLARK, D. (1984) *Making a Go of It: A Study of Stepfamilies in Sheffield*, London: Routledge and Kegan Paul.
BURKE, G. (1981) *Housing and Social Justice*, London: Longman.
BURNETT, J. (1986) *A Social History of Housing 1815–1985*, London: Methuen.
BYRNE, D. S., HARRISSON, S. P., KEITHLEY, J. and McCARTHY, P. (1986) *Housing and Health: The Relationship Between Housing Conditions and the Health of Council Tenants*, Aldershot: Gower.
CALVOCORESSI, P. (1979) *The British Experience 1945–75*, Harmondsworth: Penguin.
CAMPBELL, B. (1984) *Wigan Pier Revisited: Politics and Poverty in the Eighties*, London: Virago.
CAMPBELL, B. and SEDLEY, S. (1988) 'A Family Tragedy', *Marxism Today*, July, 32: 16–19.
CASHMORE, E. (1985) *Having To*, London: Counterpoint.
CENTRAL STATISTICAL OFFICE (1985) *Social Trends 15*, London: HMSO.
CENTRAL STATISTICAL OFFICE (1988) *Social Trends 18*, London: HMSO.
CENTRE FOR POLICY ON AGEING (1984) *Home Life*, London: CPA.
CHALLIS, L. and BARTLETT, H. (1988) *Old and Ill*, London: Age Concern.
CLARK, D. (1987) 'Changing partners: marriage and divorce across the life course', in Cohen, G. (ed.) *Social Change and the Life Course*, London: Tavistock.

CLEEVE BARR, A. W. (1958) *Public Authority Housing*, London: Batsford.
CLOUGH, R. (1981) *Old Age Homes*, London: Allen and Unwin.
COLEMAN, A. (1985) *Utopia on Trial: Vision and Reality in Planned Housing*, London: Hilary Shipman.
COOPER, S. (1985) *Public Housing and Private Property 1970–1984*, Aldershot: Gower.
CORNWALL, J. (1958) *Hard-Earned Lives*, London: Tavistock.
COWAN, R. (1985) 'The industrial revolution in the home', in McKenzie, D. and Wajcman, J. (eds) *The Social Shaping of Technology*, Milton Keynes: Open University Press.
COWAN, T. (1985) *Beyond the Kitchen: A Dreamer's Guide*, Poole: Blandford Press.
CRAWFORD, M. (1972) 'Retirement and role-playing', *Sociology*, 6: 217–36.
CROW, G. and ALLAN, G. (1989) 'Constructing the domestic sphere: the emergence of the modern home in post-war Britain', in Corr, H. and Jamieson, L. (eds) *The Politics of Everyday Life*, London: Macmillan.
CSIKSZENTMIHALYI, M. and ROCHBERG-HALTON, E. (1981) *The Meaning of Things: Domestic Symbols and the Self*, Cambridge: University Press.
CULLINGWORTH, J. B. (1979) *Essays on Housing Policy: The British Scene*, London: Allen and Unwin.
DALLEY, G. (1988) *Ideologies of Caring*, London: Macmillan.
DARLEY, G. (1975) *Villages of Vision*, London: Paladin.
DARROW, M. H. (1979) 'French noblewomen and the new domesticity 1750–1850', *Feminist Studies*, 5: 41–65.
DAUNTON, M. J. (1983) 'Public place and private space: the Victorian city and the working-class household', in Frazer, D. and Sutcliffe, A. (eds) *The Pursuit of Urban History*, London: Edward Arnold.
DAVIDOFF, L. (1976) 'The rationalisation of housework', in Barker, D. L. and Allen, S. (eds) *Dependence and Exploitation in Work and Marriage*, London: Longman.
DAVIDOFF, L., L'ESPERANCE, J. and NEWBY, H. (1976) 'Landscape with figures: home and community in English society', in Mitchell, J. and Oakley, A. (eds) *The Rights and Wrongs of Women*, Harmondsworth: Penguin.
DAVIDOFF, L. and HALL, C. (1987) *Family Fortunes*, London: Hutchinson.
DAVIES, A. (1984) *Where Did the Forties Go? A Popular History*, London: Pluto.
DAVIES, B. and KNAPP, M. (1981) *Old People's Homes and the Production of Welfare*, London: Routledge and Kegan Paul.
DAVIS, A. (1981) *The Residential Solution*, London: Tavistock.
DEEM, R. (1985) 'Leisure, work and unemployment: old traditions and new boundaries', in Deem, R. and Salaman, G. (eds) *Work, Culture and Society*, Milton Keynes: Open University Press.
DEEM, R. (1986) *All Work and No Play? The Sociology of Women and*

Leisure, Milton Keynes: Open University Press.
DENBY, E. (1941) 'Plan the home', *Picture Post*, 4 January, 21–3.
DENNIS, N., HENRIQUES, F. and SLAUGHTER, C. (1969) *Coal is Our Life*, London: Tavistock.
DEPARTMENT OF EMPLOYMENT (1986) *Family Expenditure Survey 1984*, London: HMSO.
DEX, S. (1987) *Women's Occupational Mobiity: A Lifetime Perspective*, London: Macmillan.
DEX, S. and SHAW, L. B. (1986) *British and American Women at Work*, London: Macmillan.
DHSS (1974) *Report of the Committee on One-Parent Families*, London: HMSO.
DHSS (1986) *Low Income Families 1983*, London: HMSO.
DICKENS, C. (1971) *Bleak House*, Harmondsworth: Penguin.
DOBASH, R. E. and DOBASH, R. (1980) *Violence Against Wives: A Case Against the Patriarchy*, London: Open Books.
DONNISON, D. V. (1967) *The Government of Housing*, Harmondsworth: Penguin.
DONNISON, D. V. and UNGERSON, C. (1982) *Housing Policy*, Harmondsworth: Penguin.
DUNLEAVY, P. (1981) *The Politics of Mass Housing in Britain 1945–1975*, Oxford: Clarendon.
EDGELL, S. (1980) *Middle-Class Couples*, London: Allen and Unwin.
EEKELAAR, J. and MACLEAN, M. (1986) *Maintenance After Divorce*, Oxford: Clarendon.
ELSHTAIN, J. (1981) *Public Man, Private Woman: Women in Social and Political Thought*, Oxford: Martin Robertson.
EVASON, E. (1980) *Just Me and the Kids: A Study of Single Parent Families in Northern Ireland*, Belfast: Equal Opportunities Commission.
FERRI, E. (1976) *Growing Up in a One Parent Family*, London: National Foundation for Educational Research.
FINCH, J. (1983) *Married to the Job*, London: Allen and Unwin.
FINCH, J. (1984) 'Community care and the family: developing non-sexist alternatives', *Critical Social Policy*, 9: 6–18.
FINCH, J. and GROVES, D. (eds) (1983) *A Labour of Love: Women, Work and Caring*, London: Routledge and Kegan Paul.
FRANCIS, S. (1984) 'Housing the family', in Matrix Book Group (eds) *Making Space: Women and the Man-Made Environment*, London: Pluto.
FRANKENBERG, R. (1969) *Communities in Britain*, Harmondsworth: Penguin.
FRANKENBERG, R. (1986) 'Time for the subject? Time of the subject? Time in the subject: medical anthropology and clinical medicine disentangled', American Anthropological Association paper, Keele University: Centre for Medical Social Anthropology.
GASKELL, E. (1979) *Mary Barton*, Harmondsworth: Penguin.
GAVRON, H. (1968) *The Captive Wife*, Harmondsworth: Penguin.
GERSHUNY, J. (1983) *Social Innovation and the Division of Labour*, Oxford: Oxford University Press.
GERSHUNY, J. and JONES, S. (1987) 'The changing work/leisure balance

in Britain 1961–1984', in Horne, J., Jary, D. and Tomlinson, A. (eds) *Sport, Leisure and Society*, Sociological Review Monograph 33, London: Routledge and Kegan Paul.

GILBRETH, L. (1930) 'Efficiency methods applied to kitchen design', *Architectural Record*, March, 291–4.

GILMAN, C. P. (1980) 'The home: its work and influence', in Malos, E. (ed.) *The Politics of Housework*, London: Allison and Busby.

GINSBURG, N. (1979) *Class, Capital and Social Policy*, London: Macmillan.

GITTENS, D. (1982) *Fair Sex: Family Size and Structure 1900–39*, London: Hutchinson.

GITTENS, D. (1985), *The Family in Question: Changing Households and Familiar Ideologies*, London: Macmillan.

GLENDINNING, C. and MILLAR, J. (eds) (1987) *Women and Poverty in Britain*, Brighton: Wheatsheaf.

GLYPTIS, S. and McINNES, H. (1987) *Leisure and the Home*, London: Sports Council/ESRC.

GOFFMAN, E. (1968) *Asylums*, Harmondsworth: Penguin.

GOFFMAN, E. (1971), *The Presentation of Self in Everyday Life*, Harmondsworth: Penguin.

GOLDTHORPE, J. H. (1988) 'Intellectuals and the working class in modern Britain', in Rose, D. (ed.) *Social Stratification and Economic Change*, London: Hutchinson.

GOLDTHORPE, J. H., LOCKWOOD, D., BECHHOFER, F. and PLATT, J. (1968) *The Affluent Worker: Industrial Attitudes and Behaviour*, Cambridge: University Press.

GOLDTHORPE, J. H., LOCKWOOD, D., BECHHOFER, F. and PLATT, J. (1969) *The Affluent Worker in the Class Structure*, Cambridge: University Press.

GRAHAM, H. (1983) 'Caring: a labour of love', in Finch, J. and Groves, D. (eds) *A Labour of Love: Women, Work and Caring*, London: Routledge and Kegan Paul.

GRAHAM, H. (1987) 'Being poor: perceptions and coping strategies of lone mothers', in Brannen, J. and Wilson, G. (eds) *Give and Take in Families*, London: Allen and Unwin.

GREENBAUM, J. (1981) 'Kitchen culture/kitchen dialective', *Heresies*, 3: 59–61.

GULLESTAD, M. (1984) *Kitchen-Table Society: A Case Study of the Family Life and Friendships of Young Working Class Mothers in Urban Norway*, Oslo: Universitetsforlaget.

HALL, C. (1980) 'The history of the housewife', in Malos, E. (ed.) *The Politics of Housework*, London: Allison and Busby.

HALL, S. (1984) 'The Culture Gap', *Marxism Today*, January, 28: 18–21.

HANDLIN, D. (1973) 'Efficiency and the American home', *Architectural Association Quarterly*, Winter, 50–4.

HARDY WILSON, W. (1919) 'Building "Purulia"', in Ure Smith, S. and Stevens, B. (eds) *Domestic Architecture in Australia*, Sydney: Angus and Robertson.

HARRIS, C. C. (1987) *Redundancy and Recession*, Oxford: Basil Blackwell.

HARRISON, P. (1983) *Inside the Inner City*, Harmondsworth: Penguin.
HASKEY, J. (1986A) 'Recent trends in divorce', *Population Trends*, 44: 9–16.
HASKEY, J. (1986B), 'One-parent families in Britain', *Population Trends*, 45: 5–13.
HAYDEN, D. (1981) *The Grand Domestic Revolution*, Cambridge, Mass: M.I.T. Press.
HELLER, A. (1984) *Everyday Life*, London: Routledge and Kegan Paul.
HESS, J. E. (1981) 'Domestic interiors in northern New Mexico', *Heresies*, 3: 30–3.
HILL, M. (1987) *Sharing Child Care in Early Parenthood*, London: Routledge and Kegan Paul.
HOBSON, D. (1978) 'Housewives: isolation as oppression', in Women's Study Group, Centre for Contemporary Cultural Studies, *Women Take Issue*, London: Hutchinson.
HOGGART, R. (1957) *The Uses of Literacy*, London: Chatto and Windus.
HOLE, H. V. and ATTENBURROW, J. J. (1970) 'The home', in Butterworth, E. and Weir, D. (eds) *The Sociology of Modern Britain*, London: Collins.
HOLME, A. (1985a) *Housing and Young Families in East London*, London: Routledge and Kegan Paul.
HOLME, A. (1985b) 'Family and homes in east London', *New Society*, 12 July, 43–6.
HOROBIN, G. (1957) 'Community and occupation in the Hull fishing industry', *British Journal of Sociology*, 8: 343–56.
HUNT, P. (1978) 'Cash transactions and household tasks', *Sociological Review*, 26: 555–71.
HUNT, P. (1980) *Gender and Class Consciousness*, London: Macmillan.
HUNT, P. and FRANKENBERG, R. (1981) 'Home: castle or cage?', in the Media booklet for the Social Sciences second year course, *An Introduction to Sociology*, 16–23, Milton Keynes: Open University.
IMRAY, L. and MIDDLETON, A. (1983) 'Public and private: marking the boundaries', in Gamarnikow, E., Morgan, D., Purvis, J. and Taylorson, D. (eds) *The Public and the Private*, London: Macmillan.
JACKSON, B. (1968) *Working Class Community*, London: Routledge and Kegan Paul.
JEPHCOTT, P. with ROBINSON, H. (1971) *Homes in High Flats*, Edinburgh: Oliver and Boyd.
KERR, M. (1958) *The People of Ship Street*, London: Routledge and Kegan Paul.
KING, A. D. (1984) *The Bungalow*, London: Routledge and Kegan Paul.
KING, J. and STOTT, A. (1977) *Is This Your Life?*, London: Virago.
KITZINGER, S. (1978) *Women as Mothers*, London: Fontana.
KLEIN, J. (1965) *Samples From English Culture*, Vol. 1, London: Routledge and Kegan Paul.
KNEVITT, C. AND WATES, N. (1987) *Community Architecture*, Harmondsworth: Penguin.
KNIGHT, I. (1981) *Family Finances*, OPCS Occasional Paper No. 26, London: HMSO.

LAING, S. (1986) *Representations of Working-Class Life 1957–1964*, London: Macmillan.

LAING, W. (1987) *Laing's Review of Private Healthcare*, London: Laing and Buisson.

LAND, H. (1980) 'Tha family wage', *Feminist Review*, 6: 55–77.

LASLETT, P. (1969) *The World We Have Lost*, Cambridge: University Press.

LAYARD, R., PIACHAUD, D. and STEWART, M. (1978) *The Causes of Poverty*, Royal Commission on the Distribution of Income and Wealth, Background Paper No. 5, London: HMSO.

LEE, L. (1988) 'How to get your man to help in the house', *Australian Women's Weekly*, May, 125–6.

LEONARD, D. (1980) *Sex and Generation*, London: Tavistock.

LEONARD, D. and SPEAKMAN, M. A. (1986) 'Women in the family: companions or caretakers?', in Beechey, V. and Whitelegg, E. (eds) *Women in Britain Today*, Milton Keynes: Open University Press.

LEONARD, S. (1986) 'Bed linen: big busines in fashion stakes', *Courier Mail*,. 8 October, 13.

LEWIS, J. (ed.) (1986) *Labour and Love: Women's Experience of Home and Family, 1850–1940*, Oxford: Basil Blackwell.

LEWIS, J. (1988) 'Anxieties about the family and the relationships between parents, children and the state in twentieth-century England', in Richards, M. and Light, P. (eds) *Children of Social Worlds: Development in a Social Context*, Cambridge: Polity.

LIELL, P. (1981) *Council Houses and the Housing Act 1980*, London: Butterworth.

LOCKWOOD, D. (1966) 'Sources of variation in working-class images of society', *Sociological Review*, 14: 249–67.

LOGAN, F. (1987) *Homelessness and Relationship Breakdown*, London: National Council for One-Parent Families.

LOWREY, S. and BRIGGS, R. (1988) 'Boom in private rest homes in Southampton: impact on the elderly in residential care', *British Medical Journal*, 296: 541–3.

MacARTHUR, J. (1984) 'The family and the suburb', unpublished lecture delivered at the University of Queensland, Brisbane.

MACK, J. and LANSLEY, S. (1985) *Poor Britain*, London: Allen and Unwin.

MACKINTOSH, J. M. (1952) *Housing and Family Life*, London: Cassell.

MALPASS, P. and MURIE, A. (1982) *Housing Policy and Practice*, London: Macmillan.

MANSFIELD, P. and COLLARD, J. (1988) *The Beginning of the Rest of Your Life? A Portrait of Newly-Wed Marriage*, London: Macmillan.

MARSDEN, D. (1969) *Mothers Alone: Poverty and the Fatherless Family*, Harmondsworth: Penguin.

MARSHALL, G., VOGLER, C., ROSE, D. and NEWBY, H. (1987), 'Distributional struggle and moral order in a market society', *Sociology*, 21: 55–73.

MARTIN, J. and ROBERTS, C. (1984) *Women and Employment: A Lifetime Perspective*, OPCS, London: HMSO.

MARWICK, A. (1982) *British Society Since 1945*, Harmondsworth: Penguin.

MASON, J. (1987a) *Gender Inequality in Long-Term Marriages*, Unpublished Ph.D. Thesis, University of Kent.

MASON, J. (1987b) 'A bed of roses? Women, marriage and inequality in later life', in Allatt, P., Keil, T., Bytheway, B. and Bryman, A. (eds) *Women and the Life Cycle*, London: Macmillan.

MASON, J. (1988) ' "No peace for the wicked": older married women and leisure', in Talbot, M. and Wimbush, E. (eds) *Relative Freedoms*, Milton Keynes: Open University Press.

MASS OBSERVATION (1943) *An Enquiry into People's Homes*, London: Advertising Services Guild.

McDOWELL, L. (1983) 'City and home: urban housing and the sexual division of space', in Evans, M. and Ungerson, C. (eds) *Sexual Divisions: Patterns and Processes*, London: Tavistock.

McKEE, L. and BELL, C. (1986) 'His unemployment, her problem: the domestic and marital consequences of male unemployment', in Allen, S., Waton, A., Purcell, K. and Wood, S. (eds) *The Experience of Unemployment*, London: Macmillan.

McKEE, L. and O'BRIEN, M. (1982) *The Father Figure*, London: Tavistock.

MERRETT, S. (1979) *State Housing in Britain*, London: Routledge and Kegan Paul.

MERRETT, S. with GRAY, F. (1982) *Owner Occupation in Britain*, London: Routledge and Kegan Paul.

MILLAR, J. (1987) 'Lone mothers', in Glendinning, C. and Millar, J. (eds) *Women and Poverty in Britain*, Brighton: Wheatsheaf.

MILLER, E. J. and GWYNNE, G. V. (1972) *A Life Apart*, London: Tavistock.

MINISTRY OF HOUSING AND LOCAL GOVERNMENT (1961) *Homes for Today and Tomorrow*, London: HMSO.

MOGEY, J. M. (1956) *Family and Neighbourhood: Two Studies in Oxford*, London: Oxford University Press.

MOORE, B. (1984) *Privacy: Studies in Social and Cultural History*, New York: Sharpe.

MORGAN, D. H. J. (1975) *Social Theory and the Family*, London: Routledge and Kegan Paul.

MORGAN, D. H. J. (1985) *The Family, Politics and Social Theory*, London: Routledge and Kegan Paul.

MURCOTT, A. (1983) 'Women's place: cookbooks' images of technique and technology in the British kitchen', *Women's Studies International Forum*, 6: 33–9.

MURDOCH, O. (1986) 'What your home says about you', *Good Housekeeping*, October, 88–91.

MURIE, A. (1983) *Housing Inequality and Deprivation*, London: Heinemann.

NAHA (1985) *Registration and Inspection of Nursing Homes: A Handbook for Health Authorities*, Birmingham: National Association of Health Authorities.

NISW (1988) *Residential Care: A Positive Choice*, (The Wagner Report),

London: National Institute for Social Work.

OAKLEY, A. (1974) *The Sociology of Housework*, Oxford: Martin Robertson.

OAKLEY, A. (1976) *Housewife*, Harmondsworth: Penguin.

OAKLEY, A. (1979) *Becoming a Mother*, Oxford: Martin Robertson.

O'CONNOR, J. and WALSH, M. (1986) *It's Our Home: The Quality of Life in Private and Voluntary Nursing Homes*, Dublin: The Stationery Office.

OPCS (1984) *General Household Survey*, London: HMSO.

PAHL, J. (ed.) (1985) *Private Violence and Public Policy*, London: Routledge and Kegan Paul.

PAHL, J. (1988) 'Earning, sharing, spending: married couples and their money', in Parker, G. and Walker, R. (eds) *Money Matters*, London: Sage.

PAHL, R. E. (1984) *Divisions of Labour*, Oxford: Basil Blackwell.

PAHL, R. E. and WALLACE, C. D. (1988) 'Neither angels in marble nor rebels in red: privatization and working-class consciousness', in Rose, D. (ed.) *Social Stratification and Economic Change*, London: Hutchinson.

PAPANEK, H. (1979) 'Family status production: the "work" and "non-work" of women', *Signs*, 4: 775–81.

PARKER, B. and UNWIN, R. (1901) 'Of co-operation in building', in Parker, B. and Unwin, R. (eds) *The Art of Building a Home*, London: Longman.

PARKER, S. (1980) *Older Workers and Retirement*, OPCS. London: HMSO.

PARSONS, T. and BALES, R. F. (1955) *Family, Socialization and Interaction Process*, New York: Free Press.

PASCALL, G. (1986) *Social Policy: A Feminist Analysis*, London: Tavistock.

PATEMAN, C. (1987) 'Feminist critiques of the public/private dichotomy', in Phillips, A. (ed.) *Feminism and Equality*, Oxford: Basil Blackwell.

PEACE, S. (1982) 'The balance of residential life: a study of 100 old people's homes', paper given to the British Sociological Association Study Group on Sociology and Environment, Mimeo.

PEACE, S. (1986) 'The forgotten female: social policy and older women', in Phillipson, C. and Walker, A. (eds) *Ageing and Social Policy: A Critical Assessment*, Aldershot: Gower.

PHILLIPSON, C. (1987) 'The transition to retirement', in Cohen, G. (ed.) *Social Change and the Life Course*, London: Tavistock.

PHILLIPSON, C. and WALKER, A. (1986) *Ageing and Social Policy: A Critical Assessment*, Aldershot: Gower.

POLLERT, A. (1981) *Girls, Wives, Factory Lives*, London: Macmillan.

POPAY, J., RIMMER, L. and ROSSITER, C. (1983) *One Parent Families: Parents, Children and Public Policy*, London: Study Commission on the Family.

PYM, B. (1980) *Excellent Women*, Harmondsworth: Penguin.

RAVETZ, A. (1968) 'The Victorian coal kitchen and its reformers', *Victorian Studies*, 11: 435–60.

REDMOND, H. (1988) 'Kitchens: pointers to give you ideas', *Better Homes and Gardens*, 14 February, 42–57.

REIGER, K. (1985) *The Disenchantment of the Home: Modernising the Australian Family 1880–1940*, Melbourne: Oxford University Press.

RILEY, D. (1983) *War in the Nursery: Theories of the Child and Mother*, London: Virago.

ROBERTS, E. (1985) *A Woman's Place: An Oral History of Working-Class Women 1890–1940*, Oxford: Basil Blackwell.

ROBERTS, M. (1984) 'Private kitchens, public cooking', in Matrix Book Group (eds) *Making Space: Women and the Man-Made Environment*, London: Pluto.

ROBERTS, M. (1986) *The Modernisation of Family Life? Sexual Divisions in Architecture and Town Planning 1940–1957*, Unpublished Ph.D. Thesis, University of Wales.

ROBERTS, R. (1973) *The Classic Slum*, Harmondsworth: London.

ROSSER, C. and HARRIS, C. C. (1965) *The Family and Social Change*, London: Routledge and Kegan Paul.

ROYAL AUSTRALIAN INSTITUTE OF ARCHITECTS (1959) *Buildings of Queensland*, Brisbane: Jacaranda Press.

RYBCZYNSKI, W. (1988) *Home: A short History of an Idea*, London: Heinemann.

SAUNDERS, P. (1984) 'Beyond housing classes: the sociological significance of private property rights in means of consumption', *International Journal of Urban and Regional Research*, 8: 202–27.

SAUNDERS, P. and WILLIAMS, P. (1988) 'The constitution of the home: towards a research agenda', *Housing Studies*, 3: 81–93

SEELEY, J. R., SIM, R. A. and LOOSLEY, E. W. (1956) *Crestwood Heights: A study of the Culture of Suburban Life*, Toronto: University Press.

SHORT, J. R. (1982) *Housing in Britain: The Post-War Experience*, London: Methuen.

SILTANEN, J. and STANWORTH, M. (1984) 'The politics of private woman and public man', in Siltanen, J. and Stanworth, M. (eds) *Women and the Public Sphere*, London: Hutchinson.

SIMON, E. D. (1986) 'Rebuilding Britain: the long-term programme, 1945', in Pope, R., Pratt, A. and Hoyle, B. (eds) *Social Welfare in Britain 1885–1985*, London: Croom Helm.

SLATER, E. and WOODSIDE, M. (1951) *Patterns of Marriage*, London: Cassell.

SKED, A. and COOK, C. (1983) *Post-War Britain: A Political History*, Harmondsworth: Penguin.

SPIGEL, L. (1986) 'Ambiguity and hesitation: discourses on television and the housewife in women's home magazines 1948–55', paper to the Second International Television Studies Conference, Institute of Education, University of London.

SPRING RICE, M. (1981) *Working-Class Wives*, London: Virago.

SHORTER, E. (1979) *The Making of the Modern Family*, London: Fontana.

STACEY, M. (1960) *Tradition and Change: A Study of Banbury*, London: Oxford University Press.

STACEY, M. (1980) 'The division of labour revisited or overcoming the two Adams', in Abrams, P., Deem, R., Finch, J. and Rock, P. (eds) *Practice

and Progress: British Sociology 1950–1980, London: Allen and Unwin.
STACEY, M. and PRICE, M. (1981) *Women, Power and Politics*, London: Tavistock.
SWENARTON, M. (1981) *Homes Fit for Heroes*, London: Heinemann.
SZINOVACZ, M. (ed.) (1982) *Women's Retirement*, Beverly Hills: Sage.
THOMPSON, P. (1975) *The Edwardians*, St Albans: Paladin.
TOWNSEND, P. (1962) *The Last Refuge*, London: Routledge and Kegan Paul.
TOWNSEND, P. (1963) *The Family Life of Old People*, Harmondsworth: Penguin.
TOWNSEND, P. (1979) *Poverty in the United Kingdom*, Harmondsworth: Penguin.
TOWNSEND, P. with CORRIGAN, P. and KOWARZIK, U. (1987) *Poverty and Labour in London*, London: The Low Pay Unit.
TUNSTALL, J. (1962) *The Fishermen*, London: MacGibbon and Kee.
UNGERSON, C. (1985) 'Women and housing policy', in Ungerson, C. (ed.) *Women and Social Policy*, London: Macmillan.
UNGERSON, C. (1987) *Policy is Personal: Sex, Gender and Informal Care*, London: Tavistock.
UNGERSON, C. and KARN, V. (eds) (1980) *The Consumer Experience of Housing: Cross-National Perspectives*, Farnborough: Gower.
VANEK, J. (1980) 'Time spent in housework' in Amsden, A. H. (ed.) *The Economics of Women and Work*, Harmondsworth: Penguin.
WADE, B., SAWYER, L. and BELL, J. (1983) *Dependency with Dignity*, London: Bedford Square Press.
WALBY, S. (1986) *Patriarchy at Work*, Oxford: Basil Blackwell.
WALKER, C. R. (1950) *Steeltown*, New York: Harper and Brothers.
WALLACE, C. (1987) *For Richer, For Poorer: Growing Up In and Out of Work*, London: Tavistock.
WALLMAN, S. (1986) 'The boundaries of household', in Cohen, A. P. (ed.) *Symbolising Boundaries: Identity and Diversity in British Cultures*, Manchester: University Press.
WALSH, D. (1980) *Break-Ins: Burglary from Private Houses*, London: Constable.
WATSON, S. (1987) 'Ideas of the family in the development of housing forms', in Loney, M. (ed.) *The State or the Market*, London: Sage.
WATSON, S. with AUSTERBERRY, H. (1986) *Housing and Homelessness: A Feminist Perspective*, London: Routledge and Kegan Paul.
WEARING, B. (1984) *The Ideology of Motherhood*, London: Allen and Unwin.
WEIGERT, A. (1981) *Sociology of Everyday Life*, London: Longman.
WENGER, G. C. (1984) *The Supportive Network*, London: Allen and Unwin.
WILKIN, D. and HUGHES, B. (1987) 'Residential care of elderly people: the consumers' view', *Ageing and Society*, 7: 175–201.
WILLCOCKS, D. M., PEACE, S. M. and KELLAHER, L. A. (1982) *The Residential Life of Old People: A Study of 100 Local Authority Homes*, London: Polytechnic of North London.
WILLCOCKS, D. M., PEACE, S. M. and KELLAHER, L. A. (1987)

Private Lives in Public Places, London: Tavistock.
WILLIAMS, P. (1987) 'Constituting class and gender: a social history of the home 1700–1901', in Thrift, N. and Williams, P. (eds) *Class and Space*, London: Routledge and Kegan Paul.
WILLIAMS, R. (1975) *The Country and the City*, London: Paladin.
WILLIAMS, R. (1976) *Keywords: A Vocabulary of Culture and Society*, Glasgow: Fontana.
WILLIAMS, R. G. A. (1983) 'Kinship and migration strategies among settled Londoners', *British Journal of Sociology*, 34: 386–415.
WILLMOTT, P. and YOUNG, M. (1960) *Family and Class in a London Suburb*, London: Routledge and Kegan Paul.
WILSON, E. (1977) *Women and the Welfare State*, London: Tavistock.
WILSON, E. (1980) *Only Halfway to Paradise: Women in Post-War Britain 1945–68*, London: Tavistock.
WOODROFFE, C. and TOWNSEND, P. (1961) *Nursing Homes in England and Wales*, London: NCCOP.
WRIGHT, G. (1975) ' "Sweet and clean": the domestic landscape in the progressive era', *Landscape*, 20: 38.
WRIGHT, G. (1981) *Building the Dream: A Social History of Housing*, New York: Pantheon.
WYNN, M. (1964) *Unmarried Mothers*, London: Martin Joseph.
WYNN, M. (1972) *Family Policy*, Harmondsworth: Penguin.
YEANDLE, S. (1984) *Women's Working Lives: Patterns and Strategies*, London: Tavistock.
YOUNG, M. and WILLMOTT, P. (1957) *Family and Kinship in East London*, London: Routledge and Kegan Paul.
YOUNG, M. and WILLMOTT, P. (1975) *The Symmetrical Family*, Harmondsworth: Penguin.
ZWIEG, F. (1961) *The Worker in an Affluent Society*, London: Heinemann.

Index